The Black Church in America

D1603581

Religious Life in America

The Black Church in America
by Michael Battle

Baptists in North America
by William H. Brackney

Methodism in America
by Douglas Strong

The Black Church in America

African American Christian Spirituality

Michael Battle

Blackwell Publishing

© 2006 by Michael Battle

BLACKWELL PUBLISHING
350 Main Street, Malden, MA 02148-5020, USA
9600 Garsington Road, Oxford OX4 2DQ, UK
550 Swanston Street, Carlton, Victoria 3053, Australia

The right of Michael Battle to be identified as the Author of this Work has been asserted in accordance with the UK Copyright, Designs, and Patents Act 1988.

First published 2006 by Blackwell Publishing Ltd

1   2006

Library of Congress Cataloging-in-Publication Data

Battle, Michael, 1963–
    The Black church in America : African American Christian spirituality /
Michael Battle.
       p. cm.
    Includes bibliographical references and index.
    ISBN-13: 978-1-4051-1891-0 (hardcover : alk. paper)
    ISBN-10: 1-4051-1891-1 (hardcover : alk. paper)
    ISBN-13: 978-1-4051-1892-7 (pbk. : alk. paper)
    ISBN-10: 1-4051-1892-X (pbk. : alk. paper)   1. African Americans—
Religion.   2. African American churches—History.   I. Title.
BR563.N4B38 2005
277.3'0089'96073—dc22

                                                          2005017386

A catalogue record for this title is available from the British Library.

Set in 10.5/12.5pt Sabon
by Graphicraft Limited, Hong Kong
Printed and bound in Singapore
by Fabulous Printers Pte Ltd

The publisher's policy is to use permanent paper from mills that operate a sustainable forestry policy, and which has been manufactured from pulp processed using acid-free and elementary chlorine-free practices. Furthermore, the publisher ensures that the text paper and cover board used have met acceptable environmental accreditation standards.

For further information on
Blackwell Publishing, visit our website:
www.blackwellpublishing.com

For
Raquel Battle,
my wife and model of community

Contents

Acknowledgments

A number of readers provided useful comments about the structure and content of this book. To the following I owe deep gratitude. To Rebecca Harkin, thank you for the confidence in me for this project. To the faculty and students at Duke University Divinity School, especially Deans Greg Jones and Willie Jennings my mentor and colleague Stanley Hauerwas, and members of the Black Church Studies Department (Esther Acolatse, J. Kameron Carter, Emmanuel Katongole, Tiffney Marley, William Turner, Daphne Wiggins, and Tammy Williams), thank you for making Black Church Studies a requirement in the curriculum. To President and Dean, Martha Horne, thank you for your gracious invitation to join the dynamic community of Virginia Theological Seminary. To Dr. Deotis Roberts, thank you for your rich contributions toward the discovery of the nature of the Black Church. To Archbishop Desmond Tutu, thank you for teaching me the catholic nature of the Black Church. To Bishop Gary Lillibridge, thank you for providing the setting needed for me to finish this work.

The author and publisher also gratefully acknowledge the permission granted to reproduce the copyright material in this book:

Maya Angelou, "Passing Times," from *Oh Pray My Wings Are Gonna Fit Me Well* by Maya Angelou. © 1975 Maya Angelou. Used by permission of Random House Inc.
David Frazier, for lyrics from *I Need You to Survive*, performed by Hezekiah Walker. Used by permission of David Frazier Ministries.
Becky Huguley for her letter to Dr. Michael Battle of November 15, 2000.

Every effort has been made to trace copyright holders and to obtain their permission for the use of copyright material. The publisher apologizes for any errors or omissions in the above list and would be grateful if notified of any corrections that should be incorporated in future reprints or editions of this book.

Introduction: An Amphibious Worldview

Your skin like dawn
Mine like musk
One paints the beginning
of a certain end.
The other, the end of a
sure beginning.
(Maya Angelou, "Passing Time")[1]

Maya Angelou invites my dilemma of dual identities. I am a Christian, and I care deeply about this identity. Likewise, I am an African American or some would say, an American of African descent, and I continue to make sense of these dual identities. In order to understand this book, the reader will need to know these interrelated identities and confessions. Angelou's insight is into how physiognomic differences can easily create barriers and limitations. Therefore, any discussion of a "Black" Church already invites limitation and exclusion.

For those who may be deterred from the outset about why there is a need for a Black Church, perhaps you may take comfort in the fact that most of my life has been spent in the discovery of how African American identity and Christianity combine to facilitate communal spirituality. It is through such communal spirituality that I present what I see as the essence of the Black Church in America. Although the particularity of the Black Church may suggest exclusive identity, the essence of its spirituality has always been about finding healthy patterns of community. As we will learn in this book, the original leaders in the Black Church did not seek an exclusive Church; indeed, they fought hard to stay in the corporate Church of the dominant race. In many ways, the Black Church was forced into existence – perhaps, even into exile.

So, my confession of who I am throughout this book need not create a barrier between the reader and writer because my personal voice seeks to engage how the Black Church may one day realize more fully its communal spirituality. Herein is my thesis: that despite its historical oppression, the Black Church has always sought relationality and the embodiment of community.

I started this discovery of seeking the nature of relationality with Archbishop Desmond Tutu, an exemplar of communal spirituality who embodies African and Christian identity without such identity becoming exclusive of others. Tutu also opens up a larger worldview of who the Black Church is. By imprinting on Tutu during my formative years of theological education, my self-understanding has deepened, as I now realize my amphibious status in the United States of being a Black Episcopalian, a strange identity for many in the Black Church. For you see, the Black Church is comprised mainly of members of the so-called seven major historic Black denominations:[2]

African Methodist Episcopal (AME)
African Methodist Episcopal Zion (AMEZ)
Christian Methodist Episcopal (CME)
National Baptist Convention, USA Incorporated
National Baptist Convention of America, Unincorporated
Progressive National Baptist Convention
Church of God in Christ

Later, I sketch the emergence of these historical denominations in the Black Church after slavery, but the reader must note that these denominations do not solely define who comprises the Black Church. Again, my own biography of being a Black Episcopalian illustrates the complexity of defining who is the Black Church.

In order to glean patterns of a communal spirituality, however, I will concentrate on what most people assume the Black Church to be. These seven Black denominations came mainly from Methodist, Baptist, and Pentecostal traditions, but other ties to the Black Church exist such as American Catholicism, Anglicanism, the United Methodist Church, and a host of other Pentecostal traditions. My sketch of the historical turns of the seven main Black denominations can only offer an overview of how the Black Church emerged from slavery in the American context with its spirituality of community intact.

In addition to these more classical denominations of the Black Church, those American Church traditions emerging from at least two Great Awakening periods (1730–60 and 1800–30) produced what we now understand as the Pentecostal Church – a spiritual tradition that would seem more intuitive in explicating the Black Church. My colleague at Duke University, Grant Wacker, is helpful here. Wacker contends that Pentecostals were more or less a "cross section of the American population."[3] He argues at length that the "social profile" of the "typical Pentecostal leader," when pitted against that of the "average Southern Methodist or Southern Baptist leader," came off "surprisingly well."[4] In making this argument, Wacker challenges the interpretations of those who draw starkly different conclusions about early Pentecostals' social status – usually of low esteem.[5]

In many ways, my argument in this book is similar to Wacker's perspective – that of challenging the stereotype of the Black Church. Hopefully, my Black Episcopalian perspective will prove new and instructive in the discussions of African American spirituality, especially as to its scope and breadth. The goal of this book is that we may work through it together by learning to make sense of ourselves differently than before. By doing so, we will offer living perspectives that seek a common identity that can be called African American spirituality. Despite itself, the Church of the dominant White race has an opportunity to learn a new identity, so sorely needed in the demise of mainline churches. Gardiner Shattuck helps me explain why I add the caveat "despite itself." He states:

> Episcopal leaders had been generally unmoved by abolitionist rhetoric and – unlike the Presbyterians, Methodists, and Baptists – had maintained a unified church during the bitter national controversy over slavery in the 1830s and 1840s. Abhorring ecclesiastical schism more than the suffering of people held in bondage, white Episcopalians had argued that slavery was a purely political question and, as such, beyond the church's concern.[6]

Despite the tendencies of mainline churches holding on to religious practices that mimic the dominant society, there are always opportunities in which to practice how to lead the dominant society. Here is a case in point. Centuries later, the Episcopal Church (hewn from the Anglican tradition of civil religion) now finds itself on the verge of another national controversy that threatens to tear the Church apart: the full inclusion of gay and lesbian persons. It is because of the abhorrence of schism in the Anglican tradition that I predict the Episcopal Church will not split over its current crisis of full inclusion of gay and lesbian persons because of its propensity to stay unified "despite itself."[7] Where Anglicans can be leaders is in the display of how all persons are God's children and should never be legislated against.

The Black Church has such a commitment to protect the rights of all people living into the image of God's children. It is not by accident that the civil rights movement developed out of the Black Church in America. Members of Black Churches preached and heard sermons about how all people are God's people. In such sermons and Sunday School lessons, one could hear that God will even redeem white people. Perhaps the reader may now begin to understand my own propensity toward a coherent category understood as African American Christian spirituality – that despite the obvious conflicting descriptors of such spirituality, such spirituality still seeks a unified whole of God's creation.

Instead of offering another sociological or historical work, as has already been well done by others,[8] I offer the reader a study of what I see as the theological character of the Black Church in America – that is, communal spirituality. Even more, I offer a much different view of the Black Church as has been studied because I seek the catholic (universal) nature of the Black Church instead of exclusivist views of her nature. For some, a catholic (i.e., unified) Black Church is an oxymoron, especially a Black Church made available to the world on the basis of race. For such people, the Black Church is then seen as only for herself and her own needs. This oxymoronic Black Church is not whom I seek in this book. Instead, I seek a catholic Black Church that is not only for herself, but for others.[9] A catholic Black Church presents an additional dilemma, however. Harold Lewis is helpful in describing this dilemma when he discusses the role of bishops:

> The Episcopal Church, especially in the South, where there continued to be for several decades after the [Civil War] a *stated* desire to bring more persons of African descent into the fold, found itself on the horns of a dilemma. It believed, in principle, that a black bishop could do much to evangelize people of his own race, but despaired that "under existing church law individual dioceses elected bishops to supervise church work in their regions, which would mean that a Negro bishop would have jurisdiction over both Negro and white churches," a concept that was not appealing even to the more liberal Northern dioceses. Understandably, then, blacks were desirous of the episcopate for the very reasons that the largely white Church would have barred their access.[10]

The dilemma of a Black bishop over "both Negro and white churches" presents the additional dilemma of how Christianity is increasingly a religion of the Southern hemisphere. This means that instead of Europeans comprising the dominant Church, African, Asian, and Hispanic cultures are becoming the dominant voices interpreting Christianity. The irony has become real: missionaries from Africa now need to evangelize a "pagan" Europe.

Understanding the Black Church, therefore, is more complicated today. Lewis helps us see such complexity through the innate desire of those of African descent in America always seeking a catholic Church.

Such a catholic nature contributes toward the understanding of why the Black Church became (and remains) a leader in nonviolent resistance, not just in the United States, but in the world, a fact that has been neglected for too long.[11] Herein, I maintain my allegiance to Tutu because he has profoundly negotiated how catholic Christianity helps us better see practices of peacemaking and reconciliation. Such an exemplar has led me to think that one of the unnerving issues of the Black Church in America is how provincial some views of the Black Church have become, lacking any global vision. Such provinciality leads me to the organizing theme of this book as that focus on what the Church has called spirituality.

I define spirituality in the African context of Christianity as the formation of self through communal being or relationality. For me, spirituality means a rite of passage or a way of practicing a better life. This means that at the heart of Christian spirituality is prayerful personhood seeking mutuality with God and neighbor. So I invite the reader into the discovery of African and African American Christian spirituality through my particular lens, although to make such exploration is difficult because there are few academic paradigms of such a spirituality.[12] In order to offer such a paradigm, I invite the reader to learn about the role of the Black Church in the American context; to become acquainted with its theology; to grow in the awareness of the social and political development of the Black Church in America. My argument in exposing the reader to all of this is that the essence of the Black Church is its spiritual movement of community. Therefore, the nature of the beliefs and practices of the Black Church can be summarized in the phrase *communal spirituality*.

This book exposes the reader to African American Christian spirituality through the thesis that the nature and future of the Black Church in America is constituted and maintained through its communitarian sensibilities. In other words, the essence of African American Christian spirituality is community. My essential question is this: what hermeneutics do Africans from the continent of Africa, or African Americans in the diaspora, bring to bear on the interpretation of Christian spirituality? My short answer is: communal spirituality. Such an approach offers the reader an interesting and challenging reference by which to view and study not only African Christian spirituality but also the Black Church in America. Such an answer does not go without challenge, as John Pobee illustrates: "African Americans are different from Africans from the continent of Africa."[13] Because of this legitimate concern, a program is needed to "tease out" African character that is also solvent for African diasporan identity.

My argument that the Black Church seeks always to maintain interpersonal balance is tied to African cultures around the world, especially in the particularity of African Christian understandings of God, prayer, humanity, and the created universe. After reading this book, one should gain both a breadth of knowledge of the Black Church in America and an emerging sense of its connections to the wider world as it seeks to describe how individual and communal destiny are bound together. Because of my argument for the continuous flow of African spirituality into the Black Church, I present the reader with an unusual approach to the Black Church rather than that which has often been described as a unilateral relationship with Africa (e.g., Back to Africa).[14] The goal of this book is to discover together how to make sense of ourselves differently than before. We can discover this through the simple fact that Christian spirituality was present on the African continent before the so-called Black Church in America came to be. Because of this fact, we no longer have to assume a patronizing relationship between Black and White Christians – as if African identity owes her discovery of Christ to British missionaries. I am excited that this project has gained your attention; and it is my desire that it will prove both interesting and useful for students and scholars working in this area.

When I was contacted to write this volume, I thought deeply about how I could contribute to the already rich resources on the Black Church in America. Keeping the reader in mind, I discerned that my deepest desire was to unfold an argument about the nature and future of African American spirituality based upon communal sensibilities. Stereotypically, such sensibilities are thought to be summarized in notions of emotionalism or kinetic forms of worship. My goal is to correct such stereotypes and instead inform the reader of the profound insights of African Christian spirituality as they pertain to community and relationality. For example (as I argue in more detail in chapter 4), African American Christian worship is much more diverse than many give it credit for, and yet it is just as communally committed. As such discoveries are made, it is my hope that the reader will find this book to be both interesting and challenging as we cover the basic historical framework of the Black Church, as well as her theme of communal spirituality.

Methodology

My argument is that African American Christian spirituality is communal in nature. I seek to display this argument through the history, theology, practice of worship, and social and cultural contexts of the Black Church in America. The development of the Black Church presents the twofold methodological aim of my book. It is both to provide a broad picture of the Black Church, so as to enrich the reader's knowledge, and display my thesis that there is an inherent communal spirituality that expresses African American spirituality.

Too often, books with spirituality in the title rarely discuss what spirituality really means. African American spirituality displays communal practices of the divine life, even in the face of the harshest oppression. History does not credit the Black Church enough for its miracle of holding on to communal spirituality when faced with the extremist violence of slavery. And little work has been done to show how the Black Church helped other societies face violent oppression with healthy communal practices, leading to more lasting solutions of justice and peace. Such a nonviolent spirituality has even spread to wider societies.

In terms of a chronological understanding of the development of the Black Church, I seek a historical framework in which the reader understands why the Black Church developed in a particular way. It is in such a framework that I present my thesis of communal spirituality, one that invites the reader into the book and one that anticipates objections from other views of the Black Church. In chapter 1, I attempt to contrast Western and African spiritualities relative to self and community in order to gain a better sense of what is African. Chapter 2 suggests an engaging taxonomy of African American spirituality and its components. Chapter 3 discusses in more detail how such spirituality developed despite the horrors of slavery. Chapter 4 shows how the Black Church did not merely survive, but flourished in worship and denominations. In Chapter 5 we engage the discussion above for how the miracle of community became an invitation for others to become Black. Here, African American spirituality matured through conversation with African spirituality to indeed expand what community should look like. Chapter 6 builds on preceding chapters by looking at what has come to be the global gift and contribution of the Black Church: the civil rights movement. This is a movement to increase true community among people and nations. Lastly, in chapter 7, I conclude that African American spirituality cannot be static in nature, but must be constantly reimagined to maintain true community among all people. I discuss this through the eight convictions of the Black Church.

In conclusion, I believe that African understandings of community not only survived the harshest of oppression, but also became a revolutionary appeal for communal spirituality for all people. This revolutionary communal spirituality is the essence of the Black Church in America.

There are those who have painted a different picture of what comprises the essence of the Black Church. Some argue that what most exemplifies the rich spiritual life of African American Christian spirituality is seen through the different forms of communal worship found within the Black Church in America. Others argue that survival and resistance make up the heart of the Black Church.

Most of these counter-arguments come out of an essentially historical study of the Black Church. This book, however, is not in essence a historical study. Rather, my approach to African American spirituality seems in one sense to cover a very broad spectrum in relationship to the development of the communitarian sensibilities of the spirituality of the Black Church. One may even raise the concern that my spectrum is limited to the goal of the civil rights movement. Both are legitimate concerns. However, I focus on communal spirituality that leads to the civil rights movement and beyond because both accentuate an understanding of balanced destiny between individual and community.

In order to understand the Black Church, one may be more interested in how slavery and freedom, instead of nonviolence and the civil rights movement, should shape such a study. The focus on slavery and freedom is only part of the narrative of the Black Church. My argument is that nonviolence and civil rights embody the heart of African American spirituality, from which one may predict the future character of African American spirituality – those who balance individual and communal needs. Indeed it is true that the civil rights movement cannot exist without its historic antecedents of slavery, reconstruction, Jim Crow, and migration. As a result of such antecedents, spirituality in the African American Church context has had to contend with the reoccurring themes of repression and freedom within the context of a community that although communitarian, did not always agree with the methodology of achieving this African American Christian spirituality. There are other scholars who provide the multifaceted historical context of the Black Church. My focus here is on the discovery of what could be distinctively described as African American Christian spirituality; therefore, my goal for the reader is to benefit from this approach written not by a historian, but by a theologian.

The reader is challenged through my conclusion to see the Black Church differently. The social and political context of the Black Church operates communally and collaboratively within American society, but the Black Church's roots are in African spirituality. This is why attention is given to essential tenets of African spirituality in the beginning.

It is my hope that this methodology offers the reader a certain degree of fluid discourse in which to envisage African American spirituality, while also gaining understanding of African spirituality. For this reason, I have attempted to write in an accessible and lively way so that the reader can explore the interrelation of history, philosophy, theology, practice of worship, and social and cultural context of the Black Church in America.

Notes

1   Maya Angelou, *The Compete Collected Poems of Maya Angelou* (New York: Random House, 1994), p. 67.
2   For a current look at Black Church demographics, see Michael Dash and Christine Chapman, *The Shape of Zion: Leadership and Life in Black Churches* (Cleveland: Pilgrim Press), 2003.
3   Grant Wacker, *Heaven Below: Early Pentecostals and American Culture* (Cambridge, MA: Harvard University Press, 2001), p. 199.
4   Ibid, p. 205.
5   For example, see Robert Mapes Anderson's *Vision of the Disinherited: The Making of American Pentecostalism* (New York: Oxford University Press, 1979).
6   Gardiner H. Shattuck Jr., *Episcopalians and Race: Civil War to Civil Rights* (Lexington: University Press of Kentucky, 2000), p. 9.
7   The Episcopal election of Gene Robinson, an openly gay bishop from New Hampshire, on November 4, 2003, has thrown the Anglican communion into turmoil and threat of schism.
8   For an excellent sociological study of the Black Church, see C. Eric Lincoln and Lawrence H. Mamiya, *The Black Church in the African American Experience* (Durham, NC: Duke University Press, 1990). For an excellent historical survey using primary texts, see both Milton Sernett, ed., *Afro-American Religious History: A Documentary Witness* (Durham, NC: Duke University Press, 1985), and Albert J. Raboteau, *Slave Religion: The "Invisible Institution" in the Antebellum South* (New York: Oxford University Press, 1980).
9   Here, Dietrich Bonhoeffer's ecclesiology is especially helpful. See Dietrich Bonhoeffer, *Life Together* (New York: Harper, 1954), and his earlier work, *The Communion of Saints* (New York: Harper and Row, 1963).
10 Harold Lewis, *Yet With a Steady Beat: The African American Struggle for Recognition in the Episcopal Church* (Valley Forge, PA: Trinity Press International, 1996), p. 66.
11 Only recently have I seen any attempt to rectify this situation: see Marvin Berlowtiz et al., *Reflections of African-American Peace Leaders: A Documentary History, 1898–1967* (Lewiston, NY: Edwin Mellen Press, 2003).
12 Peter Paris offers an extraordinary study, but his self-avowal is that his particular work "is a study in religious social ethics." See Peter Paris, *The Spirituality of African Peoples: The Search for a Common Moral Discourse* (Minneapolis, MN: Fortress Press, 1995), p. 162.

13   John S. Pobee, "Afro-Anglicanism: Quo Vadimus?" *Anglican Theological Review*, 77: 4 (1995).
14   See such a unilateral treatment in Anthony Pinn, "The Church and Its Relationship to Africa," in his book, *The Black Church in the Post-Civil Rights Era* (Maryknoll, NY: Orbis Books, 2002), p. 4ff.

Chapter 1
Emergence of What is African

*All of us are bound to mother Africa by invisible but tenacious bonds
... All of us have roots that go deep into the warm soil of Africa; so that
no matter how long and traumatic our separation from our ancestral
home has been, there are things we are often unable to articulate, but
which we feel in our very bones, things which make us, who are different
from others who have not suckled the breath of our mother, Africa.*

Desmond Tutu[1]

In this chapter I set forth my argument that the Black Church is
constituted by a communal spirituality. I do this first by contrasting
"African" and "Western." Secondly, I briefly explore the sociohistorical
context in which the Black Church emerged. My primary concern with
such a context is to see the vital essence of community and its corres-
ponding meaning to African sensibilities.

African Warnings

I began with a first warning. Western readers in search of what is African
must beware of the perspective that they may bring to this text. I think
the non-African[2] reader and the reader of African descent can benefit
from learning about African American Christian spirituality that moves
beyond European Enlightenment categories of individualism. When
Western persons, formed in the worldview of the sole importance of
personal responsibilities, encounter a person formed in the sensibilities
of African spirituality, they meet therein someone whose experience of
the self is distinctly different. What I mean is this. In contrast to Western
persons, African persons do not exist apart from the community. The
classic phrasing of this intrinsic relationship was started by John Mbiti
and carried on by Desmond Tutu. I call it an Ubuntu sensibility, namely
"I am, because we are; and since we are, therefore I am."[3] The person is
part of the whole, and personal identity flows from corporate experience

and never in isolation from it, since it is the community which defines who one becomes, and who one becomes defines community.

My continued use of Tutu's Ubuntu doctrine will make sense to African Americans only in the context of a communitarian understanding of making connections and moving between different worldviews. Ubuntu is a crucial African concept that displays the symmetry between African culture and Christian conceptualizations of God and humanity. Herein is the thesis of my book: African American Christian spirituality inherits from African spirituality practices and a worldview for how the uniqueness of each person is affirmed and acknowledged in community. Such inheritance informs the Black Church in America – how one's own individuality and freedom are always balanced by the destiny of the community (e.g., the civil rights movement).

The Black Church in America believes this after all, because such communal spirituality is the very Christian image of the triune God, whose persons create monotheism through the interrelation of three persons (Father, Son, and Holy Spirit). In other words, God's image is community rather than the typical individualistic notions of God spread throughout Western Christianity. The Black Church tries to live into a different *imago Dei* through the balanced destiny between individual and community displayed in worship, theology, and the civil rights movement. In Chapter 6 I discuss the impact of the civil rights movement, in particular through Martin Luther King, Jr.'s concept of the Beloved Community.

A second warning concerns the concept of the communal. What are the phenomenological practices or lifestyles that make the African American church community a more communally based church? Some may argue that my answer to this question resides in the abstraction that African Christian understandings of God, prayer, humanity, and the created universe maintain interpersonal balance within the community, but that they simply remind us of a cosmology of community, instead of being its essence. This becomes a crucial worry of the book. How does one discuss the nature of community within the Black Church context and then expand this outward into cogent examples?

One way to address this problematic is through discussions of the retention of African practices by the slave community (Africanisms).[4] Therefore, I spend a good deal of time teasing out how Africanisms carry over into African American Christian spirituality. One vivid example of such Africanisms is the Garifuna peoples of Central America. Although these discussions within African American studies are largely resolved to some degree, I will take into account the historic debates of African retentions versus their destruction in relationship to spirituality.

By taking into account a stronger communal focus, my study increases the "diversity" of the African American church experience, as opposed to the monolithic Black Church moniker so commonly written about in historic studies. In using such an approach, we are able to imagine the deep contributions of the Black Church's nature to welcome the stranger. Wendy Haight illustrates this aspect of the Black Church through her developmental psychology of the African American community, often harassed and called "You dirty, black niggers!" She concludes: "I often wondered how children of any ethnicity could develop optimally within racist communities. As I listened more closely, it became clear that, for Mrs. Hudley [a 73-year-old African American woman], human development is rooted in spirituality."[5] My observation that Black spirituality is communitarian – as opposed to the Western outlook, which is mainly individualistic – is more of a basis upon which connections to other worldviews can be made.

My notion that Black Christian spirituality is communally oriented is essential to this reasoning of making connections to other worldviews. Perhaps this is why I chose to describe my introduction as "amphibious," as the genius of the Black Church is in her ability to move between worldviews (e.g., Western and African, Black and White). Howard Thurman's spirituality may also be described in this way, as it makes connections across worldviews in the form of "a practical mysticism."[6] Making connections between spirituality and social witness is key to understanding the communal nature of African American spirituality. Thurman was the mentor of Martin Luther King, Jr. on spirituality, resulting in King's deep connections between a Beloved Community and nonviolence. King is even said to have carried Thurman's book in his briefcase as he traveled.

By means of this amphibious sensibility of the Black Church to make connections and move between worlds, I argue that there is a direct relationship between African American Christian spirituality and the struggle for racial and social justice in the US. Such a relationship between spirituality and justice includes the change in systemic health issues relating particularly to African Americans. The communal sensibility of the Black Church cannot prevent her nature from continuing to make connections and build bridges, so that new identity can emerge from oppressive formations of identity.[7] This book will do more than suggest these connections. The importance of the subject of this book for global justice is apparent. Until Western people realize the connectedness of religious experience beyond privatistic and individualistic experiences, the problem of religious wars and so-called terrorism will not be solved. Other black theologians have been in general agreement on this position that European Enlightenment religion will have to wake up to a diversity of worldviews, most of which contain communal notions of existence. The onus of this research is to pay more attention to how and why African American Christian spirituality lends itself to communitarian sensibilities in some referenceable framework. To this end there needs to be an appeal to scholarly reflection, both in Africa and her diaspora.

A third warning is in the obvious exchange of terms between "Black" and "African American." Are we talking about Black Church studies or African American Church studies or even African Church studies? Some would say it is an extraneous discussion to use the constant reference and repetition of the difference between "White American" and "Black American." Since the historical context of African American spirituality contains within itself this tension of description between Black and African, it becomes redundant to remind the reader of a Black and White Church. As I learned from my relationship with Desmond Tutu, Black identity becomes further complicated in its extrapolation in contexts outside of North America.[8] The seeming shift from Black identity in the United States to African American identity is a case in point. Although I use the terms "Black" and "African American" interchangeably, an interesting dilemma develops when white South Africans (especially Afrikaners – which means African) immigrate to the United States. Could their identity one day be conceived of as African American? If not, what prevents such fluidity in the character of being African American?

South Africa's Truth and Reconciliation hearings in the 1990s produced a transfiguration that has carved out a new national identity based no longer on race but on geography. The goal now is how to be a nation-state instead of a dominant race. My study of the South African context teaches me that descriptions of Black and White do not accurately describe the complex communities that these names seek to describe. Black and White relationships cannot easily translate into other contexts that have multilayered identities couched not only in race but also in cultural and linguistic groupings. In other words, there are at least twelve Black identities in South Africa and two White identities.

I hold up African identity, especially as crafted in South Africa, primarily for the purpose of arguing that African American identity can prove to be just as Western as European identity if there is no particular connection to Africa. The genius of African American identity can be seen in the way the American Dream is always wrestled out of individualism by the "African" focus of communal spirituality. African American identity has allowed more positive responses to the question: "What does it mean to be an American?"

In light of this third warning, I am aware of the difficult connection between the African and the African American worldviews. For example, black scholars have long argued that African cultures did not survive slavery. E. Franklin Frazier states:

> In studying any phase of the character and the development of the social and cultural life of the Negro in the United States, one must recognize from the beginning that because of the manner in which the Negroes were captured in Africa and enslaved, they were practically stripped of their social heritage. Although the area in West Africa from which the majority of the slaves were drawn exhibits a high degree of cultural homogeneity, the capture of many of the slaves in intertribal wars and their selection for the slave markets tended to reduce to a minimum the possibility of the retention and the transmission of African culture.[9]

In this book I contest the premise that African culture did not survive the North Atlantic slave trade. As an African American myself, who lived for two years in South Africa with frequent returns, I have learned through primary experience the survival of African culture in the Western world. In fact, much of the attention of this book is given to the diverse contexts of how African spirituality has survived in African American spirituality per se. African Americans came from the center of Africa, by means of the Middle Passage. The typical notion is that it was during slavery that those who eventually became known as African Americans encountered or further embraced the Christian faith. I argue, however, that to some extent the North Atlantic slave trade was not the first time Africans encountered Christianity. In fact, the heart of Christian spirituality developed in Africa as the desert tradition developed.[10] The collective memory of this Christian history is crucial to Black experience and our sense of identity as a people. In other words, more careful thought needs to be given to why African Americans embraced Christianity so readily.

The knee jerk argument that Christianity was forced on African slaves does not hold in light of current trends in the Southern hemisphere, which is increasingly Christianized. What makes many other peoples around the world convert to Christianity who are not forced into slavery?[11] Regardless of whether or not this was the first encounter between Africans and Christianity, the fact remains for those who emerged as African Americans that their Christian religious experience developed largely in a Eurocentric context. This leads to the problematic of what can be named innately as African American Christian spirituality.

While Christian experience is assumed in African and African American spirituality, I assume that a particular communal spirituality develops among African American Christian spirituality. Such a communal sensibility makes African American spirituality well suited to be a leader in peacemaking and reconciliation. It is here that I think the problematic of what is innately African American spirituality is named through a communal spirituality of nonviolence and reconciliation. Such spirituality, however, did not develop without African roots.[12]

Because of this communal spirituality rooted in Africa, African American spirituality can never be defined as exclusive or for black people only. Many of the older generation of black theologians have had to study and lecture in several African countries, thereby causing them to revise exclusivist hermeneutics in Black theology. This occurred in the course of direct dialogue with African thinkers such as Mbiti, Pobee, Tutu, and other African Church persons and scholars. However, the understanding of African Christian spirituality as being inherently communal meant connection with the excellent sources which African American religious scholars have already produced. Therefore, I will not reinvent the wheel in an endeavor to unearth what is in fact African/African American spirituality. Instead, I offer a more systematic look at the communal nature of African/African American spirituality. In those cases where the reader wishes a more detailed historical study of other aspects of this spirituality, I will point them in the direction of work already done. This will be especially important for those who seek more of a comparative religious or phenomenological approach to African spirituality.

A fourth warning has to do with "spirituality," a difficult term to define. Instead of looking for spirituality only in interior places, my goal is to provide readers with an understanding of what spirituality in community means in the African American context. Black theology, African American religious history, and African American literature have only recently fit into the "acceptable" academic canons of universities and colleges. What remains to be accepted is the study of Christian spirituality as it relates to African cultures. I argue in this book that Christian spirituality broadly seeks to express the theory and practice of the communal Christian life.[13] This theory and practice necessarily shows the maturity of individuals and communities through historical, cultural, and environmental change. Herein is the problem, however.

The approach of traditional Christian spirituality implied an agreed upon theological language in reference to the Christian life which no longer applies. For example, Denise Ackerman recounts how the Dutch Reformed Church in the Cape Colony was faced with a dilemma in the early nineteenth century. It was able to solve its dilemma through its own common understanding over against the understanding and practices of the indigenous people:

Race proved to be stronger than religion. In 1857 the synod of the Dutch Reformed Church passed the following resolution:
The [Dutch Reformed] Synod considers it desirable and scriptural that our members from the Heathen be received and absorbed into our existing congregations wherever possible; but where this measure, as a result of the weakness of some, impedes the furtherance of the cause of Christ among the Heathen, the congregation from the Heathen, already founded and still to be founded, shall enjoy its Christian privileges in a separate building or institution.

For "the weakness of some" read the racism of some white settlers. Thus the separation of believers along race lines began, a separation which ultimately led to the theological justification of apartheid.[14]

What is commonly understood to be the Christian life today is drastically different from what was commonly understood to be the Christian life yesterday. No longer is it publicly tolerated in mainline Protestant and Roman Catholic churches that Christian faith be determined by European culture. The epistemology of salvation is no longer in the control of white people. Thus, the catholic (universal) church is currently in the throes of debate as to what Christian spirituality looks like across cultural boundaries.

It is my contention that African spirituality offers a definition of Christian spirituality that is relational and communal. Christian spirituality that is relational and communal (in addition to personal and interior) is much needed, as Ackerman notes: "For those of us who have been used to dominant power or whose souls and minds are closed by rigid ideologies and fear of the other, an epiphany is needed. Without an epiphany we live in a state of solipsism – quite literally as the sun of our own individual universe. Reality is merely and only the reality of my own consciousness."[15] I want to go a step further and claim the epiphany to be African Christian spirituality. The diasporic community of Africans encompasses Africans and African Americans, and these populations from the Caribbean to Europe, the Americas and other areas, play the crucial role in discovering new meanings and practices for Christian spirituality.

What I mean by spirituality is meant to engage contemporary issues facing the world, both in Christian and non-Christian settings. As already indicated, one needs to be very careful not to juxtapose fixed definitions of spirituality (i.e., Black or White Christian spirituality). Even more, spirituality must recover from its insular definition in the context of the Western world as intelligible only in a personal way.[16] Until now, the primary focus on interior Christian spirituality has mainly been influenced by European and Asian cultures. The primary focus of this book, however, is on how those of African descent contribute toward the definition of communal Christian spirituality.

When one reads any scholarly book one reads not simply one person's view but a collaboration of ideas which, in turn, can achieve a synthesis of ideas and concepts and lead to new insights. This is my hope for readers here, for we will interact with how various sources pertaining to African American spirituality have informed my structuring of this book. The goal is collaboration, although my thesis surrounding the particularity of African Christian spirituality may disturb some. For example, a scholar may base her assumptions on Gayraud Wilmore's *Black Religion and Black Radicalism*, in which scholars who hold to a high Christology may have difficulty being in full collaboration with other scholars with less of a Christology or no Christology at all. Not to fully incorporate more "confessional" research into the conversation, however, would cause readers to miss out on the rich tradition of Christian spirituality that scholars like myself bring to the conversation about spirituality and community. While still bearing in mind my admonition about spirituality, I aim to seize upon a neglected area of contemporary theology as expressed among black theologians. Seldom do we find in theological research conducted in major academies any focused attention on spiritual commitments and practices. The volatile subject of religion post-September 11, 2001 requires that research academies revisit the premise that theology is never done objectively, but always from a particular perspective. Honest work that considers how spiritual commitments and practices need not lead toward disparate worldviews or worse – legitimation of violence – is crucial for peacemaking and stable societies.

This particular perspective has grown out of my own experience as a theologian and Episcopal priest. I have selected a particular aspect of African American Christian expression which is lifted up in my own ministry and teaching; namely, spirituality. Many books have been written by (black) scholars in the last three decades on religion and theology, but there is a scarcity of volumes on this vital aspect of African American spirituality. In this endeavor to maintain my own spiritual commitments and practices while pursuing the vital work of connecting them to other worldviews, I think it wise to delimit this study by stressing the centrality of communal Christian spirituality. There are those who are Islamic, Jewish, humanistic, etc., who claim a "spiritual" dimension to their experience and who can offer a more thorough perspective of spirituality from their worldview. This study, however, covers the segment of African American believers shaped and formed by the revelation of Jesus Christ in the triune God. I know of no other study like this from the perspective of a Black Episcopalian.[17] To a fault, much of the Black Church is understood only in her Protestant sensibilities. My Anglican worldview enables theological discourse that increases connections to many others who seek intercultural, ecumenical, and interreligious dialogue. In short, much of Black Church studies has never been catholic (global) in scope. I attempt to open such a global window.

The black philosopher-theologian Howard Thurman devoted his long career to Christian spirituality that sought connections to other worldviews. Thus far we have not seen a theologian-successor to Thurman. Perhaps this book can make an in-depth contribution to his work. Thurman received much of his inspiration from Indian (Hindu) mysticism, the Quakers, and Black slave songs (the spirituals). Like Thurman, I propose a holistic treatment of African American spirituality in light of the particularity of communal sensibilities surviving from African cultures. This treatment of African American Christian spirituality is consistent with African Americans who continually seek our "African roots," as I seek to appropriate the nature of spirituality in communal ways of knowing reality and God.

In sum, I believe that this study is unique and very much needed, not just in the African American church and community but also in the world at large. As a priest and theologian I seek to make the crucial connections between community and spirituality as displayed in the African American community. I hope that this book, as well as the Blackwell series to which it belongs, can make a real contribution toward understanding spiritual practices that are often neglected in the US and the world community. My prayer is that it will become a welcome addition to an often ignored and neglected dimension of religious experience. My principal argument – that the Black Church in America is largely defined by a symmetry between the personal and communal – is certainly not meant to be an exclusivist thesis that leaves out those uncommitted to Christian spirituality. Rather, I hope only to remind many of the brilliance of a Black Church that seeks to connect people to the notion of community. The fact that this book is part of a series on religion in America presumes major reliance on scholarly forebears. Classic African American religious texts by Gayraud Wilmore, C. Eric Lincoln, Vincent Harding, Peter Paris, and others, as well as the writings of African thinkers John Mbiti and Desmond Tutu, established the notion of community in the dialectical relationship between the "I" and the "we." Clearly, however, I intend to be even more attentive to the interpersonal than has typically been the case in most works on Black religion in America.

The question that has to be answered is this: to what degree does African American Christian spirituality address the balance between the personal and the communal? This question is crucial and controversial because it recognizes and acknowledges that the Black Church has not in all times and in all circumstances lived up to or out of the best practices of community.[18] In other words, there will be challenges to the thesis that African American Christian spirituality is by nature communal. I rely on my ongoing interests in African communal notions (especially Ubuntu) to respond to these complexities. One prominent black intellectual recently told me that the Black Church in America has waxed and waned on meeting the needs of its people and the wider world. Some say that at its best it has been the exemplar of the faith in the United States and the moral compass of a nation. At its worst it has simply mirrored the foibles of the Church at large. I argue, however, that Christian spirituality has sustained the Black Church through time and region, both with respect to her inner dynamics and external tensions.

The overall structure of the book aims for a communal view of African American Christian spirituality and its varying impacts. It cannot be stated strongly enough, however, how important it is to illuminate the Black Church as a fluid entity, constantly wrestling with the tensions of her inherent sense of purpose, manifested sometimes magnificently, and other times failingly. The emphasis in Chapter 4 will bear this out, although I may not convince everyone that the Black Church's purpose is to create community, especially between the Western and African worlds. Certainly, however, most readers will agree, not to the exclusion of events in the African and non-Western world in general (formation of independent states, symbolic meaning of Ethiopia, etc.), that more work can be done on understanding the connections between the non-Western world and Africa.

Chapter 7 is tremendously important and subtly speaks to the kind of shadings needed throughout. It broaches a number of current needs and concerns. Issues of Christian commitments and health are terribly vital. By discussing eight convictions of the Black Church, I commend sensitivity as I embark upon the contemporary relevance of the Black Church for her future existence. An additional item should not be overlooked: the relationship between the Black Church and youth culture, the hip-hop generation, which in many respects is forming its own set of spiritual criteria, drawing upon but not limiting itself to the Christian tradition. To some extent Chapter 6 addresses the relationship between African American Christian spirituality and contemporary music, but extensive work remains to be done. This leads me to return to my earlier question in a different form: can African American Christian spirituality be contained within the confines of the institutional Black

Church? Has it ever been? This is a vital question to ponder in light of numerous sectarian movements and the increasing attraction of African-derived traditions and Islam, etc., which have permeated the community for at least the last century. I propose that within such particularity there also exists the universal. Thus, readers from all backgrounds are invited to see relevant interconnections for how all people are made in the image of God. Remembering that "the personal is political" will also help us remain true to the "balance" of community broadly defined as African Christian spirituality. This means identifying the historic and creative tensions between the sociopolitical and the individual that have always been present, no less than the conflict between institutions and personal manifestations of faith.

In Chapter 2 I set forth my argument that the Black Church is constituted by communitarian and interpersonal spirituality. I do this first by briefly exploring the sociohistorical context in which the Black Church emerged. In the West, especially from the time of the Enlightenment, the self has been understood as a distinct individual, with unique value and distinct rights. Persons have the right to make something of their lives, to take responsibility for their life direction, to use their talents and gifts to the full. Such emphasis puts supreme value on the right of self-determination, self-achievement, and self-satisfaction. What is weak in this dimensional worldview, according to African American Christian spirituality, is the bonding of the person with the community. Particularly in White America, individual self-determination has been exalted over the needs of the community, giving rise to the "individualism" which found its most skewed expression in the "Me Generation" – my needs above all else. This racial and cultural value has profoundly influenced all facets of North American life, including spirituality.

In Chapter 3 I offer a contrasting cosmology to that of Western spirituality, through the emergence of slave religion in America and its new particularity of worship. Such worship demonstrates that the meaning of human life in the Black Church flows from the community to the person; whereas in White America there is often an inverse flow of meaning originating in the individual that sometimes leads to community. Instead of the latter Cartesian epistemological method, worship in the Black Church constitutes new identity, in which the individual becomes conscious of herself only through social interaction. It is from such communal epistemology that I construct a more communal way to understand the Black Church, one of the great legacies of American religious experience.

Chapters 4 and 5 discuss the profound effect of Black theology in relation to how African American Christian sensibilities have tended toward the correct relation of personhood. Radical, moderate, and conservative voices in Black theology all sought consensus of thought for how black people could relate fully to fellow human beings in light of the oppression of racism in America. African Christians would not allow African American Christians to become disconnected from the communal pursuits of Christian spirituality. Such consensus from African Christians comes from a spirituality in which persons act in concert with the community and not apart from it. Despite the arguments even among Black Christians about how racism should be addressed, there remained a consensus of Christian identity that demanded the following spiritual practices: confession, forgiveness, and repentance. There was an understanding that when good was done, it was good for the whole community, including all socioeconomic contexts; and when evil was committed, the shame affected the same.

In Chapter 6 I discuss the political impact of the Black Church in America. Because the spirituality of the Black Church is interpersonal and communal, the civil rights movement was a natural action derived from the history, worship, and theology of the Black Church. Seldom known, however, is that many of the major Black Church leaders (who de facto were leaders of the civil rights movement) were also inspired by communitarian spiritualities coming out of the Eastern world, such as Gandhi's Satyagraha movement and more currently the Dalai Lama's concept of compassion for all. This leads me to believe that the communitarian sensibilities of the Black Church extend beyond the United States. Will the Black Church continue to be the major context from which major civil rights leaders emerge, especially in light of some of the more radical political voices of some African Americans? The extent to which the Black Church in America continues to explore how individual and communal fulfillment are inextricably tied together is the extent to which the Black Church in America can continue to be a light to the nations.

What is African?

The link between community and African spirituality becomes obvious in the discovery of human identity. Although I seek to make such a discovery in more of a theological sense, a great deal of positive work has already been done in connecting Africa to human identity.[19] Of course, such positive work has been done through the efforts of paleoanthropologists (the study of human origins), who agree with Desmond Tutu that human origin derives from Africa.

One of the most hotly debated issues in paleoanthropology focuses on the origins of modern humans, *Homo sapiens*. Roughly 100,000 years ago the world was occupied by a morphologically diverse group of hominids. In Africa and the Middle East there was *Homo sapiens*, in Asia *Homo erectus*, and in Europe *Homo neanderthalensis*. Around 30,000 years ago this taxonomic diversity vanished and humans everywhere had evolved into the anatomically and behaviorally modern form. The nature of this transformation is the focus of great deliberation between two schools of thought: one that stresses multiregional continuity developing out of Africa, and the other that suggests a single origin for modern humans out of Africa. The one thing each school agrees upon is that there is a common link for humanity: African ancestry.[20]

Instead of the often shortsighted debate about the validity of evolution in Western Christian churches, it seems to me that theological discourse as it relates to African Christian spirituality has a great deal to learn from this paleoanthropological assumption. Most of all, what we have to learn is that human identity cannot be separated from the fullness of African identity. I describe such identity as fullness because of its variegated and dynamic nature. I want to recover both the fullness of African identity and relate such fullness not just to "black" people, but to the deeper understanding of human and divine community. In this sense, African American Christian spirituality does not exist for itself alone, but in a real sense, displays a catholic reality of interrelational spirituality.

What does the fullness of African identity look like? I assume here that any attempt at definition requires contrasts. My contrast of Western and African views of the human person does not seek mutual exclusion; rather, it attempts to invite the reader into understanding the wider view of the communal person in the African perspective, instead of the naturally assumed Western worldview. No doubt, some will be unsympathetic to this contrasting of Western and African worldviews, thinking that such determinations are much more complicated than I can display. (This is a worthy criticism that subsequent chapters will seek to address.) For example, an initial reviewer accurately noted that a "Western Enlightenment worldview" is certainly different from a "Western" view. My method of contrasting African and Western sensibilities, however, attempts to show why human identity can never be separated from communal identity. The following question makes our discussion more concrete: does Augustine count as an African – or is he Western? This is a crucial question for me because Augustine is often identified as initiating the "Western" Christian view of the self. My answer, in light of my thesis for a catholic Black Church, is that

Augustine is both Western and African. So, when we encounter the contrast between Western and African, mutual exclusion is not assumed. In light of the above example and my desire toward the fullness of African identity, my account of African spirituality must find congruent relationship to other Western treatments of the "self," such as Charles Taylor's, whom we discuss below. What this book seeks to affirm is that communal spirituality and its links to Africa can no longer be treated as accidental and peripheral, especially in Christian theology. Let us now delve into this discussion.

As discussed above, in the West, especially from the time of the European Enlightenment, the self has been understood in ways lacking relationality. Such emphasis puts supreme value on the right of self-determination, self-achievement, and self-satisfaction. What is weak in this dimensional worldview, according to African American Christian spirituality, is the bonding of the person with the community. To illustrate what I mean, here is correspondence from a student at my African Christian Spirituality class at Duke University:

Dr. Battle
Yesterday as you spoke on African Christian spirituality that must be embodied, contrasting it with a Western disembodied spirituality, I thought about Jungian psychology, of which I know very, very little. (Want to do some reading there one day.)
(1) Is the Jungian idea of a collective consciousness a disembodied spirituality?
(2) Given that African spirituality is embodied, and that God(s) exist throughout creation, where was God in "the beginning" – before creation? Or am I not clearly separating "spirituality" (which seems to me to be practicing the presence of God) with "spirit being," that could be "seen" like the invisible man movies – if sprayed with powder, would be more visible?
(3) Is the ultimate end of the idea of physical embodiment of spirituality that God is within us collectively, and not also among us collectively? Are we talking about a shift in thought about the transcendence of God? Again, I realize that I could be confusing God as spirit with spirituality. And yet we as Christians are to exhibit the radiance/fragrance of God, are we not? That's pretty embodied.
(4) Are these questions tangential to your point and I am not even in the ballpark of what you're setting forth? Is it easier for you to see it, despite a westernized upbringing and education, because you've experienced Africa in more than a touristy way?
Thanks and have a great day!
Blessings.
Becky[21]

Becky's questions are in response to the difficult dilemma of the White Western mind trying to understand the African worldview. Some say that this dilemma between the individual and community is illustrated by Western narcissism. Once upon a time, a beauty named Narcissa committed the sin of being choosy. As punishment, the gods had her fall in love with her own reflection, thus wasting a perfectly good wardrobe, as she was the only one to admire it. A thousand years ago, when the earth was reassuringly flat and the universe revolved around it, the ordinary person had no last name, let alone any claim to individualism. The self was subordinated to church and king. Then came the Renaissance explosion of scientific discovery, humanist insight and, as both cause and effect, the rise of individual self-consciousness. All at once, it seemed, the Western self had replaced God at the center of earthly life. And perhaps more than any great war, invention, or feat of navigation, this upheaval marked the beginning of our modern era. There are now 20 times as many people in the world as there were in the year 1,000. Most have last names, and many of us have a personal identity or reasonable expectation of acquiring one.[22]

Counter to the narrative of Narcissa, Charles Taylor, the Canadian philosopher, and Stanley Hauerwas, the American theologian, help me articulate the need for the communal self not only in African cultures but also for Western ones. Taylor's method helps me keep my African claims modest and descriptions concrete. What I use Taylor to show are the strong connections between a sense of identity and a concept of relationality.[23] He describes how identity became separated from frameworks and sources as procedural reason and an Enlightenment view of nature marginalized sources like theological worldviews. For example, Taylor shows that when William James made theology, philosophy, and ecclesiology secondary, he never gave intelligibility to his discussion of the religious experiences of individuals.[24]

A similar point is made throughout Stanley Hauerwas's Gifford lectures. For Hauerwas, natural theology divorced from a full doctrine of God cannot help but distort the character of God and thus of the world in which we find ourselves. Taylor gets to this same point differently. Where Hauerwas criticizes the natural theologian from a narrative approach to theology, Taylor criticizes the natural theologian from a more philosophical approach. That is to say that while both Hauerwas and Taylor criticize those caught in extreme individualism, Hauerwas argues that they (like William James) need more of a narrative display of communal spiritual experiences so that individuality becomes intelligible.[25]

Taylor critiques the problematic of modern self-understanding and instead argues for the deeper human desire to be a part of a community.

He writes: "Talk about 'identity' in the modern sense would have been incomprehensible to our forebears of a couple of centuries ago."[26] Taylor's perception of forebears may be solely European. Desmond Tutu's claim in the epigraph to this chapter that we are all African by virtue of human origin in the continent of Africa expands the meaning of Taylor's insight to see a deeper communal self. This helps my argument for an African communal self that does not repeat the mistake of assuming the primacy of European forebears. Just as Taylor refutes reductive claims of knowing self-identity without reference to the context of "a self" in a good society, so too African Christian spirituality resists claims of knowing that do not take into account how true selfhood can only be known in communal settings. Perhaps this is why so many African societies were conducive to the "other" coming to them through colonialism and missionary movements.

Taylor uses the terms "self" and "identity," each of which has been defined in multiple ways by sociologists, psychologists, and theologians, as well as by philosophers. Like Taylor's, my work does not attempt to be a sociological or psychological analysis of the self. Although Taylor tends to slip into European causal explanations of the development of modern self-identity though his history of ideas, this is not his conscious intent. No doubt, the reader could say the same of my writing – that I slip into African American causal explanations, though this is not my intention. Thus, you, the reader, are extremely valuable in interpreting my intentions from my blatant mistakes. So, too, we must all find deeper appreciation of those traditions outside of our own. For example, African cultural worldviews could greatly enhance Taylor's argument for a more communal self.

Taylor organizes his book *Sources of the Self* in three parts. He begins by outlining his philosophical-moral framework. This framework puts moral evaluation at the center of human identity. Persons understand who they are in large measure by evaluations they make about what is good, and how that understanding will direct their lives. He ends the book with a twofold assessment of the modern situation: (1) a consensus on morals such as universal human rights, the demand to reduce suffering, the ideals of freedom, equality, and self-determination; and (2) a lack of moral sources or agreed upon constitutive goods to undergird that consensus. Taylor devotes the bulk of the book to a historical development of three themes that influence the modern identity: (1) a radical turn inward, (2) the affirmation of ordinary life, and (3) a view of nature as a source for moral evaluation and self-identity.[27]

In exploring these themes Taylor shows how the notion of self changes through Western history. In the modern era, identity and the good commingle, but major developments change the character of both. This occurred because of the idea that reason, as a proper procedure of thought, became unrelated to a reliable world of order. Reason itself was now divided, as practical reason became subject to one's personal world alone. In the modern era, communal truth, so necessary to earlier theistic views of the self, could no longer be assumed, but now had to be related to one's inward journey. It is important to realize that when Taylor discusses the modern era, he is attempting to describe both a consensus on morals and a poverty of moral sources.

Taylor outlines three options for developing moral sources for the modern ethic: (1) a no-longer-assumable theistic basis, (2) the power and dignity of the human person, and (3) expressivistic resonances within the self. He encourages the search for moral sources especially in the expressivist area, combining deep personal insight with visions of the good that may connect with outside sources. While we may lack a public consensus on moral sources, moral sources indexed to a deep personal vision could be convincing for some. At the same time, Taylor wonders if modern moral sources can be sustained without a vision of hope or a religious dimension, "a love of that which is incomparably higher than ourselves." Having jettisoned traditional theism as a moral source, moderns are left with disengaged reason alone to search for a metaethic.

Taylor thinks that the modern moral predicament is dangerous. He suggests that the gap between moral sources and their articulation must be closed in order to provide strong reason to be a good person. Part of our humanity, he argues, is denied by the modern tendency to reject and deny deep spiritual aspirations and intuitions. Without deeper moral sources, benevolence exacts a high cost, both in commitment and in a sense of guilt for not living up to its high ideals. On the other hand, linking an ethic of benevolence to religious or nationalistic ideology has led to destructiveness, not only in past centuries but also in our own. Taylor insists that avoiding this problem is impossible; we must risk one danger or the other, and neither choice is without cost. On the one side we risk stifling the human spirit, and on the other we risk the potential dangers of the power of religious faith.

Taylor's task is an important one for understanding my project to describe the context of the Black Church. He astutely follows the center of the discussion about identity and the good through its carriers in theology, philosophy, philosophy of science, literature, and the visual arts. Taylor also works against a sense of chaos and disintegration in modern life by finding moral threads and weaving them together. His book celebrates rather than laments modernity, offering creative insights into furthering the search for moral sources.

However, are there other sources that Taylor neglects? Any rendering of history is selective and gaps should be pardonable in such a vast work. But the absence of anything on African spirituality leaves the reader without connecting links between Europe and Africa. Taylor limits his apprehension of moral sources in another way by tracing the history of a monological self. Although he is aware that (to put it in his own terms) "the community is also constitutive of the individual" and that "common meanings are embedded in our institutions and practices,"[28] somehow in this work he loses touch with the communal dimensions of moral self-interpretation. Although he refers to communities and moral practices, the modern moral sources he points to focus on a disengaged individual self. This is where the Black Church could help him.

Taylor wants to utilize personal resonances of the modern self in order to get in touch with an outside order, since no public consensus on that order is possible. His hunch is that theism may be necessary for an adequate account of moral sources and this route leaves open that possibility. He stresses the individual self, although he insists that a disengaged self offers a wrong view of agency, and he agrees that the self is socially constituted. If Taylor understands this, it is puzzling that he focuses so exclusively on modern moral sources that arise from a disengaged view of the self. I suppose European history itself moves one in this direction. Or perhaps he is trying to utilize modern self-perceptions of a disengaged self as a point from which to develop new possibilities. In either case, African traditions that focus on communal understandings of the self might have opened Taylor to socially oriented moral sources. The narrative theology of African American slaves is an example.

If the dilemma of risk is as serious as Taylor claims it is (and I think it is), these additional modern moral sources must be seriously considered. An inability to articulate moral sources may result in a consensus sought through persuasion or even coercion in the absence of reasons related to moral sources. Disparate values are linked together, conflicts among goods concealed, and moral sources that could aid evaluation of those goods remain unexplored. Taylor's illumination of some of the history behind this moral predicament is a tremendous gift to those of us who would like to understand better the concept of self and the moral sources that make such identity more compelling for an understanding of the Black Church.

Dale Andrews' book *Practical Theology for Black Churches* provides the transition for how the above discussion on the problem of Western individualism affects the very identity of the Black Church.[29] For Andrews, the effect is a deepening chasm between the varying perspectives of

Black theology and Black churches for knowing the Black Church's identity. Like Taylor's display of the modern era's confusion of knowing what transcends the individual without a framework and moral sources, Andrews puts his finger on this same problem in the African American community. The resulting identity crisis looks like this. On one hand, Black theology sees only a refuge image in Black churches, in which escapism prevails. On the other hand, Andrews describes a critique of black theologians who root themselves within African American folk religion instead of faith identity. He argues that a faith identity paradigm of Black ecclesiology emerges historically as the churches interpreted their own formation and life. Hence, there should be no contradiction between pastoral and prophetic ministries in Black churches, since there is the crucial function in both ministries to maintain faith identity.

The work to resolve the identity crisis in the Black community is for Black churches to learn from black theologians to resist escapist spirituality that ends up being the effect of Western individualism. And the work of black theologians is to construct a better liberation or prophetic theology that is not detached from the spiritual life of diverse communities. I commend this work of Andrews as he tries to synthesize the prophetic and pastoral dimensions within the Black Church. His notion that the prophetic office of Black theology is now required to ground itself in practical theology is much needed. My criticism of Andrews, however, is in his simple conflation of Black churches into American individualism.

Andrews believes that as Black churches "focus preaching and pastoral ministries on personal salvation, inner spirituality, and religious piety, the ideology of American individualism invades their sense of corporate identity and communal responsibility. The irruption of corporate identity and communal responsibility only increases amid the struggles for socioeconomic advancement conditioned by individualism in a systemically racist society."[30] No doubt Andrews would have difficulty with my ubiquitous claims of communal spirituality within the Black Church (or even naming a single entity as Black Church instead of Black churches). For him, there is a great bifurcation of the Black community reflected in the emerging Black middle class, and Black urban youth or hip-hop culture. Andrews' genius is in his narrative of the complexity of the Black community in America. Such complexity of identity is especially reflected in the debates of the African American icon Bill Cosby, now known for caustic remarks against hip-hop culture. He lambasted the language of Black urban youth, decried their decorum, and panned their parenting. Needless to say, Cosby's remarks have created a stir in the United States, especially within the African American community. Were his words a legitimate reminder of a prophet's wake-up call, or a misguided attack, lacking pastoral sensitivity?[31] Black intellectual Michael Eric Dyson illustrates the other side of the debate by defending hip-hop culture.[32] Cosby's message has stirred up a whirlwind of controversy over social identity and responsibility in the African-American community. How does one get at defining such identity and responsibility?

Where I think Andrews could go deeper in his attempt at answering this question is through a questioning of his own social scientific foundation. For example, he uses Erik Erikson's life-stage analysis along with David Augsburger's quadrangular schema to form the foundation of his judgments for Black churches, Black theology, Black urban youth, and the Black middle class.[33] So, on the one hand, Andrews thinks that Black churches need the voice of prophetic inspiration to hold preaching and ministries of care accountable to the reflexive mandates of revelation;[34] on the other hand, he concludes that his "ultimate goal is to reground the liberation ethics of black theology in a prophetic role more convergent with religious folk life in African American churches."[35] He seems to assume that something nostalgic like a religious folk life may somehow be understood apart from an accompanying faith commitment. Andrews himself admits this as weakness: "What prevents this project from becoming an exercise in nostalgia?"[36] His final conclusion is helpful in validating his book as important: "I try . . . to clarify the critical impediments to mutual resolution of the dissension between black theology and black churches."[37] My only concern for Andrews is that such mutual resolution cannot occur without Taylor's pursuit of sources that sustain our self-understanding. In other words, there should be theological analysis of prayer and practice of God's presence by African American people if he is going to attempt to describe practical theology for Black churches. But there is no such display. His claim, however, that Black churches have been displaced as a central socializing force of Black humanity because of American individualism is a vital discussion that must take place (and not only for Black churches). It is to such a discussion that we now turn.

Notes

1   Desmond Tutu, *No Future without Forgiveness* (New York: Doubleday, 1999).
2   Non-African identity is a complicated description since most respected anthropologists conclude that all human beings have ancestry in Africa.

3 See Michael Battle, *Reconciliation: The Ubuntu Theology of Desmond Tutu* (Cleveland, OH: Pilgrim Press, 1997).

4 For a good treatment of the problem of Africanism, see Joseph Holloway, "The Origins of African-American Culture," in *Africanisms in American Culture* (Bloomington: Indiana University Press, 1990).

5 Wendy Haight, *African-American Children at Church: A Sociocultural Perspective* (Cambridge: Cambridge University Press, 2002), p. 4.

6 Howard Thurman, *Jesus and the Disinherited* (Boston, MA: Beacon Press, 1976). See also a more recent selection of Thurman's writings: Walter Earl Fluker et al. (eds.), *A Strange Freedom: The Best of Howard Thurman on Religious Experience and Public Life* (Boston, MA: Beacon Press, 1998).

7 For interesting work regarding the African Church for such connections, see Paul Gifford, *African Christianity: Its Public Role* (Bloomington: Indiana University Press, 1998). Gifford analyzes African Christianity against the backdrop of Africa's social ills.

8 See Battle, *Reconciliation*.

9 E. Franklin Frazier, *The Negro Church in America* (New York: Schocken Books, 1974), p. 9.

10 Not much research has been done on Christian influence coming from other African cultures, especially North Africa. See J. E. Merdinger, *Rome and the African Church in the Time of Augustine* (New Haven, CT: Yale University Press, 1997).

11 See my conversation with Philip Jenkins about his book *The Next Christendom: The Coming of Global Christianity* (New York: Oxford University Press, 2002): "Second Coming of Christianity" on National Public Radio, Wednesday, September 18, 2002 (The Connection). My comments can be accessed in the archives of www.theconnection.org.

12 It must be noted here that besides Jesus' movement, the nonviolent movement started in Africa under Mahatma Gandhi's leadership.

13 For a more thorough discussion, see my essay on "The Christian Life" in *Essentials of Christian Theology*, ed. William Placher (Louisville, KY: WJK publishers, 2003).

14 Denise Ackerman, "Becoming Fully Human: An Ethic of Relationship in Difference and Otherness," *Journal of Theology for Southern Africa* (November 1998).

15 Ibid.

16 See Michael Battle, *A Christian Spirituality of Nonviolence* (Macon, GA: Mercer University Press, 2004).

17 Historical works have been produced by Harold Lewis: see his *Yet with a Steady Beat* (Valley Forge, PA: Trinity International Press, 1996). Works of social ethics have been produced. See Robert Hood, *Begrimed and Black: Christian Traditions on Blacks and Blackness* (Minneapolis, MN: Fortress Press, 1994).

18 Examples of this are persistent struggles with patriarchy, sexism, classism, and treatment of open homosexuals.

19 I say "positive work" because a great deal of "negative work" to disassociate human identity from African identity has also been done. We will look at this problem later.

20 For more detailed discussion of this debate, see Donald Johanson, *Origins of Modern Humans: Multiregional or Out of Africa?* (American Institute of Biological Sciences, 2001); *Lucy: The Beginnings of Humankind* (New York: Simon and Schuster, 1981); *From Lucy to Language* (New York: Simon and Schuster, 1996). Johanson is best known for his discovery of "Lucy," a 3.2 million-year-old *Australopithecus afarensis* skeleton he found in 1974 in Ethiopia.

21 From Becky Huguley, November 15, 2000.

22 "The Me Millennium," *New York Times Magazine*, October 17, 1999.

23 See Charles Taylor, *Sources of the Self: The Making of the Modern Identity* (Cambridge, MA: Harvard University Press, 1989).

24 Charles Taylor, *Varieties of Religion Today: William James Revisited.* (Cambridge, MA: Harvard University Press, 2002).

25 See Stanley Hauerwas, *With the Grain of the Universe: The Church's Witness and Natural Theology* (Grand Rapids, MI: Brazos Press, 2001).

26 Taylor, *Sources of the Self*, p. 28.

27 I am indebted to Frances Adeney's review of Charles Taylor in *Theology Today* 48:2 (July 1991).

28 According to Taylor, persons can "only develop their characteristically human capacities in society. That claim is that living in society is a necessary condition of the development of rationality . . . or of becoming a moral agent . . . or of becoming a fully responsible, autonomous being." See Charles Taylor, *Atomism, Philosophy and the Human Sciences: Philosophical Papers 2*, (Cambridge: Cambridge University Press, 1985), pp. 190–1.

29 Dale Andrews, *Practical Theology for Black Churches: Bridging Black Theology and African American Folk Religion* (Louisville, KY: Westminster John Knox Press, 2002).

30 Ibid, p. 58.

31 Bill Cosby's actual interview was on National Public Radio, "Talk of the Nation," with Lynn Neary, July 7, 2004.

32 On National Public Radio's Tavis Smiley Show, May 27, 2004.

33 Andrews, *Practical Theology for Black Churches*, p. 72ff. See Erick Erikson, *Identity and the Life Cycle* (New York: W. W. Norton, 1980); David Augsburger, *Pastoral Counseling across Cultures* (Philadelphia, PA: Westminster Press, 1986).

34 Andrews, *Practical Theology for Black Churches*, p. 105.

35 Ibid, p. 107.

36 Ibid, p. 129.

37 Ibid.

Chapter 2

The Particularity of African American Spirituality

> God of Abraham, Isaac, and Ishmael,
> Deliver us from deceit.
> God of Noah, Canaan, and Ham,
> Deliver us from betrayal.
> God of Rachel and Leah,
> Deliver us from rivalry.
> Make more of us.
> Make peace of us.
> Make sense of us.
> We pray. Amen.
> **Michael Battle**[1]

So far, I have tried to reorient the reader toward the complexity of what is African Christian spirituality. Western awareness of African Christian spirituality is often ethnocentric at best. The Western lack of awareness was reinforced by the identification of Christianity with European culture. This lack of awareness, however, is changing today, as some white theologians even argue that they will only discover their identity by wrestling with the legitimacy of African identity.[2] Whites are struggling with the reality that the complexity of African Christian spirituality deepens when we turn explicitly toward the Black Church in America. Prominent Africans like Steven Biko have advocated that "Africans must inevitably exhibit African values and be truly African in style."[3] However, how does African identity mesh with African American identity? Answering this question has been an essential struggle in African and African American scholarship.[4] For example, Winthrop Hudson states: "In America blacks forged something new, the product of their own experience in a new land. An overemphasis on African survivals obscures their accomplishment."[5] Thankfully, there are other prominent African scholars like Peter Paris who understand the continuity between African and African American spirituality, particularly through the concepts of community. Paris states: "In our judgment, the clearest mark of continuity among Africans everywhere is their mutual belief in and communal devotion to a supreme transcendent being primordially related to them as creator and preserver."[6] In Paris's view, African continuity with African Americans occurred through North American slavery, in which slaves nurtured and promoted community in secret assemblies as they co-opted the religion of the slave owners. He concludes: "As a consequence, those secret meetings became the locus for the development of an alternative understanding of the Christian gospel."[7] This struggle for the maintenance of African identity produces a question for both white and black people in North America: is Africa really the home of African Americans? Or are they aliens in a strange land, dumped in America by the colonial ambitions of Europeans? Positively put, what does it mean to be a person whose ancestry and sociocultural heritage is African, but who lives in America, whose ancestors have lived in Africa, and who is committed to Africa? In short, what does it mean to be an African American Christian?

Implicit to my argument so far is that human identity emerges in the context of relationships with other persons. Ultimately, this means that African identity not only affected African Americans, but European Americans as well. Such an influence can be seen through unique forms of music (Jazz and the Blues) and other unconscious phenomena. After all, only after European Americans came in contact with African Americans did the desire for a suntan ever evolve. My argument in understanding spirituality is that through relationships with the "other," new identity emerges in relation to the new identifying distinctions, similarities, and connections. Thus, identity is never static: as an entity relates to another, the other is changed and (often unacknowledged) the initial person is changed as a result of changing the other. For African American identity, this process of change entails the creation of new ways of being that select and interpret data according to a specific set of symbols and values. This new way of being expresses past interpretations of African American identity and thus explicates and constitutes the continuity of African American identity through the process of relationality with both African and American cultures and identities. Here it may be added that although most African Americans are Christians, there is a significant segment of African Americans who adhere to Islam and an increasing movement to Buddhism. In short, African American communal experience constitutes the interaction of its members. Of course, the history of being African in America carries tragic connotations. This can be seen even today through the negative portrayal of African American identity in the media.

In *Watching Race* sociologist Herman Gray investigates Black representations in American culture – especially television – during the 1980s
and finds this period "rich with struggles, debates, and transformations
in race relations, electronic media, cultural politics and economic life."[8]
It is his contention that cultural politics are about power and cannot
be studied apart from issues of inequality in American society. Gray
provides astute commentary on the complexities of African American
identity by examining how the Reagan administration's policy makers
used the association of Black identity with welfare queens, drug dealers,
criminals, school dropouts, teenage pregnancy, and single-mother house-
holds to justify an assault upon the liberal welfare establishment. This
discourse maintained that the underclass's immorality and irrespons-
ibility were due to a lack of individual initiative encouraged by the
welfare state. This discourse could not be seen ostensibly as racist, as its
proponents could always point to the standards of individual Black
achievement exemplified in television's *The Cosby Show*. Nevertheless,
Gray argues that African American identity had to articulate a rejoinder
to the Reagan-constructed African American identity. The opportunity
for Blacks to develop this counter-hegemonic response was a product
of structural transformations within the television industry.

With the rise of media competition, the three major television networks
were experiencing a decline in viewers. In search of new markets, the
channels turned to African Americans, who – according to studies cited
by Gray – watch television at rates higher than the rest of the population. The cultural representation of Blacks on network television has
resulted in what Gray identifies as three major categories. He describes
older shows such as *Julia* and *Room 222* as assimilationist programs in
which individual Black characters are integrated into a White world.
Titles such as *Family Matters, Amen, Fresh Prince of Bel Air, What's
Happenin'*, and *Sanford & Son* are classified as pluralist or separate-
but-equal discourses. In these programs, predominantly Black casts
demonstrate that African American families have the same basic problems
as Whites. While critical of its failure to address issues of economic
inequality, Gray perceives *The Cosby Show* as a transitional program to
themes of diversity, with "the show's use of Blackness and African
American culture as a kind of emblematic code of difference."[9]

To support his argument that diverse themes analyzing and celebrating
the Black community's social and cultural traditions are more apparent
on network television, Gray devotes detailed treatment to *A Different
World* (a spin-off from *The Cosby Show* focusing on Black college life),
Frank's Place (a professor inherits a restaurant in New Orleans), *Roc*
(a working-class family deals with challenges like drug dealers), and

In Living Color (the popular Fox parody of inner-city life). However, the limitations on cultural representations are evident in the network cancellations of *Frank's Place* and *Roc*. And Gray has reservations about whether the satire of *In Living Color* tends to reinforce White stereotypes and trivialize issues of poverty. Gray writes: "*In Living Color*'s sketches about the Black poor more often than not seem [to leave] the Black poor exposed and positioned as television objects of middle-class amusement and fascination."[10]

Yet Gray refuses to leave his readers and the African American community with a pessimistic conclusion. He acknowledges that hegemonic political orders seek to celebrate individuality and incorporate notions of Blackness without disturbing the existing system. But he holds out hope for young Blacks who, through fashion, music, hairstyles, and dance, engage in a daily discourse with the commercial forces of America. Speaking of youth's efforts at cultural representation in the marketplace, Gray concludes: "That the dominant apparatus of representation (and circulation) has responded with attempts at incorporation, surveillance, marginalization and control tells us something about the power and potency of these expressions."[11] These experiences of being African American shape an identity that is used to describe what it means to be African American today. What led to these contemporary experiences of being black?

In the case of an African American identity, slavery and human oppression have often enshrined a worldview different from European Americans. This still surprises those liberals who feel that substantial progress has been made in race relations. As we saw with the O. J. Simpson trial and other high profile cases, however, there seems to be a separate American identity called African American. This gives us the insight that African American structures, experiences of life, and context are made available through interpreted narratives of growing up in a context of oppression. As Stanley Hauerwas's work teaches us, all communities have traditions, usually including a narrative, which define their morality, mission, and boundaries.[12] In the case of African Americans, such narratives explicate personal and communal identity through the process of surviving slavery in America.

By virtue of participating in a community that has survived slavery, African Americans are constantly reshaping Black identity. One of the methods of American slavery was to strip black people of human identity; terms like "chattel" and "property" were constantly used to identify African Americans. Among African American communities, however, counter-methods were used to maintain human identity. They were such that personal and communal identities interact with each other and define each other. These are important interactions developed by persons who know that without community there is no survival. Yet a person's identity is constituted by relationships with other people in the community. This is why the Black Church looks so different from other ways of practicing the church.

I argue here that African traditions of community survived slavery and even influenced how the Black Church negotiated new identity for Africans in America. My argument's assumption is this: African Americans always lived in an intersection of differing communities with differing traditions. These traditions interact with, contradict, modify, and coexist with each other. Thus personal identity, for African Americans, becomes the struggle to form a coherent and integrated self-understanding in the midst of pluralistic communities. As for the African American identity per se in the midst of these pluralisms, no one can develop such an identity without knowledge of the painful evolution of being black in America, which contains crises and dramatic changes. African American identity can be seen when there is a radical transformation in one dimension of identity (e.g., being African) that leads to substantial dissonance between other dimensions of identity (e.g., being American). The discovery or emergence of dissonance can lead to either a suppression of the dissonance (resulting in self-deception and delusion) or to a new integration that results in a transformation of personal identity through an experience of communal conversion. It is in this new integration that I argue the Black Church in America emerges.

Fundamental to the process of conversion is the creation of a new identity. This is why the conversion experience has played such a major role in the Black Church by creating new identity. African Americans have always sought new identity. This new identity, however, does not mean that African culture has not survived in African American identity. On the contrary, there could be no new identity without the interplay of the person and the community continually discovering a history together. At a communal level the relationships between ongoing historical narratives and spiritual behavior define the Black Christian community's character. African American Christian spirituality, therefore, may be the consequence of encountering a community with a constant, alternative narrative that leads to a radical reinterpretation of the old narrative, or the creation of a new one.

We have spoken about some of the contours of African American identity. How does one add the third description: Christian?

A Christian is a member of a community that defines her identity through baptism and by her confession of faith in the triune God (an image of God as community). But Christians, just like African Americans, are located in a nexus of competing and contradictory identities that form divergent communities (e.g., denominations). In the Black Church, for example, a person's confession of faith affirms that faithfulness to the triune God interacts with, qualifies, transforms, and at times contradicts other influences on one's identity. God's community of triune persons (Father, Son, and Holy Spirit) makes it possible for new identity to constantly emerge. Thus identity formation becomes a process of struggle and negotiation in an attempt to develop an integrated identity that reflects this ultimate loyalty to God's image of community. African American Christian spirituality practices and embodies the meaning and significance of a community's conversion process. How the African American community articulates its conversion, relates to, qualifies, transforms, and contradicts other dimensions of self and other is the focus of this book.

In a pluralistic context like the United States, my focus on African American Christian identity is thus central to the theological task.[13] The interaction of identity and spirituality becomes particularly intense in the context of an identity crisis in which there was at one time only a negative understanding of African American identity. The struggle over human identity for African American Christian spirituality has been to make such a dominant understanding of negative identity obsolete, through mutual and integral practices of becoming what is now understood as a Black Church. In other words, the Black Church did not emerge because it wanted to; instead, it emerged out of the necessity to redefine African American identity – especially in the peculiar context of European identities. It is in this peculiar context of Africans and Europeans that racism, as we know it today, emerged.

Racial identity became associated with the people of Europe, who sought to colonize the world. In particular, white bodies and white minds sought to dominate black bodies and white minds. Such domination became the fabric of the Enlightenment worldview that created theological and legal boundaries of inclusion and exclusion. Those "included" within the boundaries of power were based on the continuum of light and darkness or white and black. Those of whiter complexion were more likely to experience the benefits of power and privilege. In addition to the contrast of light and darkness, those who shared "European" bodily features formed concepts of beauty antithetical to African bodies. Thus, the relationship between European identity and African identity was defined in so competitive a fashion that Christian identity was affected. While Whites had a vocation to bring "Christian civilization" to the people of Africa, they also encountered the reciprocal response of a new Church formed on the basis of race – hence, the emergence of the Black Church in America.

Strangely enough, one's baptism and faith in God were now second-ary to racial identity. As we will later discuss, with the formation of the main expressions and denominations of the Black Church, such a double standard would not be tolerated. In the context of a society structured as a racial hierarchy, those who shared "European" features controlled political and economic power and used it for the benefit of their community. The Black Church emerged as one of the only communities Europeans could not control. And although Europeans enjoyed the benefits of creating their own worlds, it was soon realized through the emergence of the Black Church that some things could not be controlled.

White identity was shaped by identification with Europe and dis-tinction from Black and African identity, and yet the Black Church raises at least the subliminal understanding in America that there could no longer be complete separation between Black and White identity. In other words, if Christian identity is primary identity, there would have to be some theological justification for slavery and African oppression. This pattern of having to justify dominant White Christian identity merged around European colonies. For example, in South Africa, those of European ancestry even claimed African identity (the Afrikaners) as a theological duty of trusteeship. For many Afrikaners, they were no longer at home in Europe, to the extent that they constructed their own African identity – to redeem it in their image and likeness. This leads to an interesting question for African American identity – namely, to imagine the possibility of a white South African who expatriates to the Americas. Could they ever be described as an "African American"? A recent docu-mentary explains why such a new identity is hard to imagine.

In six hours of dramatic storytelling, *This Far By Faith: African American Spiritual Journeys* examines the African American religious experience from the arrival of the early African slaves, through the Civil War, reconstruction, Jim Crow, the Great Depression, the civil rights era, and into the twenty-first century.[14] The documentary describes how those traditions particular to being African American were sustained in the struggle for community, and how, out of that struggle, the very cultural, political, and social fabric of this nation was transformed. Each episode combines rich archival photography, compelling music, inspiring interviews, and vibrant recreations to shed light on a population that has confronted adversity and clung to hope since the first enslaved peoples arrived on American shores in 1526.

Similar to what this book seeks to do, *This Far by Faith* also explores how African American Christian spirituality sustained black people and empowered them to change a society. The first hour, "There Is a River," begins with the stories of Sojourner Truth and Denmark Vesey (d. 1822). Both were born into slavery, and both used Christian faith to shape their new identities; however, both used their voices in very different ways – one chooses retribution and the other restoration.

Hour two, "God Is a Negro," takes place after Emancipation (1863), when minister-turned-journalist Henry McNeal Turner (b. 1834) uses the Black Church to engage black people in the political realm. Denied access to the institutions of society at large, Black religious communities found and maintained their own grammar schools, universities, banks, insurance companies, printing presses, nursing homes, and hospitals.

Hour three, "Guide My Feet," begins in the Jim Crow era, when many African Americans migrated north. In Chicago, Thomas C. Dorsey, a pianist with Blues singer Ma Rainey, melds his religious faith with his musical talent to invent what we know as gospel music. In present-day San Francisco, the Reverend Cecil Williams takes his religious faith and his compassion for all people to the streets and builds the Glide Memorial United Methodist Church congregation.

Hour four, "Freedom Faith," follows the civil rights movement in the years after World War II. Ordinary people risk their lives to challenge the sin of racism in American culture and strive to fulfill the nation's promise of "liberty and justice for all." For many, the belief that God intended all people to be equal and free sustains them in the struggle.

Hour five, "Inheritors of the Faith," plots the growth of the Nation of Islam under the leadership of Elijah Muhammad. After his death, his son Warith departs from his father's teachings and leads the Nation of Islam towards a more orthodox practice of Islam.[15]

The series concludes with hour six, "Rise Up and Call Their Names," which chronicles a two-year interfaith, multiracial, multiethnic pilgrimage from Massachusetts to Africa – by way of Florida and the Caribbean – undertaken to heal the wounds of slavery. But is religious belief alone enough to hold the pilgrimage together? The ultimate answer to this question comes through the formation of human identity capable of being sustained through Christian spirituality.

This Far By Faith provides powerful imagery in which the assumed norm of White Christianity is discredited. It helps the viewer to conclude that domination of black people is neither a Christian civilizing policy nor a "good idea that went wrong." It has become normative to conclude that Black oppression is a crime against humanity; even further, it is blasphemy. Now Christian identity can be understood as primary and prior to European-constructed typologies of race.

An understanding of Christian identity must arise out of the narratives of Jesus suffering on the cross, which provokes an invitation to discover new meanings of human identity and community. The meaning of the cross is constituted by a twofold identification of God's community never giving up on human community. God identifies God's self with the crucified Jesus so that he is the special revelation of God in human history. Jesus' disciples are called to identify themselves with the crucified, and in so doing create different kinds of communities that resist violence in the same way that God does – never giving up on human community. Thus the cross defines both the Christian concept of God and the character of authentic Christian spirituality.[16] Authentic Christian identity and theology have a cruciform shape, but the meaning and significance of the cross must be reinterpreted in relation to particular contexts.[17] This brings me back to the interesting notion of a white African American. Such a notion presents the scandal of particularity.

The message of the cross is also a scandal of particularity. Its proclamation that the ultimate revelation of God in history has taken place in this event requires that all concepts of God and claims to revelation be evaluated by their conformity to it. It also means that it is the cross and not European culture that defines the particular character of Christian identity. The cross demonstrates God's abiding commitment to the world, to the point of entering into all its suffering and God-forsakenness in order to redeem it. It is thus a call to the community of disciples to become co-workers with God by taking up their crosses and following Christ into the world in order to transform and heal it. Thus the cross requires the Church to reject triumphalism and social dominance.

The cross bars any return to a pseudo-Christian hegemony in racist America. The cross declares that self-withdrawing and self-giving love is at the heart of the divine nature. Thus God's power is not power over creatures, to dominate and destroy them, but the power manifested in self-giving and self-withdrawing that empowers creatures to become what God intends them to be. To follow Christ is to reject the use of power to dominate and control and to commit oneself to reorganize identity in the service of empowering others. If the notion of a white African American expands vision beyond racist bifurcations, then such an identity may illustrate the transformation process within Christian spirituality. Hence the cross is a rejection of all hierarchies of power based on race, gender, or class. As Simon Maimela states: "God became a human being in the person of Jesus . . . in order to enter and expose the divine self to the full range of human misery; to suffer with humanity as one of the outcast, the poor, the rejected and oppressed, the humiliated and defenseless, the exploited and condemned."[18] The cross thus deepens our racial identity crisis by subverting the White and Black identification with Christianity. Significant facets of White identity, including those associated with Christianity, are implicit rejections of the cross. Yet the message of the cross also points the way forward to new identity beyond suffering for African Americans.

To lead us forward, African American identity may begin with roots in two places: the African and American worlds. The creation that grows from these roots, however, may exceed our imaginations. Thabo Mbeki, the president of South Africa, declared: "I am an African. I owe my being to the hills and the valleys, the mountains and the glades, the rivers, the deserts, the trees, the flowers, the seas and the ever-changing seasons that define the face of our native land."[19] To be African, however, does not always carry such a positive commitment. Africa is also characterized by illiteracy, starvation, and disease – situations exacerbated by oppressive governments, corruption, violence, and war. In the majority of cases it is women who are the most victimized, subjected to patriarchy and sexual exploitation. Those who take their identity from the cross are called to a costly commitment to the transformation of society through the empowerment and liberation of all human communities. This is why I think the Black Church gave such a powerful gift not only to the United States, but also to the world at large. The Black Church gave the world a civil rights movement in which the conviction was displayed that no human being can be neglected. Such a commitment entails solidarity with the victims in their struggles.

African American Christian identity ultimately leads to the conclusion that there are no "pure" monolithic cultures. Any culture comprises a mosaic of overlapping cultural entities that bear a "family resemblance" to each other.[20] They are always in a process of transformation shaped by interaction with other cultures, with new material conditions and transformations in the natural environment. All cultures are characterized by change, ambiguity, relativism, and syncretism. African cultures have interacted with and been modified by other African cultures, Arabic cultures, and American and European cultures. Elements from these cultures have been assimilated and transformed as African people negotiated an authentic African lifestyle. The interaction between the cultures of Africa and Europe contributes to a process of convergence toward a new cultural matrix which "will not necessarily be all black; but it will be African."[21] Convergence does not mean assimilation; it should include variety and particularity – again, African American identity may be rooted in particular ways, but that does not mean we have seen its final shape. Our danger is that a new sociocultural identity will be shaped by the negative rather than the positive dynamics of both cultures. This is why Christian faith must support cultures, rather than condone racist worldviews.

African American Christians must uncover the heritage of the early North African Church, Coptic Christianity, Nubian Christianity, and Ethiopian Christianity.[22] Despite its richness, this heritage has been ignored. The legacy of these ancient practices of African Christian spirituality provides significant resources for the ongoing development of an African American Christian identity. On the one hand, the life of African Christianity, with its deep awareness of relationality and religious community, facilitates creative theological reflection and should make a profound contribution to the formation of an African American Christian identity. Such creativity is extremely important in the ongoing formation of the Black Church. On the other hand, the presence of African American theologians within the African Church provides an internal critique and comment that can contribute to the flowering of African theology. Such relationality, however, must never become the assertion of the dominance of Western ways of being over African ways. It must arise out of a deep rootedness in the African context, a careful and appreciative listening to the voice of African Christians, and a commitment to the reign of God in all of the world.

In this manner African American theologians will continue to have a significant role in the development of African theology. Because of the dominance of the publishing industry in the so-called developed world, the production of theological and spiritual books and media in Europe and North America continues to dominate the global Church, despite the shift in the numerical center of Christianity to the Southern hemisphere, with a particular concentration in Africa. This is so important a shift that Andrew Walls proposes that "what sort of theology is most characteristic of the Christianity of the twenty-first century may well depend on what has happened in the minds of African Christians."[23] As African American spirituality embraces a truly kenotic vocation in the service of the African Church, then it can provide a model for the rest of the world and for the global Church. This model demonstrates how to listen to the voice of the Church of the South without neglecting the heritage of the Church of the North. It will model how the theology of the North can be enriched and corrected and become mutual with the theology of Africa.[24] In pursuing this vocation African American theologians must resist the temptation to become the spokespersons for all that is African. Inevitably, by doing so, African American theologians obfuscate the particularity of what is in fact spirituality. I will explain this through the examples of Carlyle Stewart and Peter Paris's work on African spirituality.

Invariably, believes Carlyle Stewart in his book *Soul Survivors*, all discussions about Black freedom in America focus on emancipation from external, political, and social power structures. Seldom does analysis underscore models of spiritual freedom that prevent complete enslavement of black people by whites. Stewart concludes: "It is precisely this emphasis on the internal spiritual aspects of liberation through the practice of spirituality and the creation of black culture that makes the African American paradigm of freedom unique."[25] Herein is the power and curse of Stewart's work. He wonderfully points out the tendency to polarize Black identity in political and sociological discourse, but he never fully displays African American spirituality as its own genre apart from what normally may be called African American culture. For example, he only discusses prayer briefly at the end of his book.[26] Instead, what appears often is a discussion of spirituality and Black culture which makes spirituality synonymous with culture, with little characterization of spirituality as somehow different from culture.

From my research, this is a common problem in the dearth of material on African Christian spirituality. Even Peter Paris's *Spirituality of African Peoples* minimizes his focus on spirituality per se, as he discusses the term in only two places.[27] Despite these problems of shying away from "spirituality," Stewart does mention love, mercy, and nonviolence as characteristics of African American spirituality. Paris focuses on what looks more like moral virtues (beneficence, forbearance, practical wisdom, improvisation, forgiveness, justice, and ethics). By no means are these concepts somehow separate for Christian spirituality. The problem is in how they are seldom displayed as spiritual realities. Moral characterizations help to relieve some of burden of displaying African American Christian spirituality, but they lack essential focus on what is African American Christian spirituality if they fail to show the interdependence of the Christian life.

I still recommend Stewart's work because it attempts an African American spirituality that subverts many erroneous spiritualities in American societies that focus solely on individualistic constructs of existence. I also highly recommend Paris's work, as he has inspired my own focus on seeing African American Christian spirituality as essentially a communal enterprise. African American spirituality helps us see that "the individual is a community unto himself or herself but also participates in a larger community of other selves."[28] Where I seek to contribute to this emerging discourse of African American spirituality is in looking more closely at the additional qualification of what is "Christian." Therefore, African American Christian spirituality is what this book invites the reader to explore. My argument here is that there really are no other published works that hold in tension Christian spirituality and African American spirituality. I return to Stewart's work to explain.

In the first part of *Soul Survivors*, Stewart explores the sources of African and African American spirituality and affirms their importance in informing an idea of human freedom. He proceeds to name important sources of African American spirituality, in particular, African culture and the Bible. Within his methodology, Stewart cannot conceive of Black spirituality without understanding the influence of Black culture on spirituality's nuances and narratives, texts and subtexts. He does admit, however, that "the Bible has had a central role in preventing black people from being completely domesticated and dominated by slave masters, oppressors, and other adversaries."[29] So Black culture and the Bible need not be mutually exclusive in how they positively define African American spirituality.

The primary thought of Stewart's work is that African American spirituality forms soul survivors in a seedbed of human freedom. He concludes that African American spirituality is the practice of freedom, both inward and outward, striving particularly in an American context. Interestingly, African American spirituality is a unique model of human freedom because its very essence and nature are made in the social, political, and ontological struggle to be Black in America. Hence, Stewart's work is worthwhile in spirituality discourse because the efficacy of the African American paradigm of freedom lies in its capacity to encourage black people to develop a culture of spirituality in which the freedom to create is intimately bound to the freedom to be. "By knowing that I am a child of God, a person of worth and dignity by virtue of my practice of spirituality, there is nothing my adversaries can do to instill fear and intimidation in me as a person."[30]

For Stewart, African American spirituality is the practice of freedom to create a viable Black spirituality, which both embraces and transcends Anglo society. Both movements of embrace and transcendence are needed to create a context for the emergence of African American culture. The essence of freedom, therefore, is not as socially, materially, and politically necessitated as it is in other paradigms, but it is spiritually and culturally determined. The uniqueness of the African American paradigm lies precisely in the fact that freedom is not simply an external, material goal, but equally a spiritual and cultural practice that spawns the creative implementation of freedom. "At the heart of black spirituality then is the concept of human transformation."[31]

The burden on Stewart is to deliver a particular spirituality that is African American and yet is open to future possibilities of identity. In other words, it is difficult to name African American spirituality that is both particular and receptive to others. To illustrate this dilemma, Stewart states: "The varieties of spiritual expression found in ritual ceremonies and religious precepts may be very different between black Baptists and black Episcopalians. While the religion of these two groups has a unified basis – belief in Christ – the idioms of spirituality in worship and life are largely heterogeneous."[32] Here we see the additional complexity of how otherness is also contained in what is conceived as the particular identity. This is where Christian spirituality could be helpful to Stewart, because of the long struggles of the Church to make sense of the one and the many. For some reason, he has no time to narrate such a struggle in the Church.

One value of Stewart's work, however, is in how he distinguishes and relates African experience with African American experience. Central to an African cosmology is spiritual reality, not the material. Therefore, *a priori* spiritual reality differs from *a priori* Western material reality. In other words, when an African sees an eagle, what is seen is the miracle of life as opposed to death, but a Western person sees the species and genus of a scientifically defined animal called an eagle. Stewart states: "In European thought, ideas may convey passion, but in African thought, passion more adequately expresses the force of ideas."[33] As a result of this African sensibility of passion and freedom, Stewart describes African cosmology as "cosmic spirituality," which permeates the varieties of African religious beliefs and practices. This cosmological basis of African spirituality includes the process, power, and substance of God's creative capacities in the universe, meaning that God's creativity extends and translates into the African culture and life. The freedom of God to be God and to create, infuse, and transform reality is God's image bestowed to humankind.

Stewart's display of African cosmology never fully exposes what African spirituality entails per se; nor does he relate such a spirituality that is common to the diversity of the Black Church (e.g., the Black Baptist and Black Episcopalian). As Gayraud Wilmore believes, the Black Church has the awareness in many denominations that the ordering identity in America is being black first.[34] Instead of addressing this complexity, Stewart too quickly states: "This cosmology holds that God, the Divine Spirit, or Nature is the absolute hegemonic supreme, primordial reality, which orchestrates, governs, empowers, transforms, and infuses creation with a creative soul force that is the basis and power of life."[35] Is this cosmology displayed in the same way for Black Baptists and South African Anglicans, as well as Black Episcopalians? In other words, is the creative expression of the African Methodist Episcopal Church a little more creative, even more spontaneous, than the Black Episcopal Church?

Without addressing these complexities, Stewart turns to the second part of his book and the dynamic of African American spirituality and its influence on the praxis of Black freedom. His contention is that African American spirituality not only shapes consciousness, beliefs, realities, and expectations of Black life in America, but as ritual practice it also lends itself to the formation of a living Black cultural archive and hermeneutic, which reinforces the positive values and identity formation of African American people. These functions have historical and contemporary value. They not only helped black slaves transcend the perils of slavery, but also continue to help black people face current adversities in the present context of the American experience. Stewart's onus, however, is in the move from a definition of African spirituality to African American spirituality. This is difficult because the common assumption is that "African" and "African American" are one identity, even one culture. Stewart rightly points out that black scholars must seriously explore the positive impact of American constitutional culture on the formation of Black consciousness, culture, and spirituality. This is the extent of his solution. It is not enough, however, to wonder about the positive impact of American constitutional culture on Black experience.

It is highly problematic in understanding how European American experience relates to African American experience. Stewart names part of the problem as the desire of black scholars to retrieve their African past and the nationalistic impulse to sever any hints of cultural ties to people of Anglo descent. This desire among black scholars is due to the contradictions of American constitutional culture, in that some of the original framers of the US Constitution were slaveholders who viewed blacks as inferior and exploited and dehumanized them for economic reasons. Rather than embrace the cultural influences of whites who have historically oppressed blacks, it is more appropriate for many black scholars to negate them entirely, even if that negation mischaracterizes reality. It is more fitting to denounce white oppressors entirely than to claim any aspect of their culture as a positive factor in the formation of the African American experience. Stewart states: "We curiously adopt either/or orientations despite our co-dependency as whites and blacks."[36] The problem remains for Stewart to name what is European spirituality or White spirituality as opposed to African or African American spirituality. In doing so, he would provide better definition to the term *spirituality*.

The complexity of White and Black American spiritualities creating each other leads Stewart to discuss the difficulty of Black identity, especially W. E. B. Dubois' dilemma of double consciousness or ambivalence about self (i.e., self as seen through the eyes of white people and self as seen through black life). Instead of psychosis, Stewart advocates a survival spirituality which creates a "kind of psychological dexterity" in

African American people.[37] Black people in America have had to use spirituality as a means of self-actualization and survival. They could not have survived without it in a world that continually tries to destroy their personhood, power, and inherent self-worth. Stewart states: "Black people have either chosen to look at themselves through the eyes of their white slave masters and oppressors, which brings self-devaluation and contempt, or through the eyes of God, which brings affirmation and self-aggrandizement."[38] Herein, Stewart's best definition of African American spirituality is the ability to see with feeling in the midst of chaos, hardship, and persecution, which is "the capacity to transcend the devastation of the environment and the ultimate expression of humanity."[39] For Stewart, Black spirituality is the unique freedom to create culture in response to racism and oppression.

In evaluating Stewart's work, I should remind the reader that I am in fact a black, Episcopal (Anglican) priest. It is within this context that I desire more clarification of terms from Stewart. For example, he states: "Key terms here are *spirit*, which is a dynamic, amorphous, life-giving, and sustaining force, and *love*, which is the assurance that one is needed, nurtured, and valued by others."[40] But throughout Stewart's work the term "soul" seems synonymous with spirit. He even asserts: "Soul force is synonymous with black life, culture, and spirituality."[41] If soul is the more central defining feature of the African American practice of God's presence, perhaps Stewart would be better off defining a concept I coin as *soulity*. I say this because Stewart seems to encompass spirituality within his concept of soul. What does Stewart mean by soul? First, he states: "Soul is identified with black feeling, passion, and compassion, and it allows black people to express themselves from their true spiritual center. While this is true, in a larger sense this soul functions pragmatically to shape an alternative identity and consciousness by ordering the uncertainties and complexities of life into a viable, manageable framework for black existence."[42] Secondly, he concludes: "The soul is the cosmic, spiritual, ontological, epistemological center of African American existence."[43]

Stewart is extremely helpful in understanding African spirituality when he pushes us to see that inherent in the African American soul is the process of transformation which constantly invites us to live into the image of God. This transformation is the manifestation of the Black cultural soul which can be seen in the creation of spirituals, the Blues, Jazz, sport, Rappin', Signifyin', Testifyin', Call and Response, Praising, Partying, Celebrating, Improvisation, Spontaneity, literature, humor, art, and dance. Therefore, African American soulity is cataphatic, because in the African American experience the constant struggle is to turn negative image into positive image. This is why I think Stewart should not shy away from Christian spirituality per se, because the mystical traditions of cataphatic and apophatic practices can accentuate his points.

Perhaps an exposition of soulity for black people is more appropriate for Stewart's venture, which displays the transformation of African American culture alongside other cultures. Christian spirituality claims that primary identity formation is given through the image of God. And the resulting Christian practices through history such as forgiveness, prayer, reconciliation, resistance to evil, and nonviolence are not threats to the particularity of African American spirituality. Indeed, such practices help us make better sense of African American spirituality. Christian spirituality provides practices for us not just to focus on survival, but on flourishing. This seems to be Stewart's aim as well, but he leaves the reader conflicted between transformation and survival. As Stewart believes, the soul is not only expressive but also transformative – it centers Black life in existential reality and shapes adversarial forces into liturgies for Black survival. Soulity is the African American resiliency to transform negativity into creativity. In the American context, Stewart thinks, "no other persons besides Native Americans have been as desecrated, vilified, and dehumanized as African Americans, but the practice of spirituality and faith has remarkably prevented them from harboring a lingering hatred for their tormentors."[44]

Stewart's *Soul Survivors* is worth studying because he is one of the few black spiritual writers who work from the sobriety of being black while simultaneously articulating how blackness is not the primary adjudicating feature of identity. God's image is. Stewart explains when he states that the term "black" "simply means that, contrary to popular belief, such problems are not the predominant realities shaping the consciousness and behavior of African Americans. African Americans are not primarily shaped by their problems, nor do those difficulties define their humanity. The fundamental influence is a soul force spirituality that shapes order out of chaos and disillusionment."[45] I want to go further than Stewart, however. I argue that the primary description of African American Christian spirituality is known in the dynamic context of the Black Church in America.

How we come to understand the Black Church will help us make sense of the dilemma between particularity and openness to otherness. The Black Church has struggled not just to survive for itself (which Stewart wants us to believe); rather, it has practiced a Christian spirituality in which God's image of community must remain primary. Such a practice carries with it great costs and burdens, especially when faced with the affliction of American slavery. It would be natural to form a

Black Church focused primarily on survival and defense. But what was formed in America is a Black Church that practiced the extraordinary means of nonviolence, forgiveness, prayer, and reconciliation. Such practices have not been for the Black Church alone, but have been made available to the whole world.

Notes

1   Michael Battle, "A Petition," in Malcolm Boyd and Chester Talton, eds., *Race and Prayer: Collected Voices, Many Dreams* (Harrisburg, PA: Morehouse Publishing, 2003), p. 97.
2   See David N. Field, "On being a Euro-African Theologian: Identity and Vocation in Post-Apartheid South Africa," *Journal of Theology for Southern Africa* 102 (November 1998).
3   Steven Biko, *I Write What I Like* (London: Heinemann, 1978), p. 24.
4   For example, the prominent African American sociologist E. Franklin Frazier argued that no significant remnant of African culture survived the experience of slavery. See Frazier, *The Negro Family in the United States* (Chicago: University of Chicago Press, 1939).
5   Winthrop Hudson, "The American Context as an Area of Research in Black Church Studies," *Church History* 52 (1983), p. 170.
6   Peter Paris, *The Spirituality of African Peoples: The Search for a Common Moral Discourse* (Minneapolis, MN: Fortress Press, 1995), p. 39.
7   Ibid.
8   Herman Gray, *Watching Race: Television and the Struggle for Blackness* (Minneapolis, MN: University of Minnesota Press, 1995), p. 2.
9   Ibid, p. 89.
10   Ibid, p. 144.
11   Ibid, p. 161.
12   Stanley Hauerwas, *A Community of Character* (South Bend, IN: Notre Dame Press).
13   See Kwame Bediako, *Theology and Identity: The Impact of Culture upon Christian Thought in the Second Century and in Modern Africa* (Oxford: Regnum, 1992); Tinyiko S. Maluleke, "In Search of the True Character of African Christian Identity," *Missionalia* 25 (1997), pp. 210–19; George W. Stroup, *The Promise of Narrative Theology: Recovering the Gospel in the Church* (Atlanta, GA: John Knox Press, 1981).
14   *This Far By Faith* was conceptualized by legendary filmmaker Henry Hampton. Hampton's contributions to television include *America's War On Poverty* and the Peabody and Emmy Award-winning *Eyes on the Prize* and *American Experience* "Malcolm X: Make It Plain." Before his death in 1998, Hampton wrote that it was his dream to celebrate the sweep and range of African American religious experience "in the context of the nation's struggle to realize the goals of democracy and humanity, the heart

and soul of America itself: who we are as a nation, what we believe as a people, and what we consider worth dying – and living – for."

15 For a more detailed discussion of Islam among African Americans, see C. Eric Lincoln, *The Black Muslims in America*, 3rd edn. (Grand Rapids, MI: Eerdmans, 1994); Richard Brent Turner, *Islam in the African American Experience* (Bloomington: Indiana University Press, 1997).

16 For this theme of the cross leading to community, see Rowan Williams, *The Wound of Knowledge: Christian Spirituality from the New Testament to St. John of the Cross* (Boston, MA: Cowley, 1991); Jürgen Moltmann, *The Crucified God: The Cross of Christ as the Foundation and Criticism of Christian Theology* (London: SCM Press, 1974), pp. 18–25.

17 See Douglas Hall's distinction between contextual "theology of the cross" and an a-contextual "ideology of the cross" in *Thinking the Faith: Christian Theology in a North American Context* (Philadelphia, PA: Fortress Press, 1991), p. 25, and *Professing the Faith: Christian Theology in a North American Context* (Minneapolis, MN: Fortress Press, 1993), pp. 127–9.

18 Simon Maimela, *Proclaim Freedom to My People: Essays on Religion and Politics* (Johannesburg: Skotaville, 1987), p. 15.

19 Thabo Mbeki, "Statement of Deputy President Thabo Mbeki, on behalf of the African National Congress, on the occasion of the adoption by the Constitutional Assembly of 'The Republic of South Africa Constitution Bill 1996,'" Cape Town, May, 8, 1996.

20 Family resemblances are "a complicated network of similarities overlapping and criss-crossing: sometimes overall similarity, sometimes similarities in detail." See Ludwig Wittgenstein, *Philosophical Investigations* (Oxford: Blackwell, 1967), p. 32.

21 Albert Luthuli, *Let My People Go: An Autobiography* (Glasgow: Collins, 1982), p. 206.

22 See Bediako, *Theology and Identity*; John de Gruchy, "From Cairo to the Cape: The Significance of Coptic Orthodoxy for African Christianity," *Journal of Theology for Southern Africa* 99 (1997), pp. 24–39.

23 Andrew Walls, "Towards an Understanding of Africa's Place in Christian History," in J. S. Pobee, ed., *Religion in a Pluralist Society: Essays Presented to C. G. Baeta* (Leiden: E. J. Brill, 1976), p. 183. See also Philip Jenkins, *The Next Christendom: The Coming of Global Christianity* (New York: Oxford University Press, 2002); Kwame Bediako, "Five Theses on the Significance of Modern African Christianity: A Manifesto," *Transformation: An International Journal in Evangelical Social Ethics* 13 (1996), pp. 20–4.

24 See, for example, Neville Richardson, "Can Christian Ethics Find Its Way and Itself in Africa?" *Journal of Theology for Southern Africa* 95 (1996), pp. 37–54; Peter Fulljames, *God and Creation in Intercultural Perspective: Dialogue between the Theologies of Barth, Dickson, Pobee, Nyamiti and Pannenberg* (Frankfurt am Main: Peter Lang, 1993).

25 C. Fielding Stewart, III, *Soul Survivors: An African American Spirituality* (Louisville, KY: Westminister John Knox Press, 1997), p. 23.

26   Ibid, pp. 115–18.
27   Peter Paris, *The Spirituality of African Peoples: The Search for a Common Moral Discourse* (Minneapolis, MN: Fortress Press, 1995), pp. 22, 35, 42. Paris defines spirituality as "the animating and integrative power that constitutes the principal frame of meaning for individual and collective experiences" (p. 22).
28   Stewart, *Soul Survivors*, p. 53.
29   Ibid, p. 10.
30   Ibid, p. 33.
31   Ibid, p. 21.
32   Ibid, p. 8.
33   Ibid, p. 50.
34   Gayraud Wilmore, *Black and Presbyterian: The Heritage and the Hope* (Philadelphia, PA: Geneva Press, 1983).
35   Stewart, *Soul Survivors*, p. 8.
36   Ibid, p. 18.
37   Ibid, p. 14.
38   Ibid, p. 17.
39   Ibid, p. 47.
40   Ibid, p. 43.
41   Ibid, p. 79.
42   Ibid, p. 12.
43   Ibid, p. 48.
44   Ibid, p. 28.
45   Ibid, p. 40.

Chapter 3
The Black Church in the Shadow of Slavery

They began to sell off the old slaves first, as rubbish. One very old man went for one dollar; the old cook sold for seventeen dollars. The prices varied from that to 1,600 dollars, which was the price of a young man who was a carpenter.

John S. Jacobs[1]

As a result of slavery the Black Church has come to see itself as falling in the "Christ against culture" category, to use the typology of H. Richard Niebuhr.[2] This means that those who called themselves the Black Church for the most part knew themselves as such because of the oppressive history of slavery in North America. Sociologically, identity is normally established between the "us" against "them" opposition. The image here is of a huddled community embraced to withstand the onslaught of many enemies. But this categorization of the Black Church is limiting and inexact. And I think it is what makes many of us think that Christian spirituality and the Black Church cannot go together.

Spiritual traditions such as contemplative prayer and spiritual direction are seldom associated with the Black Church because of the particular history of the Black Church's struggle against White hegemonic privilege. African Americans have had little opportunity to describe themselves in terms of Christian spirituality. We have usually been described by white European writers. If there were any associations of spirituality, Black churches were primarily about cathartic or emotional spirituality in which to appropriate issues like slavery and racism. Without a common enemy like racism, the Black Church often seems unintelligible, especially with regard to any notion of spirituality and spiritual practices. Some disagree with this analysis and believe the Black Church is not necessarily caught in a dialectic in which its identity is formed only counter to something else. As I argued in chapter 2, however, unless we can name Christian spiritual practices that create a primary identity for many particularities, we usually end up with survivalistic theologies. My goal in trying to articulate a discourse of Christian spirituality is to say that survival is not enough, but truer community is.

The nature of the Black Church is complex and diverse, comprised of African Christian spirituality that emphasizes communal practices of relationality. The Black Church is a fellowship of churches which, accepting God's triune image, is united in believing and practicing a communal spirituality. The term "Church" has a double sense: organized Christianity, the sum of all the separate Christian individuals; or the ecclesiastical authorities and official organs of the different denominations. I am operating here on the former sense of the Church as an organization of Christian persons. The Church for African Americans speaks for a constituency of different continents, races, and nationalities. Such a Church asserts the essential dignity of humanity as the object of a divine creating and redeeming love.

The gift that the Black Church gives to the world is in its belief and practice that when any person is mistreated or disadvantaged, an incident of supreme importance has occurred, and something sacred violated. This becomes the incredible achievement of the Black Church: to make seamless human incorporation into the pursuit of God's peace and justice demonstrated in the life, death, and resurrection of Jesus. In addition, and counter to the rhetoric of Church against culture, the Black Church helps us see that all civic responsibilities are an obligation of Christian service, not just to national political systems but also international communities. Such attention to the national and the international becomes the fruit of the struggle of knowing the difference between African and African American. The Black Church reminds the world about many of God's children, whom many are inclined to forget. And so practices from the time of slavery have been put in place to find homes for refugees, empower civil rights for victims, and restore through worship and prayer the image of God among all persons. All of this becomes an awareness of human solidarity among African American spirituality. Such spirituality belongs to the Black Church, which is not for itself, but for the other. The Black Church challenges the absolute nature of individual or competing spiritualities that imply irreconcilable rivalries. The greatest achievement of the Black Church is the awareness, in the midst of affliction and slavery, that the world is not absurd – that the harmony of divine and human work, though seemingly meaningless at times, can restore even the cruelest individual to community.

How one understands the "Black" Church has great implications for how one understands the concept of self. In order to justify slavery, whites used scripture to argue against truer communal spirituality. For example, passages of scripture such as the curse of Ham were used to designate false and privileged communities. Whites did this by advocating for the African communal curse:

Noah was the first tiller of the soil. He planted a vineyard; and he drank of the wine, and became drunk, and lay uncovered in his tent. And Ham, the father of Canaan, saw the nakedness of his father, and told his two brothers outside ... When Noah awoke from his wine and knew what his youngest son had done to him, he said, "Cursed be Canaan; a slave of slaves shall he be to his brothers." (Genesis 9:20–22, 24–25)

The beauty of the Black Church can be seen in the way it did not respond by perpetuating its own biblical texts and hermeneutics to curse others. Instead, African American Christian spirituality constructs a new politics of self based on new identity in Christ.

In Christ, African Americans join the people of God to form a new humanity. Such a new formation can be seen biblically, as Christ makes disparate identities coherent:

But now in Christ Jesus you who once were far off have been brought near by the blood of Christ. For he is our peace; in his flesh he has made both groups into one and has broken down the dividing wall, that is, the hostility between us ... So then you are no longer strangers and aliens, but you are citizens with the saints and also members of the household of God. (Ephesians 2:13–14, 19)

In Christ there is an invitation to new humanity which challenges the way individuals think about self over and against others; Christ moves individuals to be facilitators of whole and diverse communities (Matthew 28:19).

Instead of the Western preoccupation with personal salvation (which perpetuates erroneous readings of the Bible), the Black Church provides the focus of communal salvation in which Christ includes all persons, Jews and Gentiles. Such communal salvation can be seen in the Book of Acts, where persons receive God's Spirit based on Jewish hope, but which is expansive enough to include those of gentile background. For example, an Ethiopian eunuch receives salvation on behalf of his people (Acts 4:8). And in Acts 10, Peter has to relearn the meaning of messianic salvation for his people alone by breaking cultural taboos that redefine his identity in relationship to strangers and aliens. From such biblical narratives those in the Black Church have learned like Peter to be open to a new paradigm of humanity beyond racial identity. This is the great power of the Black Church in America: it sees beyond itself and has practiced a communal spirituality which invites the possibility of disparate identities to find common ground. There is no greater context in which to see this than the Black Church's ordeal with slavery.

The Scourge of Slavery

After 1702 the Society for the Propagation of the Gospel in Foreign Parts carried forward the early Protestant effort to convert slaves. This movement coming out of the Church of England (later to be known as the Anglican Church) did not oppose slavery, many of its ministers being slaveholders. Where it met resistance was in teaching slaves to read and write, which could threaten the system of slavery and subjugation. This ambivalence toward Christian salvation as truly mutual among African slaves in colonial America meant that the colonies would not experience mass conversion of Africans in the American Church until the first Great Awakening period beginning in the 1730s, sparked by Jonathan Edwards and other early evangelists.

The Anglican Archbishop of Canterbury, Rowan Williams, on a visit to a former center of the West African slave trade, spoke of the continuing challenge of "overcoming slavery in old and new forms." In remarks delivered after receiving the honorary freedom of Freetown in Sierra Leone, he said:

> Even today we are not free from the slavery of destructive patterns of human behavior. There is the slavery of poverty, the slavery of injustice, the slavery of greed – both sexual and financial – the slavery caused by the HIV/AIDS pandemic, and the slavery of violence in which bitterness and revenge can be guaranteed to keep people captive forever, unless delivered by truth and reconciliation. We must go on identifying and overcoming every kind of slavery we encounter in our society. In overcoming slaveries we learn to recognize one another as human and, in this way, we learn to see in each other the face of Christ.[3]

Williams also visited the Castle of Elmina, the center of the international slave trade which sent countless thousands of Africans to a life of slavery. Williams alluded to the anti-slavery work of William Wilberforce: "I was asked some years ago who I thought had been the greatest Briton of the last 1,000 years. With all due respect to Winston Churchill and William Shakespeare, my answer was someone whom the Church will be celebrating this coming Wednesday. William Wilberforce did more to change the course of human history in his work to abolish slavery than can easily be told."[4]

Williams helps us see the tragic circumstances of slavery when he places the greatest heroism in the context of those who challenged the worldviews that condoned slavery. This was heroic because there were strong socialization forces at work to explain and normalize African slavery as necessary, if not even God ordained. To understand the Black Church is to understand the reality that America started with slavery as a normality. Scholars differ on the number of African people lost during the Atlantic slave trade, but the average numbers mentioned are in the millions.[5] The actual process of enslavement of African people was brutal. They were captured, tied together, and marched to the coast. This brutality was relativized by White European justifications of slavery.

The first Africans to arrive in an English colony came ashore in 1619 in Jamestown, Virginia, from Dutch transport. With the growth in population of African slaves in North America during the 1600s there also came an ideology and legal system designed to tightly control the behavior of slaves. The North Atlantic slave trade officially ended around 1808, but continued despite being illegal by means of the "black market" through to 1818. By 1860 there were approximately 4.5 million slaves. Because of these numbers of slaves, the acceptance of Africans as inferior relativized moral standards in such a way that black people were treated more like animals. This history of slavery affected the form of Christianity in the US and contained at its very center the justification of racial identity. As a result, American Christianity is deeply defined by racial identity. To be white in American history was akin to being essentially human – and therefore essentially Christian. All other persons' humanity was in doubt. According to Gomes Eannes De Azurara, an early Portuguese participant in the slave trade, African people:

> lived like beasts, without any custome of reasonable beings – for they had no wine, and knowledge of bread or they were without the covering of clothes, or the lodgement of houses; and worse than all, they had no understanding of good, but only know how to live in bestial sloth.[6]

There were those, however, who resisted this kind of American Christianity in which white identity defined humanity. For example, in the Northern colonies, the Quakers made an effort to convert slaves and even end slavery through the work of white leaders like John Woolman and Benjamin Lay. Unfortunately, such white leaders were in the minority.

While white Quakers sought to convert African slaves and end slavery, Puritans usually tried to convert slaves and maintain slavery. For example, in 1693, Cotton Mather sought to give spiritual instruction to the Society of Negroes. Mather was part of that White Puritan worldview that thought God had a providential plan for African people. God allowed Africans to be enslaved by white people to increase their humanity and provide better possibility for the salvation of African peoples. Slavery became an act of mercy in this worldview. Mather states:

> It is come to pass by the providence of God, without which there comes nothing to pass, that poor Negroes are cast under your government and protection. You take them into your families; you look on them as part of your possession; and you expect from their service a support, and perhaps an increase, of your other possessions. How agreeable it would be if a religious master or mistress thus attended would not think with themselves, "Who can tell but that this poor creature may belong to the election of God! Who can tell but that God may have sent this poor creature into my hands so that one of the elect may by my means be called and by my instruction be made wise unto salvation. The glorious God will put an unspeakable glory upon me if it may be so.[7]

Initially, there was heated resistance to evangelizing slaves. Black scholar C. Eric Lincoln tells us there were three principal reasons for this: "(1) the hearing of the gospel required time that could be economically productive; (2) slaves gathered together in a religious assembly might become conscious of their own strength and plot insurrections under cover of religious instruction; (3) there was an English tradition of long standing that once a slave became a Christian he could no longer be held a slave."[8] In addition, many whites were repulsed at the suggestion that blacks could go to heaven. Morgan Godwyn, a graduate of Oxford University who served in churches in Virginia around 1665, wrote that slave masters would commonly exclaim, "What, such as they? What, those black dogs be made Christians? What, shall they be like us?"[9] Other whites continued to argue that blacks were less than human. Buckener H. Payne, in his book *The Negro*, believed there were only eight souls saved on Noah's ark, and they were fully accounted for by Noah's family. It was because black people were represented by one of the beasts in the ark that they had no souls to be saved.[10]

Despite such preposterous arguments, missionary work eventually began among the slaves in the early 1700s and many of them became Christians. The brand of Christianity that was preached to them, however, was one that justified slavery. It was argued that Paul and other New Testament writers issued specific instructions for master-slave relations, thus apparently sanctioning the practice. Moreover, as explained above, a curse of slavery was placed on the "sons of Ham" – who were interpreted to be black people. Slaves were taught from both Testaments of the Bible that the God who created them had made them to be the perpetual servants of God's superior white children. Naturally, slaves could no longer worship a racist God.[11] As slavery increasingly became normalized it amounted to a worldview for whites in which what was really occurring was the importation of unsaved heathens to a Christian land where they could hear the gospel and be saved. So normal a worldview was this that even prominent black leaders articulated it. Bishop Henry McNeal Turner of the African Methodist Episcopal Church made such an argument. In 1875 he claimed:

> God, seeing the African stand in need of civilization, sanctioned for a while the slave trade – not that it was in harmony with his fundamental laws for one man to rule another, nor did God ever contemplate that the Negro was to be reduced to the status of a vassal, but as a subject for moral and intellectual culture. So God winked, or lidded his eyeballs, at the institution of slavery.[12]

Although Christianity is said to condone slavery, there can be no such consensus unless we look at why such a reading of scripture and Christian tradition is needed. For example, even when Paul gave instructions on master-slave relations, his underlying belief was that slaves should be freed (1 Corinthians 7:21). As for slavery being a justified normal reality, this seems an absurd claim in view of the cruel, inhuman treatment of the slaves. The story of Absalom Jones certainly exemplifies the contradiction between slavery and Christianity. Jones writes of a time when he was barely seen as a human being: his desire for freedom increased, as he knew that while he was a slave his house and lot might be taken as the property of his master. This induced him to make many applications to him for liberty to purchase his freedom; and, on October 1, 1784, he gave him a manumission (liberation).[13] Jones clues us in to the fact that he was a conscious, sentient person resisting the norms of his day that forced him to become "part of the property."

Absalom Jones is celebrated as the first African American priest in the Episcopal Church. His day is observed in congregations as Absalom Jones Day on February 13. Jones made history when in 1786 the white members of St. George's Methodist Episcopal Church in Philadelphia decided that black members should sit only in the balcony. After learning about the decision, Jones and his friend Richard Allen walked out of the church and were followed by the other black members. Jones and Allen were also co-founders of the Free African Society, the first Afro-American organization in the United States, the purpose of which was "to support one another in sickness, and for the benefit of their widows and fatherless children." The Preamble, dated April 12, 1787, explains that the original intent of Allen and Jones was "to form some kind of religious society" for "the people of their complexion whom they beheld with sorrow, because of their irreligious and uncivilized state."

William White, Episcopal Bishop of Philadelphia, agreed to accept the group as an Episcopal parish and the African Episcopal Church of St. Thomas opened its doors on July 17, 1794, making it the first Black Church in Philadelphia and one of the first in the country. Jones served as the parish's lay reader until 1802, when he was ordained priest and served as the parish's rector. But the world of Absalom Jones was cruel and hard, and the strongest seemed only to survive. His world was the constant struggle to be human and not someone else's property. How easy it was for the powerful to take something – even prayer – and make it a means to an evil end and try to use it to get God to do what was only in the interest of those of European descent. George Bragg, a biographer of Absalom Jones, describes how that which is good went completely awry. Bragg writes of the pivotal moment in the life of Absalom Jones:

In the large cities ... the great body of colored people took to the Methodists. Such were most enthusiastic in the support of this new brand of religion. It was a new thing, and Methodism especially appealed to the lowly. The free Negroes of Philadelphia, attended in large numbers St. George's Methodist Church. For a while, both colored and white seemed to get along happily together. But, by and by, as Methodism began to spread rapidly among the whites, the space occupied by Negro Methodists, in the church building, was more and more in demand for the constantly increasing white congregation. The Negroes were moved from place to place, as the exigencies seemed to demand. Thus, on one Sunday morning, during the year 1787, just as divine services began, a very unpleasant scene was enacted. While at prayer, Absalom Jones, the leader of the Negro group, was pulled from his knees, and he and the others ordered some distance in the rear. Whereupon the entire group of colored worshippers arose and walked out of the Church. They never returned. They were persecuted, harassed and threatened; but they never more returned. This unpleasant and unchristian episode was the occasion which called into being the very organization among "free Negroes" of which we have any record.[14]

This narrative begins the formation of Black denominations, which we will discuss later.

As more blacks began attending white Christian churches, restrictions in seating, communion services, and property ownership caused many blacks to seek autonomy in their own congregations and ultimately in separate denominations. So, by the mid-1700s, black slaves had begun meeting in private to worship, since authentic worship with whites was impossible. There is sufficient historical evidence to conclude that themes later developed by black liberation theologians were present in these early slave meetings in at least a nascent form. For example, God was interpreted by the slaves as a loving father who would eventually deliver them from slavery just as he had delivered Israel from Egyptian bondage. Jesus was considered both a savior and an elder brother who was a fellow sufferer. Heaven had a dual implication for black slaves. Yes, it referred to the future life, but it also came to refer to a state of liberation in the present. Because of the risk involved in preaching liberation, the slave learned how to sing liberation in the very presence of the master:

> Swing low, sweet chariot [underground railroad]
> Coming for to carry me home [up North to freedom]
> Swing low [come close to where I am]
> Sweet chariot
> Coming for to carry me home
> I looked over Jordan [Ohio River – border between North and South]
> And what did I see
> Coming for to carry me home
> A band of angels [Northern emancipators with the underground]
> Coming after me
> Coming for to carry me home.[15]

It was not long before slave theology gave rise to Black activism. There are many important figures who contributed to the cause of Black liberation throughout Black history. Nat Turner (1800–31) was the most notorious slave preacher who ever lived on American soil. Turner's hatred of slavery propelled him to seek freedom by violence. Indeed, Turner killed nearly sixty white people before being captured and hanged in September, 1831. This violent revolt marked the beginning of the Black struggle for liberation. There is also Marcus Garvey (1887–1940), who is regarded by many as "the apostle of black theology in the United States of America."[16] Martin Luther King, Jr., said Garvey "was the first man on a mass scale and level to give millions of Negroes a sense of dignity and destiny, and make the Negro feel he is somebody."[17] Garvey was one of the first to speak of seeing God through black "spectacles." To be African American is to be a member of a cultural and linguistic nation (*ethnos*), defined in part by its West African cultural heritage, by its forcible removal from Africa, by its estrangement from the cultures of both its mainly white context and its own past, by the ultimately unintelligible modern European concept of "race," and by shared experiences in slavery and segregation. These factors shaped African American faith in countless ways. Above all (for our purposes), Black America retained the deep faith in a supreme God that it inherited from African religion.[18] White Christians have tended to think that Black America's African religious heritage was something that stood in the way of the gospel. In fact, it was almost the opposite. Traditional African religions usually worshipped a powerful, providential creator God, who once lived close to humanity, but withdrew to the sky after an ungrateful and accidental human act.[19] Black America's continuing communal spirituality saw it through its encounter with the racist gospel of White America, as the story of Harriet Jacobs illustrates.

Incidents in the Life of a Slave Girl: Written by Herself is an incredible epic about Harriet Jacobs (1813–97), who endured and escaped from slavery in Edenton, North Carolina. I am especially drawn to *Incidents* because I am from North Carolina. I am also a priest in the Episcopal church in which Jacobs struggled fiercely to understand God's presence in relation to her tragedy of slavery. Jacobs writes to Amy Post, her white Quaker friend: "I have . . . striven faithfully to give a true and just account of my own life in Slavery – God knows I have tried to do it in a Christian spirit."[20]

Jacobs expertly narrates her harsh life as a slave under the sexual exploitation of Dr. Flint, her North Carolina master. Technically, Jacobs was the slave of a three-year-old girl, whose father, an Episcopalian (Dr. Flint), proved to be "a licentious master." As Jacobs matured, he made her endure unrelenting sexual harassment. These tragic circumstances of a black female slave were further complicated by Jacobs' sexual relationship with a young white lawyer, with whom she had two children. This lack of "loyalty" to Dr. Flint led to even harsher treatment by her jealous master, forcing her to the extremes of escape. For example, she lived for six years hidden in a tiny crawlspace above a storeroom in her grandmother's house:[21]

> Dark thoughts passed through my mind as I lay there day after day. I tried to be thankful for my little cell, dismal as it was, and even to love it, as part of the price I had paid for the redemption of my children. Sometimes I thought God was a compassionate Father, who would forgive my sins for the sake of my sufferings. At other times, it seemed to me there was no justice or mercy in the divine government. I asked why the curse of slavery was permitted to exist, and why I had been so persecuted and wronged from youth upward. These things took the shape of mystery, which is to this day not so clear to my soul as I trust it will be hereafter.[22]

During this hiding period, Jacobs practiced writing and reading to fill up her days. Perhaps more sustaining for her during this time was the Bible, to which she makes constant reference throughout her narrative. She eventually escaped her "cell of six years"[23] and survived a sea voyage to New York, where she eventually found her freedom along with her brother, John Jacobs, whose own narrative accompanies the enlarged edition of *Incidents*.

For much of the twentieth century, *Incidents* was forgotten or thought to be an anti-slavery novel written by a white woman author. In fact, Jacobs' life is so incredible a narrative that both Yellin (editor of the expanded edition) and the original editor, Lydia Maria Child, spend a significant portion of their introductions authenticating Jacobs' authorship. It was only when Yellin stumbled on Jacobs' letters and John Jacobs' own narrative, "A True Tale of Slavery," that she put this incredible volume together. It is incredible for two reasons: a slave girl wrote it and she wrote it with a cosmology of Christian forgiveness. I turn to these reasons now and encourage readers to experience this incredible story for themselves.

First, the reader will be enthralled by a self-educated slave girl who grew up to tell her life story through compelling prose. We learn from Yellin's masterful edition of *Incidents* that much of the controversy surrounding the authenticity of Jacobs writing her own narrative concerns the fact that twentieth-century scholars of Afro-American literature assign importance not only to the role of white editors of slave narratives, but also to the authenticating documents that accompany these texts. The problem here, however, is that the authenticating documents for *Incidents* are by people in a historical setting without authority. For example, *Incidents* was not endorsed by a prominent white male but by a white woman (Lydia Maria Child) and a black man (John Jacobs). Thus, who exactly has the authority to verify the truth is a crucial aspect of what makes *Incidents* an invaluable and controversial work. Writing to Amy Post about such authentication, Jacobs says: "for I must write just what I have lived and witnessed myself, don't expect much of me dear Amy you shall have truth but not talent."[24]

Secondly, Jacobs' story is incredible because it articulates forgiveness. As a product of chattel slavery in which black women's sexuality was seen as a commodity by white men, Jacobs continues to narrate a Christian ethic of forgiveness. She does this throughout her dual oppressions as a sexually exploited black woman and as a single mother trying to nurture her children, despite the law which stated that her children were the property of another white master. Jacobs' understanding of the Christian ethic of forgiveness contained the complexity of making sense of her own sexual history in light of a legal system in which she was not in possession of herself or her children. Amazingly, Jacobs reconciles her lack of chastity in such a system:

> But, O, ye happy women, whose purity has been sheltered from childhood, who have been free to choose the objects of your affection, whose homes are protected by law, do not judge the poor desolate slave girl too severely! If slavery had been abolished, I, also, could have married the man of my choice; I could have had a home shielded by the laws; and I should have been spared the painful task of confessing what I am now about to relate; but all my prospects had been blighted by slavery. I wanted to keep myself pure; and, under the most adverse circumstances, I tried hard to preserve my self-respect; but I was struggling alone in the powerful grasp of the demon Slavery; and the monster proved too strong for me. I felt as if I was forsaken by God and man; as if all my efforts must be frustrated; and I became reckless in my despair.[25]

Jacobs' constant refrain of "do not judge" ironically becomes an indictment of us as readers in the twenty-first century. The phrase "O virtuous reader! You never knew what it is to be a slave"[26] judges current Christian piety in which contemporary freedom has seldom produced as virtuous a life as Harriet Jacobs'. Because she learned not to condemn herself, Jacobs invites the reader to understand a Christian ethic of forgiveness in which she depends on us as her future generations to help her anticipate a better world. As she states above, she could not maintain her convictions because "I was struggling alone." The power of *Incidents*, however, is that she makes us struggle with her.

We struggle with Jacobs in her context of slavery, which is akin to the extreme heat of the South: "Hot weather brings out snakes and slaveholders."[27] Most of all in this context, Jacobs teaches us to distinguish between Christianity and religion in the sense that many call themselves religious and yet – like her master Dr. Flint, a respectable member of the Episcopal church – never connect how Christian character relates to Christian actions.

> There is a great difference between Christianity and religion at the South . . . When I was told that Dr. Flint had joined the Episcopal church, I was much surprised. I supposed that religion had a purifying effect on the character of men; but the worst persecutions I endured from him were after he was a communicant . . . No wonder the slaves sing, "Ole Satan's church is here below / Up to God's free church I hope to go."[28]

In the end, Jacobs forgives. It is in this forgiveness that the reader again questions how such a story could be true. How could this woman who endured so much pain at the hands of white people still find communion and forgiveness? Again, the answer is that she no longer struggled alone: she found community. Jacobs was able to leave the United States (an adventure seldom given to an African American slave) and find Christian community in England. It is in this adventure to England that Jacobs describes her restored faith:

> My visit to England is a memorable event in my life, from the fact of my having there received strong religious impressions. The contemptuous manner in which the communion had been administered to colored people, in my native place; the church membership of Dr. Flint, and others like him; and the buying and selling of slaves, by professed ministers of the gospel, had given me a prejudice against the Episcopal church. The whole service seemed to me a mockery and a sham. But my home in Steventon was in the family of a clergyman, who was a true disciple of Jesus. The beauty of his daily life inspired me with faith in the genius of Christian professions. Grace entered my heart, and I knelt at the communion table, I trust, in true humility of soul.[29]

Some black scholars argue that most blacks accepted the slave brand of Christianity at face value. Moreover, white missionaries persuaded the blacks that life on earth was insignificant because "obedient servants of God could expect a reward in heaven after death."[30] The White interpretation of Christianity effectively divested the slaves of any concern they might have had about their freedom in the present. I believe, however, that African American slaves did not accept European Christianity per se, but transformed it to what is intelligible today as the Black Church. For example, Albert Raboteau and countless others highlight the secret meetings of slaves as the location for religious and theological developments within early black communities.[31] Peter Paris states: "Further still, their clandestine ritualistic gatherings and liturgical practices of worship became the locus for syncretizing the African and Christian worldviews into a dynamic unified whole."[32]

Slaveholders had shorn slaves and their descendants of their geographic home, their ethnic heritage, and their family relationships. In effect, they had "de-narrated" Black America and left it lacking a dynamic unified whole. Ironically, this de-narration became the foundation of new African American stories. God provided the Black Church much more than the story of having lost its story. The story of salvation was also given.

Benjamin Mays' *The Negro's God* finds three African American visions of salvation proceeding from this common center. The first, which predominated from 1760 to 1860, envisioned God's work as "liberative," accomplishing the Black struggle for freedom just as the God of Israel had lifted the Hebrews out of their Egyptian slavery. The second, which predominated from 1865 to 1914, envisioned God as no longer useful to the cause of justice and freedom for Black America. Like wandering, grumbling Hebrews, emancipated but still segregated black Americans still knew God, but no longer as a liberator. The third, which predominated from 1914 to the time of Mays' writing in 1937, envisioned God as promising divine reparation for earthly suffering.[33]

Certainly, slavery caused many blacks to doubt a Christian spirituality in which those who came to define the Black Church always advocated reconciliation and practices of nonviolence. There was a natural invitation to look forward to being separated from White America, as the Hebrews had been separated from Egypt and Canaan. I argue, however, that the essential Black Church has always awaited reconciliation with all the people of God. As the descendants of slaves became Christians, they learned to appropriate the stories in scripture for a narrative of reconciliation and nonviolence. And so, when God re-narrated black Americans, God called them not the children of Noah's cursed son Ham, not even the culturally superior children of Ethiopia, but the children of enslaved and liberated *Israel*. America was not the Promised Land after all, as the Puritans had taught. America, too, was Egypt. God was not the god of Pharaoh, but the God of Moses, the God of the disinherited.

Thus, Black America learned to see its destiny not in subjugation, but in exodus.[34] This could also be said of many white Christians who relearned their racial identity. For instance, I received a recent legislative proposal for the Episcopal Church USA regarding reparations in the aftermath of slavery. The following is a preliminary draft of a document about how the Episcopal Church should respond to slavery in America:

RESOLVED, the House of – Concurring, that this 74th General Convention of the Episcopal Church meeting in Minneapolis supports a full and complete apology to African Americans for the Church's involvement in slavery and the systemic injustice which is slavery's legacy, and be it further
RESOLVED that ECUSA will spend 5 percent of the DFMS annual budget for the 20 years beginning 2006 to fund education for the descendants of slaves, and be it further
RESOLVED that Executive Council will appoint a Reconciliation Task Force to collect the evidence of the harm that this legacy continues to exact on persons of color in our church and report to the 75th General Convention.
RESOLVED that the Washington Office of the Episcopal Church will work for a just and lasting remedy at the federal level to this historic blight on our nation, and be it further

RESOLVED that the Episcopal Church advocates access to free education through at least two graduate degrees for every descendant of a slave in the US, the funding to cover education that begins on January 1st after the legislation is enacted. It is to be understood that this resolution does not guarantee the education, only the access to education meeting routine standards of admission. It is to be further understood that "education" includes certified training schools as well as colleges and universities.[35]

This can in no way repay the price paid by so many Americans for so long, but it can begin the effort, long overdue, to compensate their descendants. It can make dreams of democracy move from rhetoric to fact. Furthermore, the initiative is not unusual. The United States has granted reparations to Native Americans, to Japanese Americans, and to several other groups that have suffered systemic disadvantages from unequal and unjust policies.

Regardless of how slavery will be finally worked through, African Americans have maintained a communal spirituality derived in response to the horrors of slavery. The collective memory of African Americans during slavery, preserved in secret meetings and the movement of slaves from the Caribbean, strengthened those early Black Christians.[36] These secret meetings began in North America when the first Africans landed in Jamestown in 1619 as indentured servants. The number of Black Christians increased as more Africans arrived, first as indentured servants and later as slaves directly from Africa or through the West Indies, where African slaves were introduced as early as 1504. With the influx of more Africans, African American Christian spirituality became entrenched in the North American colonies and later in the United States.

The Survival of Africanism

After the horrific Atlantic slave trade of African people and the subsequent 200 years or so of slavery, there has been debate as to whether African culture even survived in the United States. Are there "Africanisms" (specific African cultural practices) that were maintained through such a harsh period? The answer proposed in this book is yes.[37] The cultural memory of African practices merged with the dominant European practices of Christianity during the hardships of slavery in North America, but they were not obliterated. The "invisible institution" emerged in which Africans inculturated Christianity in such a way as to facilitate survival throughout slavery. Secret religious meetings occurred in which an appropriate form of Christian practice emerged to aid Africans in the existential crisis of slavery. Of course, these meetings were illegal in a White society and could warrant severe punishment. The secluded locations of these meetings were called hush harbors, where African slaves would hear sermons, sing spirituals, and rally to support one another. Such meetings were energetic and full of emotion, so that participants could "catch the spirit" and shout praises to God. The following serves as an example:

> An' den de black folks 'ud git off, down in de crick bottom, er in a thick'et, an' sing an' shout an' pray. Don't know why, but de w'ite folks sho' didn't like dem ring shoults de cullud folks had. De folks git in er ring an' sing an' dance, an' shout; de dance is jes' a kinder shuffle, den hit gits faster, an' faster as dey gits wa'amed up; an' dey moans an' shouts; an' sings, an' claps, an' dance. Some ob em gits 'quasted an 'dey drop out, an' de ring gits closer. Sometimes dey sing an' shout all night.[38]

Christianity developed in a different way among enslaved Africans, a way in which community meant survival. African Christianity contained a spirituality that exemplified communal practices of response and catharsis. These were responses out loud for all to hear, and a catharsis of emotion that all were experiencing. Thus, communal interaction shaped a Christian spirituality differently among Africans to make Christianity corporate, visceral, and dynamic. This is not to say, however, that such an African Christian spirituality was easy to maintain (hence the debate over whether or not Africanisms survived slavery). Maintaining a sense of community when every day African people were resisting depersonalizing laws and systemic structures was difficult to say the least. Nurturing the newly converted to Christianity was also another great feat accomplished in African Christian spirituality because to become a public Christian community among slaves was an extremely threatening enterprise in White society. Churches not run by slaveholders represented the great threat that African people would forge alternative societies no longer controllable by White society. Although African Christian spirituality faced daunting obstacles, there is some evidence that the early Church among African slaves began in the early 1700s in the South. By 1936 the Black Church had grown to represent seven major denominations, with over thirty thousand church buildings and a membership of about 5 million.[39] By the 1970s the Black Church was thought to comprise over 10 million members in the United States, with hundreds of thousands of African Christians in the diaspora. Today, the seven major Black denominations are estimated to comprise 25 million members combined. How did this African Christian spirituality not only survive slavery, but also flourish?

Chinua Achebe's *Home and Exile* is required reading for insight into how African culture survives despite colonialism.[40] Achebe's first novel, *Things Fall Apart*, was the bestselling novel in the history of African literature. *Home and Exile* is in the genre of autobiography – a multi-leveled memoir that requires iconographic reading to enter Achebe's African particularity to get to the universal themes in his novels, such as hope, restoration, and cultural integrity. It may seem strange to say that a Nigerian writer can write for everyone as a Nigerian, but the deep lesson that we learn from him is that unless one writes out of one's own particularity, nothing significant will be said. For those of us in the Church, Achebe's insight has been the important lesson gained in contextual theology over the past thirty years.

Achebe is a member of the Igbo people of southeastern Nigeria. He paints his own particular narrative, beginning in Ogidi, where his father, an Anglican priest, resettled the family at St. Philip's Anglican Church in 1935. His new childhood community named his father Mister Nineteen-Four because his father told the community about his missionary journeys that began in 1904. However, Nineteen-Four was not an endearing description because of its connotation with an oppressive British Empire. It is from this negative connotation that Achebe reflects on the complexity of being Igbo in British culture. Most significant to Achebe's acculturation process is that much of British literature presented his people as subhuman; this ultimately inspired him to develop an African voice to counterbalance British cosmology in literature. Achebe developed a profound voice and overcame the debilitating worldview of many British writers (with the exception of the celebrated Welsh poet Dylan Thomas, who praised Achebe's work early on).

The appeal in *Home and Exile* is to seek a literary voice through particularity, and by so doing enrich all of literature. As an African American professor in a divinity school, I do not make Achebe's book required reading solely for one ethnic group or one racial group, or even for one intellectual discourse. Instead, Achebe's powerful writing is required reading both for those of African descent and for other cultural and national identities. Through Achebe's textured narrative, the reader is invited into his particularity to discover their own particularity. Achebe also reflects on how such an invitation has often been abused in Africa: many European writers have intruded to tell his African story in a detached and derogatory manner.

When asked if white people could tell African stories, Achebe replied that they could tell African stories if they trod softly, because "you walk on my dreams . . . People dream their world into being. If you're a visitor remember that, and you can write as strong a story as anybody else."[41] Others can tell African stories, but Achebe appeals in his book for more Africans to tell their own stories. We learn from Achebe that African writers need to narrate Africa because Africans share a "sense that even in the most tempting moments of grave disappointment with this world, the [African] author remains painfully aware that he is of the same flesh and blood, the same humanity as its human inhabitants."[42] Interestingly enough, this does not mean that non-Africans cannot tell African stories, but when they do, they must recognize their limitations and write as a visitor to such a vibrant world. This visitation and vibrant world lead us back to where I began – namely, that Achebe's book is required reading. As we engage and enter the other's world, our emerging contexts will gradually create common vision.

Achebe teaches us that there is a fierce survival instinct to hold onto cultural identity even in the midst of colonizing forces seeking the conformity of the minority group. The further development of African spirituality in America was enhanced by (if not partially responsible for) what Gayraud Wilmore labeled the "deradicalization" of Black Churches.[43] That is, the spiritual landscape of African American communities became increasingly diversified. Consequently, the normative status of the Black Churches was now more vigorously questioned as important forms of knowledge about how to be a Black community surfaced. All of this led to the emergence of Black denominations within the Christian Church. Such an emergence was seen as the threat of schism and fracture. I will argue, however, that such diversification of Black spiritual experience suggests flexibility and fluidity by embracing various manifestations of how communal spirituality is made manifest.

The Emergence of Black Denominations

Extensive changes in America's racial Christianity did not take place until participation in the Awakening revivals of the 1700s, in which Baptists and Methodists dominated the field. American white Baptist and Methodists spread their fire, inviting both the free and the enslaved into the Church. Fiery sermons were aimed at the consciences of slaveholders who now were concerned about their own salvation and spiritual welfare in light of slavery. Raboteau reports that Methodist records show a growth in African membership of almost ten thousand between 1786 (when membership records based on race began) and 1790. Baptist churches showed an African membership of about twenty thousand.[44]

The success of Baptist and Methodist evangelists in gaining African converts was due to the communal spirit of overcoming suffering, as exemplified in the life of Harriet Jacobs. The Great Awakening revivalists did not emphasize the English traditions of Anglicanism, nor the rationalism of the Puritans. Conversion was the true emphasis. Raboteau explains:

> While the Anglican clergyman tended to be didactic and moralistic, the Methodist or Baptist exhorter visualized and personalized the drama of sin and salvation, of damnation and election. The Anglican usually taught the slaves the Ten Commandments, the Apostles' Creed and the Lord's Prayer; the revivalist preacher helped them to feel the weight of sin, to imagine the threats of Hell, and to accept Christ as their only Savior. The enthusiasm of the camp meeting, as excessive as it seemed to some churchmen, was triggered by the personal, emotional appeal of the preacher and supported by the common response of members of his congregation.[45]

The importance of the felt presence of the Holy Spirit through shouting and spirit possession relates to a similar importance placed on an Africanism of spirit possession that goes back to West African spiritual practices. Beyond this, the practices of Methodists and particularly Baptists easily meshed with the practices of traditional African spirituality. Enslaved Africans found Methodist and Baptist services appealing because the emphasis on spiritual conversion translated well into the African belief in the dynamic world of the spirit. In this sense, early revivalistic Christianity served to link an African past with a North American present.

In addition to some natural harmony with African sensibilities, the Great Awakening's theological ethos appealed to Africans because of its reliance on a "priesthood of all believers" mentality. Anyone who was saved and felt a calling to preach could do so. Because preaching the gospel was not limited to those with formal training, this allowed enslaved Africans to assume a role seldom held before this period. Throughout the geographic areas touched by the Great Awakening, and in areas without restrictions concerning black preachers, those of African descent could proclaim the gospel as authoritatively as white preachers. Both lay and ordained black ministers mark the development of new spiritual possibilities in which baptism presents a person's primary identity, rather than racial identity. However, the slave system was still in place despite the new-found spiritual "freedoms" of Africans, and there existed increasingly severe restrictions on those spiritual practices that helped to form a common Christian identity.

The first Black Church in America is known to be Baptist, founded in Silver Bluff, South Carolina in the mid to late 1770s and still active after the Revolutionary War. Independent Black Churches resulted in the South, but few slaves of the time obtained their freedom until after the Civil War, when the Christian Methodist Episcopal Church was formed by separating from the Southern Methodist Church.[46] In the North, two other Black Churches emerged: the African Methodist Episcopal Church (AME), founded in Philadelphia, Pennsylvania by Richard Allen and others in 1794, and the African Methodist Episcopal Zion Church (AMEZ), founded by James Varick and others in New York City in 1821. Both of these Black denominations emerged because of the refusal of White churches to welcome black members.

Because of the expansive institutional structure of the Roman Catholic Church, it did not split over slavery to form particular Black Church denominations as most of the mainline Protestant denominations did in the United States. In the Episcopal Church there was a massive exodus of African Americans between 1865 and 1870, while the AME, AMEZ, and Baptists experienced astounding growth. Gardiner Shattuck states:

> Since the antebellum mission to slaves made paternalism and social control indispensable adjuncts to the Christian faith, African Americans saw that the creation of independent Baptist and Methodist churches represented their best opportunity to achieve freedom from the values of their former masters, now condemned by God for having gone to war to uphold the wicked institution of slavery.[47]

In short, because of slavery, racial identities emerged in the Church in America, thereby creating only partial understandings of human identity. Those who make race the primary category by which to define the mystery of humanity inevitably fall into false notions of what it means to be human. In such understandings, the power to define humanity usually resides with those who happen to be in power at the time. In the American context, Europeans gained power to define race, especially in the need to justify the horrors of enslaving African peoples. This justification then led to the theological rationalization of a hierarchy of being, in which God made white people the trustees of creation. African people were simply part of a creation that needed to be ordered and dominated. Within the context of bringing slaves to America, Europeans could enter into a unique economic constitution of the self. They could shape their own identity in the market place. Liberty, rights, and freedom were talked about in light of these new possible markets. The indigenous people were part of the acquisition of property for these markets.

Notes

1   John S. Jacobs, "A True Tale of Slavery," in Jean Fagan Yellin, ed., *Incidents in the Life of a Slave Girl Written by Herself* by Harriet A. Jacobs (Cambridge, MA: Harvard University Press, 2000), p. 209.
2   Although Niebuhr does not explicitly address the Black Church, his typology sheds light on this view. See H. Richard Niebuhr, *Christ and Culture* (San Francisco: Harper, 2001).
3   "Archbishop condemns old and new forms of slavery," Anglican Church News Service (ACNS) 3525, Lambeth Palace, July 29, 2003.
4   Ibid.
5   See John Blassingame, *The Slave Community: Plantation Life in the Antebellum South*, revd. edn. (New York: Oxford University Press, 1979); Hugh Thomas, *The Slave Trade* (New York: Simon and Schuster, 1997); E. Lovejoy, *Transformations in Slavery* (Cambridge: Cambridge University Press, 2000); Herbert S. Klein, *The Atlantic Slave Trade* (New York: Cambridge University Press, 1999).
6   Albert Raboteau, *Slave Religion: The "Invisible Institution" in the Antebellum South* (New York: Oxford University Press, 1978), p. 97.
7   Cotton Mather, "The Negro Christianized: An Essay to Excite and Assist that Good Work, the Instruction of Negro-Servants in Christianity" (Boston, 1706), quoted by Alden T. Vaughan, ed., *The Puritan Tradition in America: 1620–1730* (New York: Harper and Row, 1972), p. 268.
8   C. Eric Lincoln, "The Development of Black Religion in America," *Review and Expositor* 70 (Summer 1973), p. 302.
9   Ibid, p. 303.
10 See Millard J. Erickson, *Christian Theology* (Grand Rapids, MI: Baker Book House, 1983), p. 543.
11 See William R. Jones, *Is God a White Racist?* (Garden City, NY: Doubleday, 1973), pp. 115–17.
12 Henry McNeal Turner, "On the Anniversary of Emancipation, January 1, 1866," in Thomas J. Brown, ed., *The Public Art of Civil War Commemoration: A Brief History with Documents*, (Boston, MA: Bedford/St. Martin's Press, 2004), p. 147.
13 George F. Bragg, *History of the Afro-American Group of the Episcopal Church* (Baltimore, MD: Church Advocate Press, 1922).
14 Ibid, p. 5.
15 Emmanuel McCall, "Black Liberation Theology: A Politics of Freedom," *Review and Expositor* 73 (Summer 1976), p. 330; cf. C. Eric Lincoln and Lawrence H. Mamiya, *The Black Church in the African American Experience* (Durham, NC: Duke University Press, 1990), p. 352.
16 Lindsay A. Arscott, "Black Theology," *Evangelical Review of Theology* 10 (April–June 1986), p. 137.
17 Quoted by Clair Drake, foreword to Randall K. Burkett, *Garveyism as a Religious Movement: The Institutionalization of a Black Civil Religion*

(Metuchen, NJ: Scarecrow Press and the American Theological Library Association, 1978).

18 See Major Jones, *The Color of God: The Concept of God in Afro-American Thought* (Macon, GA: Mercer University Press, 1987), pp. 17–20.

19 See James H. Evans, Jr., *We Have Been Believers: An African-American Systematic Theology* (Minneapolis, MN: Fortress Press, 1992), p. 56.

20 Harriet A. Jacobs, *Incidents in the Life of a Slave Girl: Written By Herself*, enlarged edn., ed. Jean Fagan Yellin (Cambridge, MA: Harvard University Press, 2000), p. xv.

21 Ibid, p. 144.

22 Ibid, p. 123.

23 Ibid, p. 144.

24 Ibid, p. xxii.

25 Ibid, p. 54.

26 Ibid, p. 55.

27 Ibid, p. 174.

28 Ibid, pp. 74–5.

29 Ibid, p. 185.

30 James H. Cone, *Black Theology and Black Power* (New York: Seabury Press, 1969), p. 121.

31 Raboteau, *Slave Religion*, section 2.

32 Peter Paris, *The Spirituality of African Peoples: The Search for a Common Moral Discourse* (Minneapolis, MN: Fortress Press, 1995), pp. 44–5.

33 Evans, *We Have Been Believers*, p. 58, quoting Benjamin Mays, *The Negro's God: As Reflected in His Literature* (New York: Atheneum, 1969).

34 "By identifying themselves with the Hebrews, African slaves declared themselves as insiders in the scriptural drama . . . While slaveholders focused on ancient Israel as a slaveholding society, the African slaves saw ancient Israel first as a nation descended from slaves." Evans, *We Have Been Believers*, p. 41.

35 Received from Louie Crew at Rutgers University, August 20, 2002.

36 See George Eaton Simpson, *Black Religions in the New World* (New York: Columbia University Press, 1978), p. 19.

37 See also Joseph E. Holloway, *Africanisms in American Culture* (Bloomington: Indiana University Press, 1990).

38 Ira Berlin, Marc Favreau, and Steven F. Miller, eds., *Remembering Slavery: African Americans Talk about Their Personal Experiences of Slavery and Emancipation* (New York: New Press with the Library of Congress, Washington, DC, 1998), pp. 195–6.

39 See Jessie Parhurst Guzman, ed., *Negro Year Book: A Review of Events Affecting Negro Life, 1941–1946* (Tuskegee, AL: Department of Records and Research of the Tuskegee Institute, 1946).

40 Chinua Achebe, *Home and Exile* (New York: Oxford University Press, 2000).

41 "Views of Home from Afar," *Publishers Weekly*, July 3, 2000.

42 Achebe, *Home and Exile*, p. 49.
43 Gayraud Wilmore, *Black Religion and Black Radicalism: An Interpretation of the Religious History of Afro-American People*, 2nd edn. (Maryknoll, NY: Orbis Books, 1983), ch. 6.
44 Raboteau, *Slave Religion*, p. 131.
45 Ibid, pp. 132–3.
46 See Walter Brooks, "The Priority of the Silver Bluff Church and Its Promoters," *Journal of Negro History* 7 (1922), pp. 172–96.
47 Gardiner H. Shattuck, Jr., *Episcopalians and Race: Civil War to Civil Rights* (Lexington: University Press of Kentucky, 2000), p. 8.

Chapter 4
Communal Worship

Almighty God, our heavenly Father
In penitence we confess
That we have sinned against you
Through our own fault
In thought, word, and deed
And in what we have left undone.
For the sake of your Son, Christ our Lord
Forgive us all that is past
And grant that we may serve you
In newness of life
To the glory of your Name.[1]

The above prayer is prayed daily by African Christians such as Archbishop Desmond Tutu. It is a fitting prayer for Tutu, who led South Africa's Truth and Reconciliation Commission. The wisdom in such a prayer points to the incessant problem in human nature: repeating the sins of the past. This is why South Africa's Constitution today reflects human rights unlike any other in the world. South Africans have vowed never again to create scapegoats and victims.

In American society, African Americans became the most obvious scapegoats and victims. Their survival depended upon the communal spirituality founded in the Black Church. In this chapter we will look more deeply at how the Black Church came into being because of the sins of racism. More particularly, we will see the emergence of Black denominations. The emergence of these denominations in America, I argue, does not have to represent schism and fracture. This is especially the case if we look at such an emergence in the context of communal worship.

African American Christian spirituality emerges through its particularity of dynamic and corporate worship. Such worship demonstrates that the meaning of human life in the Black Church flows from the community to the person, whereas in White America there is often an inverse flow of meaning originating in the individual that only sometimes leads to community. Instead of the latter, Cartesian epistemological method, worship in the Black Church constitutes new identity in which the individual becomes conscious of herself only through social interaction. It is from such communal epistemology that I construct a better way to understand the Black Church that is not homogeneous in its forms of worship.

James Washington comments on the development of early Black Churches:

> The story of independent black Baptist congregations begins in Virginia and Georgia, where some slaves who had answered the revivalists' call for repentance during the southern phase of the revivals of the 1750s covenanted to form their own churches. They believed that spiritual bondage was a greater affliction than material bondage, and that freedom from one might lead to freedom from the other . . . they knew their churches were chattel arrangements. But they stubbornly trusted in the promises of the Bible that God is a liberator.[2]

Any Christian teacher who restates the faith of the Church will have to arrange that faith in a certain way. There must be a sequence because everything cannot be said at once. This is also the case when thinking about the Black Church in America. We will inevitably say more about one thing than another, and the question of proportion occurs as we try to figure out the particularity of worship in the Black Church. The task of looking at the particularity of worship in the Black Church as it relates to the emergence of Black denominations helps us relate the dynamic nature of the Church to the praxis of African American experience. In other words, such a dynamic Black Church cannot help but express different polities and styles. The Black Church becomes increasingly dynamic in character as it draws upon its communal spirituality of a loving God, who in turn requires the Black Church to love all persons.

The Black Church is not unique in understanding how its worship shapes its character in the world. For example, the Eastern Church has long remarked that liturgy serves as the school of faith. The Church is to praise God. Such doxology in turn sanctifies believers to behave responsibly in the world. You learn what you know when you worship. And as Geoffrey Wainwright believes, it is through corporate worship that a Christian life is shaped.[3] Within African American Christian spirituality, one of the crucial ways in which to see the shape of the Christian life derived from worship is through preaching. The distinction between the Church's preaching and doctrine is found in method. The Black Church became known for its preaching because of the power of proclamation in relationship to political mobilization. For a contemporary understanding of such power, I encourage the reader to see the creative book *Power in the Pulpit*, which synthesizes twelve distinguished preachers' thoughts on preaching from the Black Church tradition in North America. Each of the preachers goes into detail about how they prepare sermons and prepare themselves for Sunday morning and other preaching engagements. For example, one of my favorite preachers in this book, Charles G. Adams, writes:

> If I begin with the words and works of others concerning the basic text, I will suppress my own spontaneity, sensitivity, and creativity. The words and works of others are so excellent, so admirable, and so compelling that they must be deferred at the start of sermonic preparation, lest I become a mere puppet mouthing the words from the seemingly closed lips of some ingenious homiletic ventriloquist.[4]

What is most intriguing about this book are the variegated styles represented among the twelve preachers. Their methodology of sermon preparation is common only insofar as they appeal to the community's involvement with the world. In this regard (and key to the value of the book) each of their methodological expositions is followed by an actual sermon they have delivered. Not only does this provide the reader extended insight into the process of preparing a sermon, it also provides an integration between the theory and practice of Black preaching. *Power in the Pulpit* is valuable not only to those in the Black Church tradition, but also to all of those who seek to understand the character of the Black Church. We learn that it is not proper to enter the pulpit and read systematic theology. There must be a proper relationship between the preacher and the Church's doctrine. Doctrine serves the person proclaiming the gospel to evangelize and preach in such a way that the proclamation is informed by the experience of encountering the divine life. (This is why I argue in chapter 6 that Martin Luther King, Jr.'s preaching and affinity for the Beloved Community and civil rights flowed out of the penchant of African American spirituality to always seek true community.) Karl Barth's theology shows how the Church's doctrine and its preaching are interlinked in such a way that the doctrine always seeks to serve the Church's proclamations.[5] In light of the abuses of European Christianity, however, the question must be raised: how does one deal with embarrassing counter-evidence to one's own community when all kinds of things were preached in the name of Christ

– including the justification of slavery? Such a question informs how the Black Church became a light for America.

The Black Church has always recognized itself as having a message with a certain character and substance. Some have characterized this message as redemption, others have named it as deliverance, and yet others see the essential message of the Black Church as a love ethic. Instead of perpetuating forms of the Church that mimic civil religion, the Black Church unashamedly shows the world its worship of God that demonstrates love of neighbor. The Black Church seeks to resemble the character of Christ, who offers prevenient love. Therefore, the particular ecclesiology of the Black Church looks like love. The African Saint Augustine states there is "No knowledge of God without love of God." The Black Church teaches a similar doctrine: that no good thing can be done without love. Our love for God makes us love the particularity of our neighbor, and all along we are not to mistake God for neighbor. Love in God always reveals proper relationship between all that should be community. In other words, God's love helps us see what is true in our relationships. Therefore, the Black Church always had spiritual authorities adjudicating relational spirituality. These spiritual authorities sought to ward off the heresy of ever having a greater commandment than loving God and neighbor.

There is concern and a need to clarify the identity of the Black Church so as to see how it coheres, what it offers, and how it answers perennial questions. Its coherence is seen through the communal nature of African American Christian spirituality. To answer the question of the particularity of the Black Church (i.e., what is the Black Church at this particular time, in this or that particular place?) we need to investigate who constitutes the Black Church in its particular experience. Any scholar of the Black Church is coming from a particular angle, limited by time, place, and human individuality. I bring to the study of the Black Church the liturgical sensibilities of an Anglican, which comprise both Catholic and Protestant ways of worship. With me, a certain pluralism is inevitable and proper. But we cannot depend on unlimited pluralism to know what the Black Church is because there will have to be ways in which the Black Church recognizes itself as well as how we recognize it.

How can the Black Church be recognized? Ultimately, it is recognized through how it worships. Such an emphasis on worship anchors the Black Church in the present and then engages and necessitates it to look at the past and the future. To see the content of the Black Church one must be able to criticize particular formulations of what came to be known as the Black Church, especially its caricatures of emotionalism and irrationality. Our critical faculties will be useful to help clear up misunderstandings and to prevent us from lapsing into stereotypes of the Black Church. Criticism for the sake of criticism is meaningless, however, without some form of basis to know meaning. This basis is provided in the Black Church's pursuit of communal prayer.

Throughout history, the Church's practice of common prayer is recognized through the particularity of tradition, and the Black Church is no exception. From what stream of Church tradition does a particular ecclesiology construct its common prayer? The answer is often recognized by means of the various individual leaderships within the Church. To which figures in the Church does a particular way of prayer possess authority? Who leads the understanding of worship? In chapter 6, I answer the former question by examining the leadership of those like Martin Luther King, Jr., who championed the particular ways of non-violence and civil rights to model common prayer. I answer the latter question concerning worship through the notable leadership of Richard Allen (1760–1831), to whom we now turn. We shall see that the Black Church includes those who lead worship toward communal harmony and balance, as King also sought through the civil rights movement.

The Controversy of Emotionalism

Kenneth Waters argues that Richard Allen's spirituality has been largely neglected because of his attitude toward emotionalism in African American worship.[6] More specifically, when Allen's hymnody is consulted, there is misunderstanding of his spiritual and cultural sensibilities as to what constitutes the Black worship experience. Allen was, of course, the founder and first consecrated bishop of the African Methodist Episcopal Church (AME, incorporated in 1816).[7] Waters calls attention to both the neglect and the misunderstanding of Allen's spirituality by examining a hymn written by Allen entitled "Spiritual Song." This hymn offers a fascinating investigation of the relationship between Allen's hymnody and his views on African American worship styles. It was originally published in Philadelphia. An original copy now resides at the William L. Clements Library in Ann Arbor (University of Michigan).[8]

Allen collected and authored hymns. He produced the first compilation of hymns specifically for African American congregations. In 1801 he published *A Collection of Spiritual Songs and Hymns Selected from Various Authors by Richard Allen, African Minister*. John Ormrod was hired by Allen to print this collection of 54 hymns drawn from the collections of Isaac Watts and John and Charles Wesley.[9] Later that year, Allen added ten more hymns and had T. L. Plowman print this enlarged edition under the title, *A Collection of Hymns and Spiritual Songs from Various Authors, by Richard Allen, Minister of the African Methodist Episcopal Church.* Allen published a pocket sized edition of this collection in 1808; and finally in 1818 he brought together 314 hymns to produce the first hymnal of the AME Church.[10] Allen himself probably authored some of the hymns in his evolving collections. He also created hymns that circulated independently. Two such hymns, "The God of Bethel heard her cries" and "Ye ministers that are called to preaching," appeared in his 1887 autobiography. "Spiritual Song" is among these independently circulating compositions. Like his other hymns, it was written without tune or melody.[11]

Dorothy Porter reproduces the hymn in her anthology of early African American writings. In her introductory comments, where she refers specifically to the second stanza, she observes: "In this religious chant [Allen] warned his congregation against loud 'groaning and shouting'; such religion, he states, is 'only a dream.' "[12] Her remarks suggest that Richard Allen was generally opposed to traditional styles of African American Christian worship with their highly celebrative, emotive, enthusiastic, rhythmic, kinetic, and vocal expressions. Kenneth Waters provides an investigation that shows that Porter's impression of Allen requires revising. According to him, one *could* argue that Allen was at least opposed to extreme manifestations of these worship styles, but this hymn, when properly interpreted, cannot be taken as evidence for such opposition.

Such a misunderstanding of Allen's position can be found in another otherwise outstanding work by John Lovell, Jr., who also refers to the second stanza of the hymn: "Richard Allen did not like shouting Methodists; he thus had his congregation sing, 'such groaning and shouting, it sets me to doubting.' "[13] Regrettably, other fine scholars appropriated Lovell's misreading of the same hymn. Wendel Whalum, for example, wrote an informative essay on the Black hymnic tradition in which he quoted Lovell: "Expressed feelings against the use of spirituals, especially shouting ones, are evident from early black church fathers. The attitude of Richard Allen . . . is described as follows: 'For example, Richard Allen did not like shouting Methodists; he thus had his congregation sing, such groaning and shouting.' "[14] In a more recently published text, Melva Wilson Costen produced an excellent work on the historical and theological roots of the African American worship tradition. Yet she also reiterates Lovell's mistaken impression of Richard Allen: "His concern for emotional restraint and the 'offensiveness' of unbridled emotions during worship is revealed in this song:

'such groaning and shouting, it sets me to doubting . . . 'Twas truly offensive to all that were there.'"[15] Thus, we have a history of interpretation spanning a number of decades that emphasizes an understanding of Richard Allen's perspective on African American worship as distinctly negative. Moreover, this interpretation relies on his own hymns as primary evidence.

"Spiritual Song" and the Emergence of Black Denominations

For Kenneth Waters, the purpose of Allen's "Spiritual Song" was to *defend* traditional, historic styles of early African American Christian worship against his contemporary assimilationist detractors. In sum, Waters argues that "Spiritual Song" is actually a dialogue between two speakers. It is an antiphony or call and response typical of the Black Church tradition. In those stanzas where traditional, historic styles of early African American worship are defended and affirmed, Allen himself is speaking. In those stanzas where these features of early African American worship are exaggerated and decried, a representative figure named brother Pilgrim is speaking. For example, Allen starts the hymn with an early morning encounter with brother Pilgrim:

> Good morning brother Pilgrim, what marching to Zion,
> What doubts and what dangers have you met to-day,
> Have you found a blessing, are your joys increasing?
> Press forward my brother and make no delay;
> Is your heart a-glowing, are your comforts a-flowing,
> And feel you an evidence, now bright and clear;
> Feel you a desire that burns like a fire,
> And longs for the hour that Christ shall appear.[16]

Waters provides a profound analysis of how Allen inquires about Pilgrim's trials, spiritual progress, and Christian hope. For example, this initial greeting, which is followed by a series of questions addressed to a second person, sets the stage for a dialogue. All that is needed is a first-person response to establish the antiphonal character of the hymn. We have such a response in the second stanza, and again in the fourth, seventh, and eleventh stanzas. Such antiphonal response is typical of the Black worship style.

In the second stanza, brother Pilgrim returns from an ecstatic worship experience to which he reacted negatively. He declares:

> I came out this morning, and now am returning,
> Perhaps little better than when I first came,
> Such groaning and shouting, it sets me to doubting,
> I fear such religion is only a dream;
> The preachers were stamping, the people were jumping,
> And screaming so loud that I neither could hear,
> Either praying or preaching, such horrible screaching,
> 'Twas truly offensive to all that were there?

Waters argues it is pivotally important to see that this second stanza, so often quoted, is *not* the voice of Richard Allen, as so frequently supposed, but that of brother Pilgrim. Allen, of course, was the author of these words, but, Waters argues, they do not represent the perspective that emotive worship is inappropriate. Rather, in the world of the hymn they represent the sentiments of those members of Allen's community who oppose the historically peculiar worship forms that were so characteristic of early African American worship. Allen's rhetorical strategy is to place their complaints in the mouth of brother Pilgrim so that he can answer them. Pilgrim's comments reflect an assimilationist tendency among some African Americans to exaggerate the features of early African American worship. Waters concludes that brother Pilgrim becomes a straw man for whom Allen builds an argument to welcome diverse forms of worship.

Allen closes his affirmation of early African American spirituality on an eschatological note. He warns brother Pilgrim that those who are not in the Spirit will nevertheless do some shouting, screaming, and crying of their own, but for mercy not for joy:

> Our time is a-flying, our moments a-dying,
> We are led to improve them and quickly appear,
> For the bless'd hour when Jesus in power,
> In glory shall come is now drawing near,
> Methinks there will be shouting, and I'm not doubting,
> But crying and screaming for mercy in vain:
> Therefore my dear Brother, let's now pray together,
> That your precious soul may be fill'd with the flame.

Pilgrim's act of contrition, concession, and confession is, of course, the indication of Allen's purpose to unify the Church.

Richard Allen is a pivotal figure in how African American Christian worship coalesced. He was concerned about the encroachment of European formalism upon the Black Church, and he encouraged dynamic worship. In a nutshell, Waters' argument is that "Spiritual Song" is easily misinterpreted because of the conflict between assimilation and inculturation. This conflict between those who affirmed a personal, heartfelt, uninhibited worship expression and those who promoted an emotionally subdued, staid, ceremonial worship life was played out in a peculiar way within the early African American religious community. Apparently, there were those who were so motivated by the desire for assimilation within a predominantly White European American culture that they abdicated their African worship heritage. They chose instead to accommodate themselves and be assimilated to White European American congregational life. High tensions arose between them and those like Richard Allen who held on to dynamic African worship.

Allen and his family were slaves of Benjamin Chew, a lawyer in Philadelphia. Influenced by the Methodists, Allen converted to the Christian faith in 1777 and was encouraged to pursue leadership in the Church. Benjamin Chew was converted also, which presented the opportunity for Allen to purchase his freedom. Francis Asbury and others encouraged Allen to preach, giving him opportunities to preach at St. George's Methodist Episcopal Church in Philadelphia, where Asbury first preached in North America.

In 1787 Allen and others formed the Free African Society in Philadelphia to address the dire needs of African slaves. Because of such community work, there was rapid growth of Africans attending St. George's. Of course, this contrasted the mores between Church society and civil society. In other words, could black and white Christians be mutual in church? Could they sit together? Could they worship together in God's house? Could the church be a refuge from an immoral society? The answer came in 1787 when Allen and others were physically prevented from praying at St. George's altar. This touchstone event made Allen and others make vows to form their own Church. Allen describes this historic scene:

> A number of us usually sat on seats placed around the wall, and on Sabbath morning we went to church, and the sexton stood at the door and told us to go in the gallery. He told us to go and we would see where to sit. We expected to take the seats over the ones we formerly occupied below, not knowing any better. We took those seats. Meeting had begun, and they were nearly done singing, and just as we got to the seats the elder said, "Let us pray." We had not been long upon our knees before I heard considerable scuffling and loud talking. I raised my head up and saw one of the trustees . . . Having hold of the Rev. Absalom Jones, pulling him off his knees, and saying, "You must get up; you must not kneel here." Mr. Jones replied, "Wait until prayer is over." . . . He came and

went to William White to pull him up. By this time prayer was over, and we all went out of the church in a body.[17]

Because of such circumstances, organizations like the Free African Society that were extracurricular to the main Church facilitated the particularity of the Black Church. There was interest at first in joining the Anglican Church (as Absalom Jones did), but Allen convinced many blacks to stay with Methodism. Allen and others purchased a blacksmith shop and turned it into a church on Sixth Street in Philadelphia. In 1794 Asbury dedicated this church as Bethel Church, and Allen was ordained in 1799. African Methodists experienced similar hardships across the country, which resulted in the official formation of the African Methodist Episcopal Church in Philadelphia on April 9, 1816.

Allen alludes to the threat of European formalism as early as the famous "Christmas Conference" of 1784 in Baltimore. He observed prophetically: "The English preachers just arrived from Europe, Dr. Coke, Richard Whatcoat, and Thomas Vassey. This was the beginning of the Episcopal Church among the Methodists. Many of the ministers were set apart in holy orders at this conference and were said to be entitled to the gown; and I have thought religion has been declining in the church ever since."[18] Parenthetically, a few years later in the *Arminian Magazine*, John Wesley (1703–91), the founder of Methodism, disclosed his own fears about the formalistic direction that the young Church was taking. Alluding to 2 Timothy 3:5, he wrote: "I am not afraid that the people called Methodist should ever cease to exist either in Europe or America. But I am afraid, least they should only exist as a dead sect, having the form of religion without the power. And this undoubtedly will be the case, unless they hold fast both the doctrine, spirit, and discipline with which they first set out."[19]

Wesley's conversion experience in 1738 made him not only concerned about the soul's condition but also about social conditions. Of course, this was not the usual position among most white evangelists, who were mostly concerned about white souls and disregarded black bodies and souls and deplorable social conditions. Wesley recognized, however, that all people, even African slaves, needed organizational structures and networks to grow spiritually. Sermons and worship were good for a time, but daily structure for spirituality was also needed. During his early years, Wesley worked out a spirituality of societies and practices (love feasts, watch-night services) intended to improve the Anglican Church in this matter of being a daily Christian. The Book of Common Prayer was used along with more energetic and emotional worship that characterized Methodist societies. Of course, such energy and emotionalism was not common in the Church of England at that time. The emotional energy of the Methodists, a spirituality of daily conversion, and an evangelical nature made Methodism very attractive to African Christians. Conversion was especially important for African Christian spirituality because it meant that a paradigm shift could occur and worldviews could change. It was now shown through conversion and salvation that no one was immune to improvement – rich, poor, slave, or master – and no one had greater access to heaven than through spiritual conversion through Jesus Christ. The sacrament of baptism also illustrated conversion into a new identity beyond human fabricated ones.

John Wesley wanted to maintain links with the Church of England, but experienced a rift in 1791. The more prominent rift occurred in 1784 when he appointed three superintendents responsible for the growing Methodist societies in North America. By doing so he usurped the power of Anglican bishops to ordain others. It was under the leadership of appointees like Francis Asbury that the Methodist Episcopal Church was formed in 1784 in the United States. Herein we gain a stronger sense of Methodists interested in "saving" black people. Asbury's diary illustrates:

> It is of great consequence to us to have proper access to the masters and slaves. I had a case, a family I visited more than a year ago, a tyrannical old Welshman. I saw there he was cruel, his people were wicked, and treated like dogs. "Well," say you, "I would not go near such a man's house." That would be just as the devil would have it. In one year I saw that man much softened, his people admitted into the house of prayer, the whole plantation, 40 or 50 singing and praising God. What now can sweeten the bitter cup like religion? The slaves soon see the preachers are their friends, and soften their owners towards them. There are thousands here of slaves who if we could come out to them would embrace religion. It is of vast moment for us to send the news far and wide. It hath its influence.[20]

Asbury even believed that the work of Methodists should destroy slavery through practices of only accepting as members those without slaves. Methodism, however, gave in to compromise over such practices as White society heated up the debate over whether Black and White Christianity could be mutual.[21] The compromise was to accept in some measure the reality of African slavery and hope for freedom in the life beyond. Of course, not everyone accepted this compromise, particularly the slaves. Despite such compromise, the success of Methodism, unlike Anglicanism, was due to its willingness to go into difficult places and evangelize and convert people. Methodists went into "the highways and byways" preaching the gospel. This meant that many Methodist churches were built inland and in out of the way places, whereas Anglican churches were built in beautiful areas, often along waterways.

The Black community flocked to the Methodist Church. In 1791 there were roughly 12,000 African Methodists, with their numbers increasing. In 1861 the Methodist Church contained around 210,000 African people.[22] The success of the Methodists among Africans carried with it the objections that Methodist worship offended those of more sophisticated styles of worship (i.e., those of "high church" sensibilities). Such Methodist sensibilities may have offended fellow white people but opened the door for the "invisible institution" of African slaves to slowly become more visible and proud of who they were.

African Methodist Episcopal Zion Church

This Church developed in New York at John Street Church. The context was similar to St. George's in Philadelphia when black members faced discrimination in worship. With the permission of Francis Asbury, Peter Williams and others formed the African Methodist Episcopal Church of New York City. Later, they became known as the Zion Church. Another Church was formed known as Asbury Church. When the white leadership of these two churches left, black members petitioned for a new conference within the Methodist Episcopal Church. In 1821 this conference was formed, but the General Conference opposed it as a threat to the authority of the Methodist Church. As a result, the AMEZ Church emerged as a separate denomination. Leaders like James Hood developed resources to sustain the AMEZ Church in both the North and South.

Like the AME Church, the AMEZ Church spread outside of North America to Africa and the Caribbean. The AMEZ Church also ordained black women a lot earlier, in 1894.

Christian Methodist Episcopal Church

With the end of slavery, the Methodist Episcopal Church, South, realized that Northern African American churches would recruit in the South and take away many of its members. To maintain some of its black membership, a meeting was held in 1870 during which the Colored Methodist Episcopal Church was formed, which changed to the Christian Methodist Episcopal Church in 1956. Although the CME Church differed from the other Black denominations on political issues and refused to become involved in Reconstruction's political and social dimensions, it shared their concern for evangelizing recently freed slaves. CME Church members believed that political issues should be addressed from the political stage, and the Church's pulpits should be reserved for preaching the gospel. Before the twentieth century, the Church concentrated on establishing new churches and developing institutions of higher learning in the United States. In the mid-twentieth century it began foreign missions in Africa, and it also finally allowed women access to a full range of Church ministries through ordination.

African American Baptist Churches

The story of the Baptist Church in America begins with John Smyth, a Separatist, someone who desired separation from the Church of England on religious grounds. He was a preacher in Gainsborough, England who moved with his group to Holland because of persecution. Smyth argued that baptism should only take place when an adult has repented and made a confession of faith in Jesus Christ. Based on this doctrine, Smyth rebaptized himself and the members of his congregation in an effort to move closer to an understanding of the Church as God would have it. What resulted from this act was the development of the first Baptist church in Holland. Smyth states:

> Wee professe even so much as they object: That wee are inconstant in erroer: that wee whou'd have the truth, though in many particulars wee are ignorant of it: Wee will never be satisfied in indevoring to reduce the worship and the ministry of the Church, to the primitive Apostolic institution from which as yet it is so farr distant.[23]

This search for a purer fellowship with God and fellow Christians was not without conflict. For example, those Smyth followers who began questioning his interest in and eventual merger with the Mennonites left and developed a Baptist church outside London under the leadership of Thomas Helwys. Helwys had been a part of Smyth's group and retained the understanding of salvation as open to all who confess belief in Jesus Christ.[24] In spite of persecution, Baptist churches in England grew and developed a general assembly in 1671.

In addition to this doctrine of general salvation, there were Baptist churches in England that held to a Calvinist understanding of salvation for only an elect few. These Baptists were called Particular Baptists due to their belief in redemption for only a select group. Other Baptists were labeled General Baptists because of their belief in salvation as available to all. There were strong differences between these two groups of Baptists, but there was also a common push to transform the Church. Both communions believed in the reformation of the official Church by moving away from the compromise and corruption they saw in the Church of England and the Roman Catholic Church. So both sought a separation from communities and doctrines that prevented a full life in keeping with biblical principles and the workings of the original Church discussed in the New Testament. Some groups distanced themselves from the Church of England and its corrupt political powers, but Baptist congregations went much further by seeking a complete separation (hence the name Separatists), which is reflected in the doctrines of no ordination by Church of England bishops and no infant baptism as promoted by the Church of England. With regard to the latter point, it was reasoned based on scripture (John 3:5) that infants were too young to make a confession of faith and act upon it. Hence, only adults could fulfill the requirements of baptism. Simply put, baptism was only for believers, and only believers were the true members of the Church.

In the North American colonies a similar perspective was present in the teachings of figures such as Roger Williams. Williams believed in a "covenanted congregation" with membership strictly limited to those who are "professing and practicing Christians" and who publicly reject association with the Church of England. Williams thought the Church of England made a mistake in thinking Christendom could be defined geographically, when Christendom was rightfully defined as the community of all who confess Jesus Christ and work toward holiness. Although Williams was seemingly content in England, he left for New England and made his home in Massachusetts. His insistence on a complete break with the Church of England presented a problem for those who thought it possible to live a righteous life without a complete rejection of the Church of England because the regenerated should have no fellowship with the unrepentant. He believed true Christians should be able to interpret scripture for themselves, under the guidance of God's Spirit. As Williams moved within New England, the first Baptist church in North America was developed among the numerous religious communities based on Williams's group in 1639.

In Rhode Island, as in Europe, division developed between those who believed the death and resurrection of Christ served to redeem an "elect" group – the Calvin-influenced Particular Baptists – and the General Baptists who argued for Christ's gift of redemption for all humanity. With time, associations (groups of congregations based on region) began to develop in New Jersey and Pennsylvania and in Southern states. The Particular Baptist perspective was dominant during this early phase, but it did not prevent other perspectives. The autonomy of Baptists and the thrust for religious growth during the mid-eighteenth century fueled two major groupings of Baptists: New Light or Separate Baptists and Old Light or Regular Baptists. The development of these communions is complex and beyond the scope of this book; however, while both groups were "poor and disinherited," the Separate Baptists were revival-minded and enthusiastic in worship, while the Regular Baptists were not. Baptist churches appealed to many, including enslaved Africans who were often treated as spiritual equals, including all the accompanying opportunities and responsibilities. "The relatively disinherited, looking for a faith that would indeed give promise that they, too, might share equally in all of God's gifts, found fulfillment in the Baptist faith and polity. The church was the community of believers. Once accepted, a man was the equal of everyone else in the church."[25]

Many enslaved Africans who were permitted by their owners to attend revival services and camp meetings embraced the Baptist faith. In addition to the strong appeal of emotional worship, Baptists showed limited concern for educational qualifications for preaching and with memorizing catechisms. No doubt Africans found the preaching of these evangelists appealing because it often condemned institutions that prevented humans from fulfilling God's will, such as the slave system. In opposition to ungodly systems of oppression, Baptists preached the equality of all believers and the autonomy of local communities of the faithful. In this sense, for poor whites and enslaved Africans, the Baptist message promised full humanity and democracy despite the restrictions of the unchurched world.

By the 1800s much of the theological frictions between Separate and Regular Baptists had eased. Through this blending, Baptist churches became more acceptable in the South, but acceptability required a less consistent denouncement of the slave system. Successful evangelists had to be sensitive to the concerns of slaveholders. When slaveholders believed conversion posed no threat, they supported it; however, when it was perceived as a danger to the slave system, slaveholders prevented religious instruction. In either case, social inequality took preference over religiosity. James Smith, a former Virginia and Georgia slave, points to this White suspicion in an 1852 interview, recounted by Henry Bib:

> [James Smith] became a convert to the Christian religion, and made application to the Baptist Church one Sabbath-day to be admitted into the church and the ordinances of baptism: but the minister refused to

have anything to do with him until he could see Brother Wright (his master), who was a member of the same church, about it. After the preacher had seen his master, who consented that he should be baptized if he should be found worthy after being examined . . . On the day appointed, he was accordingly examined: many questions were asked him, to which he answered and gave general satisfaction, but before he was discharged, his master had one or two questions to ask, namely: "Do you feel as if you loved your master better than you ever did before, as if you could do more work and do it better?" "Do you feel willing to bear correction when it is given you, like a good and faithful servant . . ."[26]

In spite of White resistance and suspicion, Africans were converted. The first African Baptist on a church roll was at a church in Newton, Rhode Island, and by the early 1770s the Baptist church in Boston began to reflect African membership in its records. Africans in Northern churches, however, remained second-class members with virtually no opportunity for leadership and a limited voice with respect to the workings of the church.

The religious situation for Africans was in many respects far worse in the South. Nonetheless, the first African Baptist churches were Southern churches: the congregation on William Byrd's plantation in Mecklenburg, Virginia (1758) and the Silver Bluff Church (of Silver Bluff, South Carolina). The latter was founded by George Liele and managed by one of his converts. During the early 1800s African Baptist churches also developed in other Southern states, including Kentucky, Tennessee, Alabama, Mississippi, and Louisiana. Outside the Deep South, historians note the emergence of Black Baptist churches in Virginia as early as 1774; Massachusetts as of 1805; Pennsylvania in 1809; New Jersey in 1812; Manhattan in 1808; and Brooklyn in 1847. These are just a few examples of independent Black Baptist communities during the years prior to the Civil War. The appeal of these relatively independent Black churches – some making use of white ministers – is clear in that participation in such a church was a step toward complete personhood and freedom in an oppressive land. These churches and others like them functioned as best they could under existing social restrictions. Fear that such gatherings would result in rebellions, combined with growing pressure on slaveholders from Northern abolitionists, made the development of independent Black Baptist associations impossible. One example of the realization of this apprehension of insurrection was the rebellion organized by Baptist minister Nat Turner in 1831.

Turner was born into slavery with markings that, according to folk wisdom, signaled great abilities and a profound destiny. Impressive intellectual abilities exhibited as a child only reinforced the opinion that

Turner had been selected by God for a special purpose. For many of the more religious on the plantation, this special purpose was spoken of in terms of ministry.

Turner was drawn to scripture that focused on the coming of justice through judgment, and he came to believe that God had appointed him to bring about judgment on those who perpetuated the system of slavery. Always mindful of this sense of calling, Turner could not find peace in escaping and securing his own freedom. Visions convinced him that he had been appointed to preach the gospel and to bring freedom:

> And on the appearance of the sign [the eclipse of the sun in February 1831] I should arise and prepare myself, and slay my enemies with their own weapons. And immediately on the sign appearing in the heavens, the seal was removed from my lips, and I communicated the great work laid out for me to do, to four in whom I had the greatest confidence. It was intended by us to have begun the work of death.[27]

Turner perceived the solar eclipse as a necessary sign from God, but illness kept him from beginning the mission on July 4 as planned. In August, he received another sign – a strange coloration of the sky – and began his work of "bringing death" to slaveholders. From midnight on Sunday August 21 until Tuesday morning, Turner and those with him battled whites in the surrounding area, leaving over 120 slaves and whites dead. Unable to complete his task, Turner escaped into the woods, only to be found and eventually hanged for leading the insurrection. This rebellion and others like it resulted in resistance to Christianization of slaves by many slaveholders who did not want religion to turn their slaves into Nat Turners. Maintenance of the slave system meant securing the dominance of whites above all else.

Circumstances for African Baptists grew even worse when White Baptists underwent a North–South split over the issue of slavery. In short, those opposed to slavery questioned the right of slaveholding Baptists to serve as missionaries: could one who held others in bondage provide a proper witness to the gospel of Christ? Friction over this issue resulted in the formation of the Southern Baptist Convention in 1845 and the Baptist Missionary Union, which handled missionary activities for Northern Baptists.

The rather inconsistent conversion rate of enslaved Africans to the Baptist faith resulted from a combination of factors, including inconsistent access to plantations, legal restrictions on the gathering of slaves, and internal conflict over the issue of slavery within Baptist circles. After all, Baptists had a tenacious hold on the idea of individual freedom, but did this freedom apply to blacks? By extension, was the holding of slaves a sin? Theological questions such as these were addressed in light of the material objectives of Southern Baptist slaveholders. This was not a balanced debate. The material objectives and existing social conventions often won out, producing as a byproduct questionable missionary practices and less impressive results than might have been possible. Although the Civil War and Reconstruction would change some of this, it was not uncommon prior to 1865 for enslaved Africans to embrace the Baptist faith in spite of White Baptists. In many cases, African Baptists held a degree of independence in that their services were conducted with little supervision and monitoring from whites (as was required by law and social custom).

Notwithstanding race-based opposition, restrictions, and repression, the number of African Baptists continued to grow, reaching a total of 40,000 by 1813. This figure is rather small in light of the total African population of the South, yet it is an impressive development from the less than 20,000 Black Baptists in the South only 18 years earlier. Most of these Southern converts had no choice but to remain in White churches or plantation missions until after the end of slavery, while some made use of rare opportunities to develop their own churches. The work of this latter group was impressive. According to some estimates there were over two hundred Black Baptist churches before the end of the Civil War, mostly in the South, with a total membership of close to five hundred thousand.

In addition to this significant growth in the number of African Baptists in the South prior to Reconstruction, it is also important to note the opportunity for independent church bodies in the North. The work of bringing Africans into the Baptist fold often fell to devout persons such as Nathaniel Paul, who combined a concern for religious independence with a call for abolition. According to Paul:

> Slavery, with its concomitants and consequences, in the best attire in which it can possibly be presented, is but a hateful monster, the very demon of avarice and oppression, from its first introduction to the present time; it has been among all nations the scourge of heaven, and the curse of the earth. It is so contrary to the laws which the God of nature has laid down as the rule of action by which the conduct of man is to be regulated towards his fellow man, which binds him to love his neighbor as himself, that it ever has, and ever will meet the decided disapprobation of heaven.[28]

The perspective advocated by Paul was held by many Africans in the North, and it became a major platform for Baptist churches, including

Paul's Hamilton Street Baptist Church in Albany, New York, and Abyssinian Baptist Church in New York City (1808). The efforts of these churches were extremely important, but it was understood that a much more expansive effort was necessary, one that encompassed larger geographic areas in both the North and South.

Church collectives were important because they allowed local churches to think and act beyond their own walls, which helped start missions and also better the fate of Africans in more substantive ways. The situation in the North was far from perfect, but it was liberal enough to allow for the organizing of the first collective of African Baptists, which was called the American Baptist Missionary Convention, founded at New York City's Abyssinian Baptist Church in 1849. The harsh nature of race relations in the South before and after Reconstruction made the formation of African alliances there more dangerous, if not impossible. In the West, however, circumstances made possible the development of all-black Baptist associations as early as 1834 in Ohio (the Providence Baptist Association). When associations formed, they tended to embrace abolitionist views. Ministers and laity alike took the formation of associations as an opportunity to articulate a commitment to freedom with more power than could be mustered by single congregations. As associations and conventions formed, they recognized the value of cooperative action and developed statewide conventions able to act on the mission impulse of churches. These statewide collectives were followed by attempts to organize African Baptists beyond state associations for the purpose of advancing spiritual and educational concerns.

As with the African Methodists, this was the period between the Civil War and the end of Reconstruction (1877) that marked tremendous growth among Black Baptists, but this growth had growing pains. Unlike the African Methodists, they were unable to place their work within the context of a national organization until the nineteenth century. Should Baptists concentrate on domestic missions to the exclusion of foreign concerns? Do African American Baptists make the best missionary representatives among the recently freed? Most agreed that priority must be given to the Southern mission field and that as many African American missionaries as possible must lead the work. Yet it was more difficult to secure consensus on two issues: class-based questions revolving around the appropriateness of folk religion and practices within Baptist church worship, and the Church's best response to social attitudes and political agendas on the national level.

Concerning the first issue, missionaries in the South found themselves confronted with cultural ways that ran contrary to their Northern sensibilities, and in too many instances they responded with an attitude of paternalism and superiority. For example, some objected to the singing of spirituals as opposed to more "refined" forms of music. This attitude led to conflict between these missionaries and local preachers, and the Northern bias of missionary-sponsoring organizations only provided a further irritant. Nonetheless, representatives of black-run religious organizations provided the recently freed with an option of greater self-determination and autonomy that many found acceptable, regardless of the nagging classist and political conflicts.

Many white Baptists grew troubled with the rise of the Black Baptists, even physically attacking black churches. The autonomy enjoyed by Baptist churches was a mixed blessing in that it guaranteed freedom for local congregations regardless of size, but also made compromise difficult on issues like mission agendas, financial arrangements, and other workings of associations and conventions. This was a recipe for perpetual schisms and reorganizations.

National Baptist Convention, USA

Despite several earlier attempts, Baptists did not succeed in developing a national organization until 1895, when three regional conferences joined forces to form the National Baptist Convention, USA. Using its ability to reach much farther than smaller conventions and individual churches, this convention concerned itself with the spiritual health and social development of African Americans. Two years after its formation, it had a foreign and domestic missions department as well as a publishing house. Based on voluntary association with the convention, local churches worked together to increase the reach of Baptist missions through the formation of schools and other associates with racial uplift. This relationship, however, was not free from problems, and church leaders and members fought over the proper relationship with White Baptist organizations.

Internal feuds ultimately resulted in numerous schisms, which resulted in the National Baptist Convention of America (1915) and the Progressive National Baptist Convention (1961). In 1961 Gardner Taylor (an outstanding preacher of Concord Baptist Church, New York), Martin Luther King, Jr., Martin Luther King, Sr., and several others met and formed the Progressive National Baptist Convention. They broke away from the National Baptist Convention, USA over interminable term limits and to free Baptists to become involved in the civil rights movement. But even with these developments, the National Baptist Convention,

USA maintained its presence in black communities across the country as the largest African American denomination in the country.

African American Pentecostalism

Anxiety over the spiritual condition of America became the obsession of evangelists in the late nineteenth century. As a result, these Christians took on the mission of a holiness campaign, a call to sanctification. Sanctification was a call to personal holiness by accepting Jesus as savior and being cleansed from worldliness. Salvation occurs by surrendering to the work of Jesus, who removes our sinfulness that separates us from God. Members of this holiness movement were primarily Methodists in the beginning. To be holy in this movement meant "to be in the world but not of it." Holiness preachers or evangelists preached such holiness, and if one was not living it, then repentance was called for. The first black holiness congregations developed in the late 1800s in the rural South. Friction occurred, however, between those of the holiness tradition and the Methodists, mostly due to the perceived hierarchical structure of Methodism.

According to David Barrett, 26 percent of Christians globally are what can be called Pentecostal, including 30 percent of Christians in the United States.[29] British sociologist David Martin calls the growth of Pentecostalism "the largest global shift in the religious market place over the last 40 years."[30] He conservatively estimates Pentecostalism at a quarter of a billion people and says that while it was initially a lower-class phenomenon, it is increasingly drawing middle-income people. Pentecostalism takes its name from the experience of Jesus' disciples on the day of Pentecost, described in Acts 2:4, "when they were all filled with the Holy Spirit and began to speak in other tongues, as the Spirit gave them utterance." Worldwide, Pentecostalism takes many forms – for example both as organized denominations and independent churches – but the movement is distinguished by an emphasis on the experience of the "baptism of the Spirit," often (but not always) evidenced by speaking in tongues. Pentecostals are also typically quite conservative in their theology.

Related to Pentecostalism and often referred to as "neo-Pentecostalism" is the charismatic movement. This movement shares some of Pentecostalism's enthusiasm and emphasis on spiritual experience, but it is typically a movement within established, non-Pentecostal denominations and churches aimed at revitalizing them from within. Most of the congregations that I describe here are self-consciously Pentecostal and are often independent of denominational affiliation. Some are more accurately called charismatic. All of them, however, give strong emphasis to the work of the Holy Spirit and to the believer's direct spiritual experience that develops a doctrine of holiness.

Holiness doctrine eventually became known as Pentecostal doctrine. William Seymour became one of the most famous in moving toward what is now known as Pentecostalism. Seymour was raised Baptist but moved away from his roots in Louisiana. In Ohio he encountered the Evening Lights Saints Church (also known as the Church of God). Seymour became acquainted with Charles Fox Parham's teaching that one's conversion in Jesus is followed by baptism in the Holy Spirit as taught in the second chapter of Acts. Those who embraced such teachings, like Parham, became known as Pentecostals; thus, Pentecostalism was born.

Seymour moved to California and an event occurred that forever shaped the Pentecostal movement. During one of the prayer meetings in Los Angeles on Bonnie Brae Street, Seymour had a Pentecostal experience:

> He kept on, alone, and in response to his last prayer, a sphere of white hot brilliance seemed to appear, draw near, and fall upon him. Divine love melted his heart, he sank to the floor seemingly unconscious. Words of deep healing and encouragement spoke to him. As from a great distance he heard unutterable words being uttered – was it angelic adoration and praise? Slowly he realized the indescribably, lovely language belonged to him, pouring from his innermost being. A broad smile wreathed his face. At last, he arose and happily embraced those around him.[31]

Word spread and with time the gatherings were too large for the Bonnie Brae Street location. To accommodate the group, Seymour moved his services to an old building previously owned by the AME Church at 312 Azusa Street in 1906, using this site as the home of a revival meeting that lasted more than three years. This revival eventually became an organized church in 1909, starting with a group mostly of women. The emphasis was on the recovery of the original Church seen through the Pentecost movement in the Book of Acts. Christians came from all over to experience the Baptism of the Holy Spirit as recorded in Acts. In these early stages, the Pentecostal movement was relatively free of the social hierarchy of dominant men or White control. This was the spirit of what was recorded in Acts, in which an international community formed the early Church. These original services were without musical instruments and the length of the services was long. Testimonies were heard, and prayer and speaking in tongues were the main components of the liturgy.

The difference of African American Pentecostalism was a critique of mainstream Methodist and Baptist churches that did not care adequately for migrants during the Great Migration of the late nineteenth century and the first decades of the twentieth century. Many of these poor migrants embraced the style of worship of the Pentecostal movement and had socioeconomic needs that mainstream churches seemed to be inadequate to handle. Seymour ignited a movement for the poor to find a creative intersection between their religious identity and social vision in which religion had relevance for all of life. The revival at Azusa Street caused a fire of religious commitment and fervor to spread through congregations across the country. Even at the demise of the Azusa Street experience (eventually institutionalized as the Azusa Street Mission) in 1931, nine years after Seymour's death, the impact of its work continued.

The largest and perhaps most widely recognized offshoot of the Azusa Street experience is the Church of God in Christ (COGIC), founded by Charles Harrison Mason, who was among those making their way to Los Angeles to receive the Holy Spirit. Mason was a Holiness minister whose doctrine made it difficult to maintain his relationship with Baptist churches. Mason developed his own church, now known as COGIC. His contact with Seymour's revival services changed his doctrine and created a conflict with his own congregation. Those who rejected Pentecostalism left and formed the Church of God (Holiness) USA. Under Mason's leadership, COGIC, the only incorporated Pentecostal denomination until 1914, grew as ministers ordained by Mason traveled across the country creating new churches. Ministers preached a strict interpretation of the gospel that gave priority to energetic religious experience and sanctification over formalism. After Mason's death, the denomination underwent organizational restructuring, but this did not hamper growth.

Black Worship

Daniel Alexander Payne (1811–93), a highly educated man from a Lutheran and Presbyterian background and destined in 1852 to become the sixth bishop of the African Methodist Episcopal Church, was history's driving force in the production of an educated African American clergy. Indeed, his efforts to achieve an educated black clergy can only be described as heroic. Nevertheless, when commenting upon contemporary forms of traditional African American Christian worship, he revealed a formalistic bias:

> I have mentioned the "Praying and Singing Band" elsewhere . . . After the sermon they formed a ring, and with coats off sung, clapped their hands and stamped their feet in a most ridiculous and heathenish way . . . Among some of the songs . . . I find . . . what are known as "corn-field ditties" . . . I suppose that with the most stupid and headstrong it is an incurable religious disease . . . The time is at hand when the ministry of the AME Church must drive out this heathenish mode of worship or drive out all the intelligence, refinement, and practical Christians who may be in her bosom.[32]

Although there is no evidence that Richard Allen and Daniel Payne ever directly engaged one another over worship style, it is clear that they each encountered representatives of the other's beliefs and practices. More importantly, they stood in opposite camps on the issue of worship.

Alexander Crummell (1819–98), a black Episcopal priest, was similar to Payne in his judgment upon the religious practices of his kinspeople. He particularly associated these practices with the corrupt character of rural clergy: "Good but illiterate men numbers of the field preachers were. But large numbers of them were unscrupulous and lecherous scoundrels! This was a large characteristic of 'plantation religion'; cropping out even to the present, in the extravagances and wildness of many of their religious practices!"[33] Crummell considered such worship styles of African Americans as one of the deleterious effects of slavery. He even conceded as much to his enemy, Joseph L. Tucker, a white Episcopal priest from Mississippi who accused former slaves of being morally retrograde: "We will, for Dr. Tucker's sake, make large concessions, (a) on account of the ignorance of these people; (b) for the taint of immorality, the heritage of slavery, which, doubtless, largely leavens their profession; and (c) because their religion is certainly alloyed with phrensy and hysteria, and tinged with the dyes of superstition."[34]

Francis J. Grimké (1850–1937), a Presbyterian minister, was another who would have sided with Payne. In a 1892 address to the Minister's Union of Washington, DC, Grimké was highly disparaging of the phenomenon he described as mere emotionalism in African American worship, particularly in regard to pulpiteering:

> The aim seems to be to get up an excitement, to arouse the feelings, to create an audible outburst of emotion, or, in the popular phraseology, to get up a shout to make people "happy." In many churches where this result is not realized, where the minister is unable by sheer force of lung power, and strength of imagination, to produce this state of commotion, he is looked upon as a failure. Even where there is an attempt to instruct, in the great majority of cases this idea is almost sure to assert itself, and become the dominant controlling one.[35]

Whether or not Grimké was correct in reducing contemporary African American worship expression to mere emotionalism, he compellingly warns that mere emotionalism deters authentic spirituality: "Where emotionalism prevails there will be a low state of spirituality among the people, and necessarily so. Christian character is not built up in that way."[36] It appears that Grimké had no use for the type of worship manifestations that Allen seemed to defend.

We find a more sympathetic and understanding view of indigenous African American worship in W. E. B. Du Bois (1868–1963), journalist and sociologist. For Du Bois, early African American worship style was not an aberration but a pattern typical of religious expressions since ancient times. He wrote in *The Souls of Black Folk*:

> Finally the Frenzy or "Shouting," when the Spirit of the Lord passed by, and, seizing the devotee, made him mad with supernatural joy, was the last essential of Negro religion and the one more devoutly believed in than all the rest. It varied in expression from the silent rapt countenance or the low murmur and moan to the mad abandon of physical fervor, – the stamping, shrieking, and shouting, the rushing to and fro and wild waving of arms, the weeping and laughing, the vision and the trance.[37]

All this is nothing new in the African world, but is old as religion.[38] And so firm a hold did it have on the Negro, that many generations firmly believed that without this visible manifestation of God there could be no true communion with the Invisible. Du Bois' position is reminiscent of Allen's in the ways in which he alludes to ancient precedents for African American worship style.

It is the ongoing debate over what is the proper worship style of African American Christians that makes a thoughtful consideration of Richard Allen, Daniel Payne, and others relevant for us. Intimations of the debate are detectable in the work of several writers. One of the most arresting asides to the debate was made by Martin Luther King, Jr. (1929–68) in his sermon on Luke 11:5–6 entitled "A Knock at Midnight," where he speaks of two kinds of "Negro" churches that "feed no midnight traveler" (i.e., that fall short of having a vital ministry). According to King:

> One burns with emotionalism, and the other freezes with classism. The former, reducing worship to entertainment, places more emphasis on volume than on content and confuses spirituality with muscularity. The danger in such a church is that the members may have more religion in their hands and feet than in their hearts and souls . . . The other type of Negro church that feeds no midnight traveler has developed a class system

and boasts of its dignity, its membership of professional people and its exclusiveness. In such a church the worship is cold and meaningless, the music dull and uninspiring, and the sermon little more than a homily on current events. If the pastor says too much about Jesus Christ, the members feel that he is robbing the pulpit of dignity. If the choir sings a Negro spiritual, the members claim an affront to their class status.[39]

The former type of African American church that King described may be called an "emotionalist" Black church. This type of church emphasizes a superficial emotional and sometimes hysterical expression of worship rather than a more substantial spirituality that responds to the deeper needs of the person and community. The second type of church fits the description of a Western individualistic congregation. This type of church has abdicated an authentically African American worship and religious heritage in order to adopt a White European American style of worship.

King at least alluded to yet a third type of Black church that has the "vitality" and "relevant gospel to feed hungry souls" and whose worship is a "social experience in which people from all levels of life come together to affirm their oneness and unity under God."[40] This type of church, had King described it more directly, would be an "affirmationist" congregation: a congregation that *affirms* and celebrates an authentically African American worship, congregational life, and ministry. Of course, it can not be assuredly said that King would have agreed with these labels for the types of African American churches that he describes or alludes to; nevertheless, they are helpful for the present discussion.[41]

J. Deotis Roberts informs the debate about African American Christian worship styles, commenting particularly on the issues of assimilation and accommodation in the Black Church:

Blacks who copy the religion of the White mainstream because they have really arrived at a measure of success or make believe that they have done so have no healing provisions built into their church life . . . They are less emotional and are more consciously sophisticated in their worship than Whites of the same denomination . . . The minister is to be well educated and extremely polished, but he dare not extend morning worship for more than an hour. He must not introduce any Africanisms into his service – "gospels" and "spirituals" are out. Anthems are in. The preacher must not get carried away with his message. He must present a clear, concise, logical, and cohesive message. Not only must he steer clear of emotion in his manner of delivery; he must not belabor the cause of social justice in his message. It is my impression that this is not the proper climate for the visitation of the Spirit. What cost inauthentic existence![42]

Incidentally, Roberts also addresses the problem of mere emotionalism or hysteria in Black Church worship, contending that "It is very important . . . that the mere expression of vehement emotion not be automatically taken as a manifestation of the Spirit of God."[43]

There were and still are those like brother Pilgrim or Daniel Payne who would describe African American Christian worship in negative or exaggerated emotionalist terms, but it is evident that such spirituality is more substantial than the stereotype would allow and of a type that became translated into the ministry of social healing and empowerment. After leading the exodus from Old St. George's Church, Allen and Absalom Jones established the Free African Society as a mutual aid, self-help, and burial society. Not only was this organization the precursor to Mother Bethel of Philadelphia, the first African Methodist Episcopal church congregation, but it was also an embodiment of Allen's spirituality and extension of his social witness. The leadership of Richard Allen and Absalom Jones during the Yellow Fever outbreak of 1793 in Philadelphia was an extraordinary demonstration of how the religion of the heart becomes the religion of the hands.[44]

The African American style of worship proves to be variegated and dynamic, and it must be concluded that African American people have indeed adopted a wide variety of styles of worship.[45] It is only when the historic style of African American Christian worship comes under attack in deference to some supposedly "superior" or "better" style that problems arise. African aspects of worship constitute a significant resource that African Americans have retained as part of their spiritual heritage in their worship and congregational life. Such African influence also leads to other forms of African American sensibilities, such as music. For example, the genre of music known as the Blues came out of the Church.[46] Blues follow the spirituals, as Jazz follows the Blues.[47] As the prodigal brother of spirituals, the Blues are fathered by the same forces. Both traditions are born of White oppression and domestic dysfunction. Both are framed by Black theodicy's urgent question of "whether God is a white racist." Both draw on the conviction that evil really is evil, and that there is no quick fix to African American troubles. Both answer the call to tell the truth. Yet common forces also distinguish the two. First, Blues are distinct from spirituals by their home in the dreadful "not yet" of plantation life and its work songs, rather than the otherworldly "already" of the Black Church's worship gatherings. This eschatological tension is as old as Jewish worship. It inhabits the space between imprecatory psalms and enthronement hymns, between songs of lament and assurances of faithfulness, between holy despair and holy rapture, between the fasting of Jesus' waiting disciples and the feasting that anticipates his return. It haunts times of weeping and times of laughing, mourning and dancing, war and peace. It writes the songs that lurk in captives' hearts when their captors ask for songs from Zion (Psalm 137). A second force, modernity, traumatizes this eschatological tension by forcing it into the alien categories of sacred and profane.

Jon Michael Spencer points us to the Blues' own words: almost all Blues make reference to God by means of such familiar interjections as "O Lord," "Good Lord," "Lordy, Lordy," "Lord have mercy," "the Good Lord above," "my God," "God knows," "for God's sake," "so help me God," and "Great God Almighty." Yet a kind of worldliness is behind the Blues' challenge to African American spirituals. Blues sing of "the world" passing away, spirituals of a world coming.

Spencer and James Cone trace the Blues back to the revived White Puritanism of the Second Great Awakening, which introduced into Black America an alien distinction between sacred and secular, imposing the "Puritan ethos on a people whose most elegant traditions were the complete antithesis of it."[48] Slave Christianity rapidly became other-worldly, looking forward to a "crossing the Jordan" that could only happen with death's release.[49] In the Second Great Awakening grew an anti-worldly Black spirituality that left the world to the devil. Secularism came to African America from Enlightenment Christians whose otherworldly agendas dovetailed with the worldly agendas of slaveholders. The remarkable power of Blues in what Early calls our "redeemer nation of Puritan origin" is ironic, but logical. Post-Puritan secularism gave Blues the philosophical space in which to flourish and challenge its estranged brother. However, by respecting the modern dichotomy of sacred and profane, Blues and spirituals cut themselves off from both the Christian eschatology and the African spirituality that could reconcile them. They become false opposites that demand we either mourn or dance. Each trivializes the other eschatological pole of the dialectic that locates the sojourning Church. Blues life and spiritual life are too incompatible to be reconciled merely by being overlaid. Cone is still right that the Blues are an ache for human (and divine) community.[50] The Blues tradition, and Rap its successor, need be neither White fashion accessory nor the enemy of hopeful Black activism. Blues and Rap find their proper place in the greater narrative frame of Black and non-Black Christian worship.

Turning salvation into escape left the world profane and thinly narrated, and open to thicker counternarratives.[51] Great Awakening Christianity compensated for this with moralism.[52] Moralism proved as robust in the Blues as immorality. "No matter how much Blues people were opposed to the hypocrisy and self-righteousness of the churched," Spencer claims, "they still accepted [their] ethical principles."[53] This allowed them to judge the Church's hypocrites in songs like "Preacher Blues" and "Church Bell Blues."[54] It also eased conversions as Blues players planned to rejoin the Church after retiring and authorized a certain amount of clean living in the meantime, such as sabbath-keeping.[55]

Since African spirituality does not respect a dichotomy between sacred and secular, Spencer and Cone see Blues as an outlawed but necessary aspect of a healthy spirituality. Cone tells us that Blues and spirituals both respond to suffering within the theodical frame of Black epistemology. Spirituals plead for God not to leave them alone in their troubles. "The Blues people, however, sing as if God is irrelevant, and their task is to deal with trouble without special reference to Jesus Christ."[56] Cone calls this the authentic existence of a community finding transcendence in its historical experiences. Spirituals and Blues are "two artistic expressions of the same black experience."[57] Both genres represent "one of the great triumphs of the human spirit."[58] Such triumph "is real, not imagined."[59] Cone also calls such triumph "a firm hope in the possibility of black people's survival despite their extreme situation of oppression. That is why blacks also sing, 'Times is bad, but dey won't be bad always.' Why? Because times 'gotta get better 'cause dey caint get w'us.' "[60]

Spencer thinks of those who play the Blues as missionary priests. Laboring to survive in a hostile world, they "rebaptized profane space for the sake of the unchurched black community." Blues clubs offer a "communion of blues confession" by "blues priests" who preach "gospel blues."[61] Henry Townsend states: "If I sing the blues and tell the truth, what have I done? What have I committed? I haven't lied."[62] The Blues are truth telling in the Black prophetic tradition.[63]

Notes

1   *An Anglican Prayer Book* (Church of the Province of Southern Africa, Collins Publishers, 1989), p. 45.

2   James Washington, *Frustrated Fellowship: The Black Baptist Quest for Social Power* (Macon, GA: Mercer University Press, 1986), p. 8.

3   Geoffrey Wainwright, "Renewing Worship: The Recovery of Classical Patterns," *Theology Today* 48:1 (April 1991).

4   *Power in the Pulpit: How America's Most Effective Black Preachers Prepare Their Sermons*, ed. Cleophus J. LaRue (Louisville, KY: Westminster John Knox Press, 2002), p. 15.

5   Karl Barth, *Prayer and Preaching* (London: SCM Press, 1964).

6   Kenneth Waters, "Liturgy, Spirituality, and Polemic in the Hymnody of Richard Allen," *North Star* 2:2 (Spring 1999). Waters provides invaluable analysis of Allen's "Spiritual Song," discussed below.

7   Daniel Coker was the first bishop-elect of the AME Church, but he resigned on April 10, 1816, the day after his election. Richard Allen was then elected and consecrated on April 11. See Daniel Alexander Payne, *History of the African Methodist Episcopal Church*, ed. C. S. Smith (Nashville, TN: AME Sunday School Union, 1891), p. 14.

8   See Dorothy Porter, ed., *Early Negro Writing 1760–1837* (Boston, MA: Beacon Press, 1971), p. 521.

9   See Eileen Southern, *The Music of Black Americans: A History*, 2nd edn. (W. W. Norton, 1983), p. 76.

10 Ibid, p. 76.

11 Ibid, pp. 76–7, 80–1.

12 Porter, *Early Negro Writing*, p. 521.

13 John Lovell, Jr., *Black Song: The Forge and the Flame* (New York: Macmillan, 1972), pp. 105–6.

14 Wendel Whalum, "Black Hymnody," in *Black Church Life-Styles: Rediscovering the Black Christian Experience*, ed. Emmanuel L. McCall (Nashville, TN Broadman Press, 1986), p. 86.

15 Melva Wilson Costen, *African American Christian Worship* (Nashville, TN: Abingdon Press, 1993), p. 95.

16 For the entire hymn, see Porter, *Early Negro Writing*, pp. 559–61.

17 Quoted in Harry V. Richardson, *Dark Salvation: The Story of Methodism as It Developed among Blacks in America* (Garden City, NY: Doubleday, 1976), p. 72.

18 Richard Allen, *The Life Experiences and Gospel Labors of the Rt. Rev. Richard Allen*, introduction by George A. Singleton (Nashville, TN: Abingdon Press, 1960), p. 22. Cf. Gayraud S. Wilmore, *Black Religion and Black Radicalism: An Interpretation of the Religious History of Afro-American People*, 2nd edn. (Maryknoll, NY: Orbis Books, 1984), p. 80: "[Richard Allen] shared with the Wesleys, Asbury, and other Methodist fathers a bias for personal, noninstitutional religion . . . He saw that the formal churchmanship that was gaining ground among whites of the northern cities, as the new middle class began to dominate churches such as St. George's, was not for poor blacks."

19 John Wesley, *Selections From the Writings of the Rev. John Wesley, M.A.*, ed. Herbert Welch (Nashville, TN: Abingdon Press, 1942), p. 205.

20 Francis Asbury, journal, vol. 3, February 11, 1797, p. 160.

21 See Donald G. Matthews, *Slavery and Methodism: A Chapter in American Morality, 1780–1845* (Princeton, NJ: Princeton University Press, 1965).

22 See A. J. Raboteau, *Slave Religion: The "Invisible Institution" in the Antebellum South* (New York: Oxford University Press, 1978), pp. 131, 175; Dwight Culver, *Negro Segregation in the Methodist Church* (New Haven, CT: Yale University Press, 1953), p. 50.

23 Quoted in W. Clark Gilpin, *The Millenarian Piety of Roger Williams* (Chicago: University of Chicago Press, 1979), p. 50.
24 See James Melvin Washington, *Frustrated Fellowship: The Black Baptist Quest for Social Power* (Macon, GA: Mercer University Press, 1986), pp. 4–5.
25 Michel Sobel, *Travelin' On: The Slave Journey to an Afro-Baptist Faith* (Westport, CT: Greenwood Press, 1979), p. 88.
26 Ira Berlin, Marc Favreau, and Steven F. Millier, eds., *Remembering Slavery: African Americans Talk about Their Personal Experience of Slavery and Emancipation* (New York: New Press, 1998), pp. 276–7.
27 Wilmore, *Black Religion and Black Radicalism*, p. 68.
28 Nathaniel Paul, "African Baptists Celebrate Emancipation in New York State," in Milton Sernett, ed., *Afro-American Religious History: A Documentary Witness* (Durham, NC: Duke University Press, 1985), p. 182.
29 David B. Barrett, George T. Kurian, and Todd M. Johnson, *World Christian Encyclopedia*, 2nd edn. (New York: Oxford University Press, 2001), pp. 3–23.
30 David Martin, *Pentecostalism: The World Their Parish* (Oxford: Blackwell, 2002), p. xvii.
31 Iain MacRobert, *The Black Roots and White Racism of Early Pentecostalism in the USA* (New York: St. Martin's Press, 1988), p. 53.
32 Daniel A. Payne, *Recollections of Seventy Years* (Nashville, TN: AME Sunday School Union, 1888). The full text is available at Documenting the American South from the University of North Carolina at Chapel Hill Libraries (docsouth.unc.edu/church/payne70/menu.html). Cf. Richardson, *Dark Salvation*, p. 111: "Today we would regard the tunes Payne opposed as indigenous folk music, possibly as precursors of the now-accepted 'spirituals.' But Payne felt that they were neither good music nor good religion, and he opposed their use. He encountered, of course, terrific opposition."
33 Alexander Crummell, *Civilization and Black Progress: Selected Writings of Alexander Crummell on the South*, ed. J. R. Oldfield (Lexington: University Press of Virginia, 1995), p. 83.
34 Ibid.
35 Francis J. Grimké, *Addresses Mainly Personal and Racial*, vol. 1 of *The Works of Francis J. Grimké*, ed. Carter G. Woodson (Washington, DC: Associated Publishers, 1945).
36 Ibid, p. 230.
37 W. E. B. Du Bois, *The Souls of Black Folk* (Greenwich, CT: Fawcett Premier, 1968), p. 191.
38 See Portia Maultsby, "Africanisms in African-American Music," in *Africanisms in American Culture* (Bloomington: Indiana University Press, 1990).
39 Martin Luther King, Jr., *Strength to Love* (Minneapolis, MN: Fortress Press, 1982), pp. 62–3.

40 Ibid, p. 63.
41 Cf. Floyd Massey, Jr. and Samuel Berry McKinney, *Church Administration in the Black Perspective* (Valley Forge, PA: Judson Press, 1982), pp. 11–12, 50–2. Massey and McKinney offer categories for identifying Black church types that I find helpful and analogous to my own. They are the "mass" or "Negro" church characterized by emotion and social isolation, the "class" or "Mulatto" church characterized by pseudo-Whiteness and social elitism, and the "mass-class" or "Black" church which achieves a vital worship and an effective social ministry. These designations have little to do with shades of skin color. They have more to do with behavior. Massey and McKinney argue, for example, that "some Mulatto churches are 'whiter' in behavior than some White churches."
42 J. Deotis Roberts, *Liberation and Reconciliation: A Black Theology* (Louisville, KY: Westminster Press, 1971), p. 125.
43 Ibid.
44 Allen, *Life Experiences*, pp. 48–65.
45 See a more comprehensive survey of Black worship styles in C. E. Lincoln and L. H. Mamiya, *The Black Church in the African American Experience* (Durham, NC: Duke University Press, 1990), pp. 377ff.
46 Larry Neal, "The Ethos of the Blues," in *Sacred Music of the Secular City: From Blues to Rap*, ed. Jon Michael Spencer (Durham, NC: Duke University Press, 1992), p. 37.
47 See LeRoi Jones, *Blues People: Negro Music in White America* (New York: William Morrow, 1963), p. 70.
48 Jones, *Blues People*, p. 126.
49 Ibid, p. 40.
50 James H. Cone, *The Spirituals and the Blues: An Interpretation* (Maryknoll, NY: Orbis Books, 1991), pp. 117–22.
51 Spencer, *Sacred Music*, pp. 42–4.
52 Dena J. Epstein, *Sinful Tunes and Spirituals: Black Folk Music to the Civil War* (Urbana: University of Illinois Press, 1977), p. 208.
53 Jon Michael Spencer, *Protest and Praise: Sacred Music of Black Religion* (Minneapolis, MN: Fortress Press, 1990), p. 123.
54 Ibid, p. 115.
55 Spencer, *Protest and Praise*, pp. 123–30.
56 Cone, *The Spirituals and the Blues*, p. 113.
57 Ibid, p. 130.
58 Ibid, p. 130.
59 Ibid, p. 123.
60 Ibid, p. 124.
61 Spencer, *Protest and Praise*, p. 113.
62 Cone, *The Spirituals and the Blues*, p. 106; Spencer, *Protest and Praise*, p. 123.
63 See Spencer, *Protest and Praise*, pp. 121–4.

Chapter 5
Inviting Others to Be Black

I need you, you need me.
We're all a part of God's body.
Stand with me, agree with me.
We're all a part of God's body.

It is his will, that every need be supplied.
You are important to me, I need you to survive.
You are important to me, I need you to survive.

I pray for you, you pray for me.
I love you, I need you to survive.
I won't harm you with words from my mouth.
I love you, I need you to survive.

It is his will, that every need be supplied.
You are important to me, I need you to survive.[1]
Hezekiah Walker, "I Need You to Survive"

The African context in America is one in which cultural conquest and Christian faith have lived in tension. Within this context the image of the Christian God was assumed to be European and white. It is only recently that such an image has been contested and the war begun as to the color of God. I posit that the Black Church in America faced severe choices between a warring image of God or an image of God reflecting human interrelationship. In the end, the beauty of the Black Church in America is in its common sight of God's image in both black and white people. As Hezekiah Walker states in his beautiful gospel song, "I need you to survive."

For quite some time into the twentieth century, there was no common theological anthropology to which both black and white people could assent. For example, it is often forgotten that Martin Luther King, Jr.'s famous "Letter from a Birmingham Jail" was not addressed to civil rights advocates but to church officials. Nor did he send it to the segregationists who had jailed him. The letter was written to church leaders. Therefore, using the model of communal spirituality inherited by African Americans, I argue that the Black Church did make a decision, one toward the eventual inclusion of all of God's children. This invitation for others to become black would be King's Beloved Community in which African American Christian spirituality would display its particularity in relationship to white people. And there would be no threat in doing so.

This conciliatory character of African American Christian spirituality invites criticism by black theologians such as Itumuleng Mosala who think that "African" or "black" people have courageously struggled in an apartheid society in which European and American epistemologies provide little relevance. According to Simon Maimela, communal spirituality naturally elicits contradictory perceptions.[2] My method of displaying these perceptions is to situate to some extent communal spirituality in Black and African theology that invites others to become black.

Over 130 years after Nat Turner was hanged, Black theology emerged as a formal discipline. Beginning with the Black Power movement in 1966, black clergy in many major denominations began to reassess the relationship of the Christian Church to the Black community. Black caucuses developed in the Catholic, Presbyterian, and Episcopal churches. Charles Hamilton states: "The central thrust of these new groups was to redefine the meaning and role of the church and religion in the lives of black people. Out of this reexamination has come what some have called a 'Black Theology.' "[3] For the first time in the history of Black religious thought, black clergy (primarily educated, middle-class black clergy) and black theologians began to recognize the need for a completely new "starting point" in theology. They insisted that this starting point must be defined by people at the bottom and not the top of the socioeconomic ladder. So, black theologians began to reread the Bible through the eyes of their slave grandparents and started to speak of God's solidarity with the oppressed of the earth.

The formative phase of Black theology lies in the civil rights movement of the 1950s, which grew on the religious faith and activism of the masses of black Christians. However, by the mid-1960s many black pastors and clergy had grown increasingly disenchanted with the demand of Martin Luther King, Jr. for absolute commitment to nonviolent protest and suffering love. James H. Cone wrote and published his first book in this phase, and formally started Black theology to discern, understand, interpret, and impart the word of God and its meaning for the historical, religious, cultural, and social life of the Black community.

Black theology burst on the scene as the heir to an entire tradition of responding to slavery in America. Its theologians reclaimed and rejected various strands of their heritage, answering questions and retelling old stories in widely diverse ways. They overwhelmingly revived and intensified the liberationist strand of African American faith that had predominated before the Civil War. James H. Evans, Jr. summarizes Black theology in one word: "liberation."[4] Practically every writer in James H. Cone's and Gayraud S. Wilmore's two-volume historical survey embraces liberation as the overriding category of salvation. J. Deotis Roberts is an exception to the rule, not because he denies liberation as a central concern of Black theology, but because he goes so far as to place reconciliation alongside it as a necessary dimension to liberation.[5] The full story of God's deliverance of African Americans in slavery reflects a Black American faith that speaks faithfully and truly from its perspective on God. But not all black scholars agree as to what is faith, especially in light of the Black Church that has suffered so deeply.

In the 1980s some black theologians were concerned that Black theology had become too concerned to prove itself to the White academy, thereby legitimating a "universalism" that clouded its interpretation of the Black experience. Also within this period, Black theology was seen as displaying an uncritical acceptance of Black Power.

Eric Lincoln and Laurence H. Mamiya undertook a ten-year statistical study of the Black Church in America. They published their findings in a volume called *The Black Church in the African American Experience*. In a 1990 questionnaire asked of 1,531 urban churches about their theology and influences, only 34.9 percent of the urban black clergy said they had been influenced by Black theology. The Black Church and Black liberation theology have both failed to penetrate the Black community in order to empower the poor. The US Census Bureau released its most recent study of income and poverty on September 3, 2003. For the second consecutive year, the poverty rate and the numbers living in poverty rose. Almost 35 million Americans (12.1 percent) made less in 2002 than the extraordinarily modest federal poverty threshold of $18,500 for a family of four. About 17 percent of the children living in the US are poor. The numbers are even worse for black (24 percent) and Latino (22 percent) children. Responses to the urban questionnaire in 1990 were also quite revealing. Only 34.9 percent of urban Black clergy said they had been influenced by Black liberation theologians, as opposed to 65.1 percent who said they had not. Little more than one-third of the black pastors interviewed claimed any influence from this movement! Lincoln and Mamiya discerned that age and education were among the most significant variables in determining clergy responses:[6]

Clergy who are forty and under claimed to be more strongly influenced by black liberation theology than those who are older. Education was also very strongly associated with knowledge of black liberation theology. Pastors with a high school and less educational background said that they were minimally influenced by liberation theology, while those with a college education have the most positive views of the movement. The majority of the less educated pastors have neither heard of the movement nor of the names of theologians associated with it. Among educated clergy familiar with the movement, James Cone has the highest name recognition.[7]

These differences are not that surprising, Lincoln and Mamiya claim, since Black liberation theology is a relatively recent intellectual movement "occurring largely among the educated elite of the black clergy."[8]

Another significant variable was found to be denominational affiliation. According to Lincoln and Mamiya, the Black denominations with higher educational levels among their clergy – such as the African Methodist Episcopal Church – are the major proponents of liberation theology. "The fact that the Pentecostal ministers of the Church of God in Christ, which has the largest sector of lower-class members among the seven [major Black] denominations, have been scarcely influenced by this theological perspective suggests some of the class limitations of this movement."[9] This would seem to indicate that the formulators of Black liberation theology have not been able to move beyond their middle-class origins, even though Black liberationists have sought to do theology from the "bottom up" – that is, from the perspective of the oppressed in American society.[10]

Based on their nationwide field experience, Lincoln and Mamiya have observed that the majority of black clergy are educated as apprentices – learning "on the job" under the direction of senior clergy. What little academic education they receive is usually at the level of the local Bible school. Moreover, most of their reading is denominationally oriented. "It is this local level of clergy education," Lincoln and Mamiya suggest, "that the new black liberation theology has thus far failed to penetrate."[11] They close with this warning: "Unless the movement of black liberation theology reaches beyond its present location in an intellectual elite and gives more attention to a mass education of clergy and laity in the churches, the movement will continue to have minimal influence among its key constituencies."[12]

Lincoln and Mamiya are probably correct. However, the problems of Black liberation theology go much deeper than a simple failure to reach the masses.

African American Christian spirituality challenges those coercive ideologies that construct the framework within which the majority culture deprives others of their human identity. However, some like Itumeleng Mosala think that communal models of African Christian spirituality fail in their task of representing the complexity of African cultures: "I contend that, unless black theologians break ideologically and theoretically with bourgeois biblical-hermeneutical assumptions, black theology cannot become an effective weapon of struggle for its oppressed people."[13] Mosala argued that as an African Christian, the greatest difficulty in withstanding the oppression of apartheid is the fact that the oppression of black people was theologically justified. African theologians like Mosala therefore saw the need for additional hermeneutical weapons with which to combat European religion. Such a recognition among African/black theologians became common, as Takatso Mofokeng explains:

> Black Christians, pastors and theologians were called upon to respond theologically to counteract and restrict the mental damage to black Christians. They had to join hands with black sociologists, economists, psychologists and other scientists.[14]

Due to the incommensurate views of Christianity of African theologians, and secondarily influenced by the school of Black theology in the USA, African theologians arose to give careful thought and voice to the task of empowering the oppressed majority in South Africa. The great resource for such African theologians is James Cone. Indeed, there is a lot to be learned from Cone, especially his thesis that because Christianity had often been co-opted by universal notions of White Christianity (e.g., the *imago Dei*) it has been used to justify racism, in that God's image assumed White identity. In order to counter this implicit understanding of Western Christianity, there needs to be more particular authorizing criteria with which to claim racial oppression as immoral. Therefore, Cone claims God is black.

The problem with Mosala's response is that as a result of countering apartheid structures ordained by white theologians, African and African American theologians have increasingly grown dependent on secular authorizing criteria by which to adjudicate theological truthfulness. One can see this played out in contemporary struggles via the work of Anthony Pinn (discussed in chapter 6). I conclude that objectors to the communal nature of African Christian spirituality as modeled by Desmond Tutu misunderstand such spirituality because they provide no space for the intelligibility of the desert tradition in which African spirituality sought community with God. However, there still remains the problem – deeply influenced by Cone's powerful voice in Black theology – as to whether or not African American spirituality is more effective in the context of the USA than in Africa.

Tutu's impact in South Africa offers an uncharacteristic model of African Christian spirituality, which does not necessarily exclude historically the structures of the Anglican Church. Tutu explains:

> It is true to say that most of what is subsumed under the heading "African Theology" is the result of a reaction against cultural and ecclesiastical colonialism. Most of it certainly predates the agitation and struggle for Africa's liberation from colonial domination. But the two movements are very intimately linked.[15]

Instead of constructing African spirituality as defined by Mosala's conflictual model in order to reveal that the dominant ideas of every society are in fact the dominant ideas of the dominant class, Tutu operates from a transformative, ascetical theological model by which to facilitate the movement of historically oppressive structures into supportive structures from which Christian identity (Black and White) may be practiced in common.[16] Therefore, for Tutu, the struggle for the Church to *be* the Church in South Africa is not necessarily defined by, for instance, Mosala's criterion of a derivation of Marxist dialectical sociology, or Cone's basis of Black theology, but from *anachoresis*, the faithfulness of the peoples of God in practicing the presence of God through an alternative community called the Church in a naturally oppressive world.[17]

African vs. Black: Dialectic Tension

In the 1970s, influenced by African Americans, Steven Biko founded the Black Consciousness movement in South Africa. In this movement, Church leaders like Allan Boesak became adept in the rhetoric of the Black Power movement by affirming the language and conceptualization of Blackness already developed in North America.[18] It is a complex task, however, to marry the Black Power movement to the Black Church. We can see this through Martin Luther King's struggle. What did Black Power mean to King? First, for King, Black Power is a cry of disappointment. The slogan was born from the wounds of despair and disappointment. Second, Black Power, in its broad and positive meaning, is a call to black people to mount political and economic strength to achieve their legitimate goals. Power is defined, therefore, as the ability to achieve purpose. King's contention is that power without love is reckless and abusive and that love without power is sentimental and anemic. There must also be a pooling of black financial resources to achieve economic security. Third, Black Power is a psychological call to humanity.[19]

Because Black Power tended toward violence, King did not believe that it could become the basic strategy for the civil rights movement. He characterized it as a nihilistic philosophy born out of the conviction that the Negro cannot win. Black Power is an implicit and often explicit belief in Black separation. King completely rejected Black Power's unconscious and often conscious call for retaliatory violence. He believed it dangerous to organize a movement around self-defense.[20] King believed that "If every Negro in the United States turns to violence, I will choose to be that one lone voice preaching that this is the wrong way."[21] King also responded to white liberals who wanted him to relinquish his pacifistic tendencies:

> The white liberal must see that the Negro needs not only love but also justice. It is not enough to say, "We love Negroes, we have many Negro friends." They must demand justice for Negroes. Love that does not satisfy justice is no love at all. It is merely a sentimental affection, little more than what one would have for a pet. Love at its best is justice concretized. Love is unconditional. It is not conditional upon one's staying in his place or watering down his demands in order to be considered respectable. He who contends that he "used to love the Negro, but . . ." did not truly love him in the beginning, because his love was conditioned upon the Negroes' limited demands for justice.[22]

More recently, South African thinkers such as Itumeleng Mosala have questioned this kind of response to Black consciousness. Mosala sees incongruity in North American Black theology's inability to become an autonomous weapon in the hands of the oppressed and exploited black people of South Africa.[23] He thinks that Black theologians like Desmond Tutu and James Cone are caught between espousing a Black, revolutionary rhetoric against White social discrimination and simultaneously adhering to a colonial Christian identity which will always bring African identity into crisis because of the privileges of White culture.[24] Mosala grants that this current consciousness in South African Black theology is inherited from James Cone, whom he sees ironically in the same light as Tutu, as they both concede hermeneutical privilege to the dominant political sectors of society. For Mosala, what is good about Cone's pioneering Black theology in the Western world is that it exposed the cultural assumptions of a dominant, White theology and demonstrated the hermeneutical marriage between Christianity and White racial identity. In this way, Cone facilitated the demythologization of an idolatrous faith which was assumed to possess no cultural or ideological conditioning.

Mosala reacts against notions of communal spirituality because the European dominance in theology entails a surreptitious conditioning to hold to some sort of objective method by which to proceed in theological discourse. Thus, he sees Tutu's theology as even more problematic than Cone's, in that Tutu perpetuates contradiction within his goal of reconciliation of identity by conceding a political reading of the Bible to the hegemonic sectors of society. Instead of Mosala's antagonistic approach to theology, Tutu adheres to a conciliatory model of Christian spirituality that advocates communal existence. Christian spirituality is not about ultimate survival, but something more than that: the flourishing of creation. Tutu believes:

> The Church must face up to the possibility that it may die in this struggle, but what of that? Did our Lord and Master not tell of a seed that will remain alone unless it falls to the ground and dies (John 12:24)? We can never have an Easter without a Good Friday: there can be no Resurrection without a Crucifixion and death.[25]

Tutu is not ashamed of his European and African roots combining in this way. In fact, his spiritual model of Ubuntu displays how each person in community informs the other toward reflection of the image of God. Tutu's model of Ubuntu claims that human identities are interdependent in such a way that anyone's survival is dependent on all others. And Tutu's ascetical training forms him to act through the Church to encourage corrupted forms of human societies to see the truer image of God. He therefore rejects Mosala's conclusion that struggle is all there really is to life and seeks to move the discussion back to a normative language of Christian discourse, so that prayer becomes intelligible, and most of all, the image of God comes back into the light. This is also the movement and interdependence of Ubuntu, which instead of perpetuating disparate viewpoints, allows a theological grammar for which South African society may see that

> the evil of apartheid is perhaps not so much the untold misery and anguish it has caused its victims (great and traumatic as these must be), no, its pernicious nature, indeed its blasphemous character is revealed in its effect on God's children when it makes them doubt that they are God's children. This is why it has been of crucial importance that black consciousness should have succeeded – because it was of God – an almost

evangelistic movement to awaken in the black person the realization that s/he is a child of God. It has not been anti-white as its detractors have tried to make it out to be, but it has been pro-black, it has been affirmative of what God has done. It has said people must celebrate the fact of who they are and not accuse God of making a mistake in creating them black and looking forward to the time when they would celebrate their own culture and value system so that they could make their own distinctive contribution to the body politic. It is after all the glorious diversity among God's people which make us all interdependent because none can be self-sufficient.[26]

Influenced by the desert tradition, Tutu's theology proclaims that human identities become new through the creation of the Church in the world. And this newness is most expressed in the death and resurrection of Jesus Christ, through whom God broke the manic cycle of death and showed God's self to effect salvation. The very nature of God related in three persons becomes the Christian paradigm of Ubuntu, in which antagonistic schemes of power can no longer be tolerated, and deterministic ideologies can no longer fix human identity because the Christian God is always creating that which is new.

The comparison between Tutu and Cone proves to be a different contrast than with Mosala's Black theology. Compared to Tutu's theology, Mosala's hermeneutic of struggle has a short attention span for the concept of salvation as liberation rooted in black and white people's recognition of new identity. Even when white political opponents try to characterize Tutu's theology as radical,[27] the assumption is still to make race one's primary identity. However, Tutu aims for his society to venture only in the direction of a new identity for both black and white Christians. For Tutu, this venture is already underway in the practices of the Church, which characterize his theology in such way that it does not fit the caricature of Black theology as a radical hermeneutic. Tutu's theological model can be seen as a Black theology only insofar as we recognize that his goal is communal reconciliation of racial identity through the practices of the Church.

James Cone and Desmond Tutu

James Cone's theology is a great contrast to Tutu's. Tutu is a Xhosa archbishop, trained in the ascetical tradition of the Community of the Resurrection (a monastic order), while Cone is a Christian intellectual, contextualized by North American societies. This is not to say that their contexts distinguish the two more than their views of inclusive community. For example, Tutu has a strong affinity for African American culture:

> It is good to speak to you, my soul brothers and sisters. I address these words especially to you who are black. We have a solidarity, we here in South Africa and in Africa, with you in the USA. It is a solidarity that is like a threefold cord which is not easily snapped. First of all we have a solidarity that stems from the color of our skins . . . Secondly, the solidarity between yourselves and us blacks in South Africa stems from the fact that we are victims (in differing measure) of oppression, exploitation and racism . . . Thirdly, our solidarity as blacks in South Africa and the United States stems from our unity in Jesus Christ through our baptism.[28]

It is from this last cord of baptism that I compare Tutu and Cone.

My argument in comparing Cone and Tutu is that they operate from different epistemologies of community. Cone's epistemology is estranged from Tutu's in the sense of having difficulty making sense of Tutu's preexistent ascetical strains within a South African Anglicanism that forms Tutu's theological model. I have argued above that this asceticism is a model of Christian spirituality in which individuals practice the discipline of *anachoresis*, namely, learning to be vulnerable for the sake of the other. This means that Tutu cannot abide by Cone's exclusivist rhetoric in which God's image is black or white. A truer accounting for God's image in the world means the discovery of vulnerability, of being poured out for the other like a libation poured on the ground. This is God's *kenosis* (pouring out) in the person of Jesus, who includes not only those to whom he is first called (the Jews), but also the gentiles and all those made in such an image of God's *kenosis*. God's image in Christ is especially aimed at the tearing down of exclusionary modes of existence. Tutu states: "I worry, however, about some of Cone's exclusiveness – that, for instance, only the oppressed can form a genuine Christian koinonia."[29] But this does not mean that Tutu and Cone disagree on the meaning of Black identity. Tutu continues: "Basically, Cone is concerned about how we do theology . . . The black experience, he claims, provides the appropriate context for questions and answers concerning the divine."[30] Tutu would therefore agree that Cone's school of Black theology – criticized by Mosala as not being radical enough – is correct in demonstrating the pervasive nature of how White identity may find reconciliation with Black identity.

Racial reconciliation involves personal and political relationships. In South Africa, Tutu is known to be one of the first theologians to agree with how this pervasive nature of reconciliation may occur. Louise Kretzschmar states: "The initial criticism from a South African black theologian was voiced by Bishop Desmond Tutu, who pointed out that in South Africa the concerns of African, Black and Liberation Theology come together."[31] Tutu states:

> We cannot deny too that most of us have had an identical history of exploitation through colonialism and neocolonialism, that when we were first evangelized often we came through the process having learned to despise things black and African because these were usually condemned by others. The worst crime that can be laid at the door of the white man (who, it must be said, has done many a worthwhile and praiseworthy thing for which we are always thankful) is not our economic, social and political exploitation, however reprehensible that might be; no, it is that his policy succeeded in filling most of us with a self-disgust and self-hatred. This has been the most violent form of colonialism, our spiritual and mental enslavement, when we have suffered from what can only be called a religious or spiritual schizophrenia.[32]

In a sense, Cone's theology is compatible with Tutu's since both theologians assume an eschatological community in which a radical transformation takes place in people's identity. However, for Cone, this transformation seems to occur exclusively in the "Black Church," in which the janitor becomes chairperson of the deacon board; the maid becomes president of the steward board; everybody becomes Mr. and Mrs. or brother and sister; and (lastly and most importantly) everyone talks as if they know the truth about which they speak. Here is the beauty of Cone's work: it is this experience of being radically transformed by the power of the Spirit that defines his primary view of the transformation of human identity, not as a social theory that offers only scientific analysis of societal oppression.

For Cone, just like for Tutu, Christian identity is a spiritual vision around which the construction of a new humanity can take place.[33] In such a vision, black people are no longer defined by oppression, but by freedom.[34] The problem in all this, however, is how Cone's preference for the Black Church could ever make sense of Tutu's Anglican Church, in which Tutu was trained by an ascetical community comprised mainly of white English men. It is difficult for black American Baptists to understand black Anglicans, although in fact there are more Afro-Anglicans in the world than black National and Progressive Baptists combined.

Cone's hermeneutic comes from within this African American Church. It seems to imply a greatly different construal of the nature of the Church and salvation than Tutu's ecclesiological emphasis on sacraments and asceticism. The concern here is whether or not Black American churches are catholic in nature. To put this another way, do Black Baptists in the

United States understand the universal and global nature of the Church? I argue yes, especially through later discussions around Martin Luther King, Jr.'s concept of the Beloved Community and the active role of the Black Church in the civil rights movement. One could argue that the early work of Cone lacked this catholicity. Cone understood the Black Church as fundamentally a prophetic voice to the world, a vibrant Church centered in the prophetic call and response of singing and preaching. And though Cone is critical of his own Church's witness in the world, his vision of the Black Church is like the prophets of the Old Testament who stand and declare the judgment of God upon other kingdoms with little recourse to models of reconciliation.[35]

We are provided the best purchase on categorizing Cone's theology – formed through the African American Church – by his own question: how are we going to survive in a world in which black humanity is deemed an illegitimate form of human existence?[36] Cone's work can thus be described as a survivalist theology, whereas Tutu's spirituality is communal. Both Tutu and Cone's theology not only question the premise of rational discourse about ultimate reality, but also aim higher in being a prophetic word of God's righteousness spoken amid corrupted societal structures. More specifically, Tutu and Cone's Christian theology must abide by the tenets of a theology which conveys that what whites mean by oppression is what blacks mean by liberation. The difference between Tutu and Cone's theological approaches is that for Cone, blackness simultaneously symbolizes oppression and liberation in the Black Church, whereas for Tutu black identity represents the *imago Dei* in which God redeems white identity.

Where Tutu agrees with Cone is in the definition of "blackness" – all victims of oppression who realize that the survival of their humanity is bound up with their liberation from Whiteness as that which demonizes black human identity to denote criminality, subhumanity, and anarchy. Where Cone differs from Tutu is in Cone's ecclesiastical preference. Cone, on one hand, sees the existence of the Church, especially the Black Church, as in fundamental opposition to a dominant society that sometimes likes to call itself Christian or even "the Church":

> We cannot solve the ethical question of the twentieth century by looking at what Jesus did in the first. Our choices are not the same as his. Being Christian does not mean following "in his steps" (remember that book?). His steps are not ours; and thus we are placed in an existential situation in which we are forced to decide without knowing what Jesus would do. The Christian does not ask what Jesus would do as if Jesus were confined to the first century. He asks, "What is he doing? Where is he at work?"

And even though these are the right questions, they cannot be answered once and for all. Each situation has its own problematic circumstances which force the believers to think through each act of obedience without an absolute ethical guide from Jesus.[37]

On the other hand, Tutu would not disagree with this view of black identity in the sense of opposing a dominant society, yet he would contend that the Church is prophetic by being the people of God among the kingdoms of the world through both a sacramental and prophetic witness. Sacramentally, the Church is to model redeemed identities. Thus the Church is already "involved" in transforming a profane world by means of its very existence.

For Cone's Black Church, the nature of the Church's involvement has a different form than Tutu's Anglicanism. The Black Church gains its definition historically by being in opposition to white identity and therefore lacks the ability to model the *imago Dei* in the sense that both black and white identities must conform. What this really means for Cone is that the Black Church is better able to attend to the nature of the fragile existence of human identity in the USA than the White Church because the life of African Americans in the United States remains a very dangerous reality. And as Cone later came to see, this danger can be international, in the sense that one is under constant threat in black identity.[38] Tutu agrees that there are definite dangers involved with being black and voices these sentiments in the context of the USA's involvement in South Africa in the 1980s:

We have been deeply hurt. We have seen that when it comes to the matter of black freedom then we blacks are really expendable in the view of the mighty US. It is a case of blood being thicker than water. You can't really trust whites. When it comes to the crunch, whatever the morality involved, whites will stick by their fellow whites. At least under the Carter administration our morale was upheld by their encouraging rhetoric of disapproval . . . I am personally fond of most of [the US embassy staff in South Africa], but as my own personal little protest at the actions of the Reagan administration I no longer attend US embassy functions, nor do I see Reagan administration people.

The US government gave us an eloquent spiel on the general ineffectiveness of sanctions – that they had to be applied by several countries at the same time, etc., etc. There might have been merit in these observations, but they lost all credibility for us. Why? Well, when the Polish government applied martial law in Poland, who applied sanctions and unilaterally at that? Why, it was the self-same US that can't see its way to doing half of what it did against the Polish government and the Russians. The US government does not really care about blacks. Poles are different. They are white . . . When we are free South Africa will still be of strategic importance and her natural resources will still be of strategic significance and we will remember who helped us to get free. The Reagan administration is certainly not on that list. Will your CIA now be out to get me?[39]

Tutu's ecclesial vision serves as an important lens for organizing people for the transformation of society because black people, as oppressed people, can know through the Church that they are more than who they have been identified as by those in power. This knowledge inspires oppressed people to struggle for freedom in society by practicing the Church's life of worship. From this worship life, the Church (not just the Black Church) forms persons so as not to limit salvation to the definitions of a corrupt society, for as long as people are bound to society, they are bound to law and death.

If the oppressed, while living in corrupt economic structures, can see a future beyond this world, then "the sigh of the oppressed creature" (to use Karl Marx's phrase) becomes a revolutionary cry of rebellion against the established order. It is this revolutionary cry that is granted in the resurrection of Jesus. Salvation is not simply freedom to be Black and White societies; it is freedom to affirm that future which is beyond segregated identities. This is how the sacramental Church transforms the world. (This view of transformation will be in a book that Tutu apparently hopes to write one day called *Transfiguration*.)

God does not take the Church out of the struggle of racial identities; instead, it is to be firmly rooted in cultures of death to show that death is not the goal of history. The transcendent factor in salvation helps us to realize that our fight for justice is God's fight. Cone states: "The power to be somebody in a world that had defined Blacks as nobody is what God meant to me and many other Black people."[40] This knowledge enabled black slaves to survive despite having their identity defined for them. They were not defeated or ultimately dehumanized because the Church worshipped the eternal God of three persons in one nature who acts in the world in such a way as to favor the oppressed as they escape their limitations in history. The slaves knew or believed that death had been conquered in Jesus' resurrection. They could also transcend death and interpret salvation as a heavenly, eschatological reality.

Thus, for Cone and Tutu, the Church works for salvation, which is first reflected in the restoration of God's creation within economic, political, and social configurations. Cone's emphasis is on displaying the nature of salvation first through God's movement toward addressing unjust realities.[41] Tutu does not dispute the importance of addressing these realities yet, for him, the Church, as a redeemed community, must be the locus in which God's movement becomes intelligible and these realities first addressed. For Cone, Tutu's locus would be too narrow and idealistic in a structured society such as the USA, in which a black person must assume a certain identity that the American Church has long defined as inferior. And doubtless, Cone would critique Tutu's kenotic God in the following way: "By emphasizing the complete self-giving of God in Christ without seeing also the content of righteousness, oppressors could then demand that the oppressed do likewise."[42] By means of this critique Cone would perhaps state that Tutu's Church presupposes a social configuration that is indeed different from his own.

Perhaps the following quotation from Cone provides the most distinctive contrast with Tutu: "There is no place in black theology for a colorless God in a society where human beings suffer precisely because of their color. The black theologian must reject any conception of God which stifles black self-determination by picturing God as a god of all peoples."[43]

Cone is provocative in his display of a view of God rooted in the experience of the Black Church in which one gains access to the work of God to save the oppressed.[44] However, his fundamental problem is in his display of how the Church is first subject to the same economic, political, and social realities as other kingdoms, yet remains distinctive and prophetic.

Cone's strength is iconoclastic, as his Black theology creates the contrast to see how and why different racial identities "see" theology and how other ecclesiologies naturally assume the Church to be the people of God who can circumvent profane realities, but in the end often *are* those profane realities. Perhaps this double standard of profane reality is Cone's greatest criticism of Tutu's Anglican Church. Cone's weakness is in failing to acknowledge the positive image of the Church, when it is able to pool resources and interrogate the ways in which Christian identity can itself interrogate the world.

Antony, an Egyptian who lived almost two thousand years ago, shows us that this can be done. Like Antony, Cone teaches that there can no longer be a surreptitious dominant identity defining theology for other human identities. In this respect, his theology is unparalleled in importance, as it bursts the hermeneutical dam (from which Mosala flows) and facilitates an onrush of the previously voiceless to speak and reflect in a public forum. This is Cone's invaluable contribution to theological discourse.

My criticism of Cone is that he has a weak ecclesiology because in many ways his necessary Black Church continues to promulgate profane structures of racism. No doubt Tutu would agree that black identity is victimized by white identity, but he would still advocate working and preaching through the Church's traditions and doctrines to show the original nature of the Church to be the kind of community able to contain disparate identities made one in the triune God. In other words, effort needs to be made to put clapping and shouting in the same context as incense and sung liturgy. The bane of Cone's ecclesiology is in its inevitable fall into an abyss of contextual theologians who are confined to incommensurate discourse, although there is an ostensible confession of solidarity.

For Tutu, the Church as the locus of salvation is embodied by its way of life, its practice of the presence of God by both celebrating the Eucharist and demanding that those perpetuating political injustice repent. For Cone, the Church as the locus of salvation is the involvement of a rescued, oppressed community in the interrogation and questioning of the economic, political, and social configuration of nations. If white people accept this interrogation, then salvation is near, if not already upon them. But how does Cone's Church exemplify an atmosphere in which racial classifications no longer prove what is the end of persons? And is theological reflection about grace ever provided to account for the transformation of broken human identities which may in the end be healed by participating in the sacraments of the Church? In short, the ecclesial vision of Cone lacks sufficient instrumentality in which the Church plays a significant part in a larger vision of societal restoration.

Both Tutu and Cone's strength is in their vision to see that, ironically, no ecclesiology is particular enough. This means that for both of them the relation of God to the Church, given their notions of reconciliation, remains problematic in the reality of a divided Church. Yet they both have inherited the problems of being African thinkers in European theological discourse. Their genius is located in their attempts to think out loud as to what the relation of the Church to the world should be. I privilege Tutu in this comparison because he displays the implications of the incarnation and the trinity in a volatile context like an apartheid society to model how black and white identities are in fact dependent on one another.

Both Cone and Tutu admit a dynamic nature between the Church and the state, though Cone seems more unapologetic in sometimes being unable to tell them apart. Both advocate direct action in the name of creating not only a responsible society, but also a Church that is defined beyond "White." For Cone, this has a deeper theological significance than simply a Constantinian rejection accounts for. But his theology does not lend itself so easily to theological notions such as the form of the kenotic Christ as does Tutu's, but rather assumes the nature of a new power group that seeks to dominate in terms of its particular conception of a good society. Cone's justification of such power is that it is God's manifestation for being on the side of the poor and black.

Cone might say I have misrepresented his ecclesiology and that his premise is that the Church is Black and provides the best working symbol of the dimensions of divine activity in a North American context. Therefore, Black theology must exemplify contextual language because there is no uninterpreted fact. He might continue that theology cannot be written *ex nihilo*, and it cannot be written for all times, places, and peoples. For Tutu though, the Church need not be confined to antagonistic debate and may see itself as a community of disciples trained in the politics of Jesus to be agents in the world to birth a different kingdom. Tutu's ascetical formation is important to establish how Black theology may seek to negotiate how the profane structures of the earth may be transformed into the sacred realities of the Church.

Tutu's asceticism continually questions how what we are being saved from determines the nature of the Church. Tutu and Cone both seem to be in agreement that the task of theological ethics is to specify theological language in such a way that a person's view of salvation may be seen through God's particular witness amid diverse communities that comprise the Church. Such a view accentuates the belief that at Pentecost the Holy Spirit displays how persons are dependent on other persons to be persons.

As far as how Cone and Tutu's theological convictions interact, their enterprises are successful in their attempts to understand one another, but their theologies diverge, as their views of the Church manifest. In the end, as we will see below, Cone provides an essential perspective from which Tutu is able to challenge those in power.

We, black and white South Africans, have basically totally different perceptions of our country. We think we are looking at what is the same reality but we seem to see different things . . . Most whites think that we are involved in a veritable orgy of reform which has left them breathless; whereas, the same phenomena have been dismissed by most blacks as either cosmetic or merely peripheral to the real fundamental problems of our country. We could be inhabiting different planets for all the effective communication that takes place between black and white people. When there was a state of emergency, blacks knew from better experience what that meant. Whites could well have asked, "What emergency?" After all what did they know of road blocks, of Casspirs and Hippos, of the sting of tear gas, of the slashes of the fangs of police dogs, of rubber bullets and birdshot and live ammunition? So it was possible, at the height of the emergency, for whites to be playing tennis under floodlights in their yards, as I saw happen near where I am by the zoo in Westcliff. Many whites believe that you can reform apartheid when blacks declare that it cannot be reformed – it must be destroyed.[45]

African and Black: Communal Synthesis

I have argued that Cone's Black theology is defined by the Church's awareness of the primary signifier of being black. White Christianity is the identity of Christians of European descent who exist in various churches and denominations but who are united by one implicit idea: they are not black Christians. The life of the Black Church or African Christians is absolutely essential for understanding how Christianity was distorted in the West.[46] With racial identity the danger of oppressive definitions of identity come into being, especially as economic structures are put in place as a result of the dominant group. Those who are the most powerful – white people – assume the all encompassing identity by which all others are defined. Tutu illustrates:

> I was a Native who to many did not seem to count for much – as in newspaper accounts of say a road accident reading "Three persons and a Native were injured." Then we became "non-whites," then "non-Europeans," negative entities who presumably came from somewhere called "non-Europe;" then we were Bantus, and wonder of wonders we even became "plurals," so that you probably might have a singular "plural," an urban "plural," or a rural "plural."[47]

Consciously and unconsciously, people use racial descriptions as though these were the ultimate characteristics by which to define human beings. Racial identity (e.g., White and Black Christianity) may indeed impede the progress of the Christian life. Herein, Black theology becomes helpful for Tutu because like his ascetical training, Black theology displays a way for judging authentic Christianity. As we shall soon discuss, the historical configuration of the Black Christian protest provides a ready critique of erroneous forms of Christianity, especially those justifying racism and slavery. This still raises the problematic among more radical voices in Black theology that have little patience for "traditional theology."

According to the Black theological school, "traditional theology" still assumes that Blacks are called to believe in Christ and forgive the oppressor although the power structures stay the same. In this instance, theological language of reconciliation lacks intelligibility for the oppressed. To counter these unhelpful understandings of theology, black theologians like J. Deotis Roberts (b. 1927), though committed to liberation, insist that Black theology must speak of "reconciliation that brings black[s] . . . together and of reconciliation that brings black[s] and white[s] together."[48] "It is my belief that true freedom overcomes estrangement and heals the brokenness between peoples."[49] However, Roberts argues "reconciliation can take place only between equals. It cannot coexist with a situation of Whites over Blacks."[50] Genuine reconciliation can come only if people – both black and white – commit to a view of their sisters and brothers of different contexts, seeing all people as created in the image of God (Genesis 1:26) and of infinite value to God (1 Corinthians 6:20; 1 Peter 1:18). Such a commitment guards against a "traditional theology" shaped only by those in power. In short, there is no final theology; and it is not eternal or ever will be perfect as long as persons see through a dark glass. "Of course, the true insights of each theology must have universal relevance," Tutu believes, "but theology gets distorted if it sets out from the very beginning to speak, or attempt to speak, universally."[51] There must be a plurality of theologies because we do not always apprehend the transcendent in exactly the same way, nor can we be expected to express our experience in the same way. On this point Tutu quotes Maurice Wiles:

> Theology today is inductive and empirical in approach. It is the ever changing struggle to give expression to man's response to God. It is always inadequate and provisional. Variety is to be welcomed because no one approach can ever do justice to the transcendent reality of God. Our partial expressions need to be complemented by the different apprehensions of those whose traditions are other than our own. There are no fixed criteria for the determination of theological truth and error. We ought therefore to be ready to tolerate a considerable measure even of what seems to us to be error, for we cannot be certain that it is we who are right. On this view a wide range of theological difference (even including what we regard as error) is not in itself a barrier to unity.[52]

African and Black theology is concerned with liberation because liberation often carries casualties as a result of warring identities seeing themselves as under threat and in need of rebellion. Tutu's theology, however, seeks a different reality that avoids the self-securing realities of black identity and the alternative dominant identity of white identity, couched in the guise of the personal identity of being a Christian. Instead, there is an inescapable consequence of taking the gospel of Jesus Christ seriously – that we are already reconciled in Christ. Herein is Tutu's impetus to synthesize the tenets of African and Black theology.

African theology emphasizes the relationship between Christianity and African traditional religion and culture, whereas Black theology as Black Consciousness emphasizes that blackness is not to be negated as inferior, but affirmed as part of God's creation, and draws out the implications of a Black theology for the Church. Black theology as liberation theology stresses three liberational themes: (1) a gospel of liberation in which the good news is primarily for the poor; (2) a liberation of individuals from the oppressive social structures in which they live; and (3) the creation of a new society.[53] Louise Kretzschmar states, "Individual black theologians may, as Desmond Tutu does, embrace all three of these. Others, such as Allan Boesak, emphasize Black Consciousness and Liberation, while yet others, like Gabriel Setiloane, will speak mainly in terms of African Theology."[54] Kretzschmar believes that scholarly African theology developed slowly because its leadership (i.e., in the churches and theological seminaries) was largely in the hands of white men who determined both the concerns and content of theological study and generally had a low opinion of African culture and tradition. In such an environment a distinctively African theology could not be propagated.[55] An opponent of Tutu illustrates this problem: "Why does Tutu not wear tribal garb? Who paved the way for him to receive a Western education different from his hereditary pattern?"[56]

For Tutu, African and Black theology provides a sharp critique of Western theology. Westerners usually call for an ecumenical or universal theology which they often identify with their brand of theologizing; however, Western theology is no more universal than other brands of theology can ever hope to be. For theology, as Tutu concludes, can never properly claim a universality which rightly belongs to the eternal gospel of Jesus Christ. Tutu explains the paradox of particular and eternal in this way:

> Let African theology enthuse about the awesomeness of the transcendent when others are embarrassed to speak about the King, high and lifted up, whose train fills the temple. It is only when African theology is true to itself that it will go on to speak relevantly to the contemporary African – surely its primary task – and also, incidentally, makes its valuable contribution to the rich Christian heritage which belongs to all of us.[57]

Therefore, for Tutu, theology is a human activity possessing the limitations and the particularities of those who are theologizing. It can speak relevantly only when it speaks to a particular historically and spatiotemporally conditioned Christian community; and it must have the humility to accept the scandal of its particularity as well as its transience.[58]

Tutu does not claim that his theological model is eternal or can ever hope to be perfect, for in the end there is no final theology because God will always supersede our expectations. However, for Tutu, the true insights of each theology must have eternal relevance. The sin of apartheid is this expectation: we are expected to express our experience of God in the same way.[59] For Tutu, a liberational spirituality that does not worry about indigenization encourages a facile alliance between culture and Christ. It is true that Christ comes in fulfillment of all the best aspirations of African culture, but equally Christ stands in judgment over human identity. The weakness of creating too many Christs in the interest of indigenization can be laid at the door of most theologies, "unless they are constantly on the alert not to neutralize the scandal of the gospel."[60] Therefore, Tutu admits that his theology must always submit to the scandal of the gospel. The scandal of the gospel in the African context can be seen in the following way. A serious criticism of African theology is that indigenization has tended to be far too concerned with historicity, consequently giving the impression that culture is static. African theology assumes the complicated role of taking context seriously, while at the same time holding faithfully to the truthfulness of its Christian conviction that Jesus died for the sins of the whole world. In the end, both claims must be made if it is to speak relevantly to any context. Tutu concludes: "And it is perhaps in this area that African theology has performed least satisfactorily."[61]

Tutu refers to J. C. Thomas as a model for African theologians to reflect upon in order that the process of Africanizing Christianity can occur through both the inheritance of African traditional religions and the doctrine of the Christian Church.[62] Both must be examined carefully and systematically so that the areas of agreement and conflict are made intelligible to avoid the tragedy of African theologians who produce superficial and unscholarly work. If this increases, African theology will fail to produce a sufficiently sharp cutting edge.[63] African theology performs well when addressing the split in the African soul, yet it has by and large failed to speak meaningfully in the face of a plethora of contemporary problems which assail the modern African mind. African theology seems to advocate disengagement from the hectic business of life. Evidence of this is that very little has been offered in African theology that is pertinent, say, to the theology of power in the face of the epidemic of coups and military rule, about development, about poverty and disease, and other equally urgent African issues. This is where "abrasive Black Theology" teaches Tutu.[64] Black theology helps African theology recall its vocation to be concerned for the poor and the oppressed, to be concerned for liberation from all kinds of bondage

that threaten an authentic personhood constantly undermined by a patho-
logical religiosity. And Black Theology teaches that Christ's disciples
are to be concerned about any political authority which constructs
personal freedom in its own image, and this without too much opposition
from the Church.

In the end, Black theology helps Tutu recover his prophetic calling.
African theology is improved by a radical, spiritual decolonization that
happens within each community. No longer can African theologians
remain docile and look for European permission to do theology.
Tutu asks, "Why should we feel embarrassed if our theology is not
systematic?"[65]

> We are still too much concerned to play the game according to the white
> man's rules when he often is the referee as well. Why should we feel that
> something is amiss if our theology is too dramatic for verbalization but
> can express itself adequately only in the joyous song and movement
> of Africa's dance in the liturgy? Let us develop our insights about
> the corporateness of human existence in the face of excessive Western
> individualism, about the wholeness of the person when others are con-
> cerned for Hellenistic dichotomies of souls and body, about the reality
> of the spiritual when others are made desolate with the poverty of the
> material.[66]

Tutu's theological model includes a description of African theology
in terms of its nature to be more inclusive than its counterpart, Black
theology, in the West. He explains:

> By and large, it was legitimate to generalize and speak of African as
> an inclusive term. This anthropolitical concern of African theology has
> been an important achievement to chalk up. It was vital for the African's
> self-respect that this kind of rehabilitation of his religious heritage should
> take place. It is the theological counterpart of what has happened in, say,
> the study of African history. It has helped to give the lie to the supercilious
> but tacit assumption that religion and history in Africa date from the
> advent in that continent of the white man. It is reassuring to know that
> we have had a genuine knowledge of God and that we have had our own
> ways of communion with deity, ways which meant that we were able to
> speak authentically as ourselves and not as pale imitations of others.
> It means that we have a great store from which we can fashion new ways
> of speaking to and about God, and new styles of worship consistent
> with our new faith.[67]

The main achievement of African theology is in its attention to "religious
schizophrenia" (Western and African) and its attempt to remedy it by

rehabilitating Africa's rich cultural heritage and religious consciousness. However, this attempt alone is not sufficient.

The major criticism leveled against African theology is its epistemological claim of ethnic identity as the primary form of knowledge of God. Tutu describes the complaint further: "There is only one faith and, therefore, it is a serious aberration to try to nurture a particularistic theology instead of holding out for an ecumenical and universal one."[68] This criticism is often made as well by Africans who are apprehensive that a peculiar theology will mean that theology could so easily be turned into a chauvinistic tool by unscrupulous politicians who desire a supernatural sanction for their secular mindset. African theology, for Tutu, is precarious in this regard because it must both reflect the experience of a particular Christian community and relate this experience to what God has done in Christ. Thus theology must necessarily be limited by the qualifying factors of those who are theologizing, which include ethnic, temporal, cultural, and personality conditions, but also be mindful of the scandal of this particularity as not fully descriptive of God. This means that theology must of necessity be particularistic, existential, and provisional, and eternal at the same time. Tutu concludes: "It must glory in its in-built obsolescence because it must be ready to change if it will speak meaningfully to the situation which it addresses."[69]

Tutu acknowledges the differences between African and Black theology as they develop from different contexts. Tutu believes "theology is a risky, albeit exhilarating business of reflecting on the experience of a particular Christian community in relation to what God has done, is doing and will do, and the ultimate reference point is the man, Jesus."[70] Black theology arises in a context of Black suffering at the hands of rampant White racism. And consequently, Black theology is much more concerned to make sense theologically of the Black experience, whose main ingredient is suffering made sense of in light of God's redemption in Christ. Black theology is concerned with the significance of Black existence in light of reconciliation, humanization, and forgiveness. Because of this, Black theology is much more aggressive and abrasive in its assertions, as its evangelistic zeal leads the Black community to convert black persons out of their subservient stupor to accept the vigorous responsibility of personhood.[71]

Persons once assumed as white are burned by this zeal to see the degradation into which human identity had fallen. By dehumanizing the black identity, white identity became equally corrupted – the liberation of the oppressor is equally caught up in God's delivery of the oppressed. The root of racial identity in societies makes it naive to think that only economic or political oppression matter. Therefore, for Tutu, true liberation must be understood holistically as the removal of all that keeps human identity in bondage and stunts its growth. Anything that makes human identity less than *imago Dei*, less than what God intends us to be, is apartheid.

I argue further that African Christian spirituality seeks more inclusive interpretive epistemologies in light of the reconciliation of enemies. In the end, spiritual leaders like Tutu present communal models of Christian spirituality meant to include even disparate identities. Tutu's theology and ecclesiology provide vital impetus in forging a society defined by more than race. Unlike the bane of many black theologians whose theological language prioritizes race as the sole criterion of particularity by which to adjudicate all other categories in social discourse, Tutu's theology defines black identity as one identity among others in need of God's deliverance from oppressive forces.

> Our starting points are the Christian doctrines of creation, redemption and sanctification. A tremendous assertion, quite staggering really, made about the nature and dignity of the human person, and it is an assertion of universal application . . . Our worth, our dignity, all these are intrinsic to who we are, they come as a divine gift with our creation. They come with the whole package of being human. Our worth, our infinite worth does not depend on any extraneous attribute or achievement – it is an inalienable right which is a gift freely bestowed on us by God . . . That doctrine is thoroughly and radically subversive of our discriminations, injustice, oppression and exploitation based on race, sex, culture, status, education and whatever else we might think up as giving worth and value to persons. That was the basis – thoroughly biblical – for our structures against apartheid which said that the color or race of a person was what made you important.[72]

For Tutu, it is inconsistent with the gospel to construct a method of blackness by which to address "all" the categories of traditional theology. Instead of this approach, Tutu promotes the particularity of peoples through the catholic character of the baptized and faithful people of God who find themselves constantly in awe of the mysteries of creation, especially that of being human. In light of this qualification, Tutu states: "I thank God for Black theology in the life of the Church and in my own life."[73] Therefore, for Tutu, theology does not happen in a vacuum of racial identity, catering for the caprice of the theologian who must publish or perish.[74] Theology is the prayerful reflection of how God transforms us in such a way that the European and African may one day dwell completely in God's presence, with uninhibited relationship.

This leads us to chapter 6 and the genius of Martin Luther King, Jr.'s truth telling, which offered to the world a powerful practice emerging out of African American Christian spirituality. The spirituality of the Black Church constituted by preaching, testifying, and witnessing leads toward the model of restoring God's community through love.

Notes

1   Hezekiah Walker, "I Need You to Survive," on the album *Family Affair 2: Live at Radio City Music Hall*.
2   Simon Maimela, "Archbishop Desmond Mpilo Tutu, A Revolutionary Political Priest or Man of Peace?" In *Hammering Swords into Ploughshares: Essays in Honor of Archbishop Mpilo Desmond Tutu*, ed. Buti Tlhagale and Itumeleng Mosala (Grand Rapids, MI: Eerdmans, 1986), pp. 41–61.
3   Charles V. Hamilton, *The Black Preacher in America* (New York: William Morrow, 1972), p. 140.
4   James H. Evans, Jr., *We Have Been Believers: An African-American Systematic Theology* (Minneapolis, MN: Fortress Press, 1992), p. 152. Evans develops a soteriology that is entirely liberative, calling Jesus both "a political messiah or liberator, and spiritual mediator/healer" (p. 97). Jesus as healer and Jesus as liberator are essentially comparable categories, especially in the gospels.
5   J. Deotis Roberts, *Liberation and Reconciliation: A Black Theology* (Philadelphia, PA: Westminster Press, 1971); and "Black Theology in the Making," in James H. Cone and Gayraud S. Wilmore, *Black Theology: A Documentary History, Vol. 1: 1966–1979*, 2nd edn. (Maryknoll, NY: Orbis Books, 1993), Vol. 1, pp. 118–19.
6   See www.census.gov.
7   C. E. Lincoln and L. H. Mamiya, *The Black Church in the African American Experience* (Durham, NC: Duke University Press, 1990), pp. 178–9.
8   Ibid, p. 179.
9   Ibid, p. 180.
10 Ibid, p. 180.
11 Ibid, p. 180.
12 Ibid, p. 181.
13 Itumeleng J. Mosala, *Biblical Hermeneutics and Black Theology in South Africa* (Grand Rapids, MI: Eerdmans, 1989), p. 3.
14 Takatso Mofokeng, "Black Theology in South Africa: Achievements, Problems and Prospects," in *Christianity Amidst Apartheid: Selected Perspectives on the Church in South Africa*, ed. Martin Prozesky (New York: St. Martin's Press, 1990), p. 50.
15 Desmond Tutu, "Whither African Theology?" In Edward Fasholé-Luke et al., *Christianity in Independent Africa* (London: Rex Collings, 1978), p. 364.

16 For more of an analytical perception of a model like Mosala's by an Anglican theologian, see John Milbank, *Theology and Social Theory: Beyond Secular Reason* (Oxford: Blackwell, 1991).

17 See Desmond Tutu, "Called to Unity and Fellowship." In M. Nash, ed., *The Church and the Alternative Society: Papers and Resolutions of the Eleventh Conference of the South African Council of Churches* (Johannesburg: SACC, 1979).

18 See Allan Boesak, *Black and Reformed: Apartheid, Liberation and the Calvinist Tradition* (Maryknoll, NY: Orbis Books, 1984). Boesak dedicates this book: "For Desmond Tutu, Prophet of God, Shepherd of his people, Brother and Friend in whom God's gifts are seen and admired."

19 See Martin Luther King, Jr., *Where Do We Go from Here: Chaos or Community?* (Boston, MA: Beacon Press, 1967), pp. 51–77.

20 Ibid, pp. 51–77.

21 Ibid, p. 73.

22 Ibid, p. 105.

23 Itumeleng Mosala, a biblical scholar, is now a key political leader in the new South African government.

24 In addition to Tutu, Mosala also critiques James Cone and Alan Boesak.

25 Desmond Tutu, "God's Strength – In Human Weakness." In M. Nash, ed., *Your Kingdom Come: Papers and Resolutions of the Twelfth National Conference of the South African Council of Churches* (Braamfontein: SACC, 1980), p. 23.

26 Desmond Tutu, "Jesus Christ: Life of the World," keynote address for 48 hour Women's Colloquium, June 17, 1982.

27 See the "Report of the Commission of Inquiry into Mass Media" (1982) under the chairmanship of Judge M. T. Steyn. Volume two deals with African, Black, and liberation theology. This report quotes from Tutu's address at the 1977 conference in Accra where he argues that in South Africa, Black theology and African theology come together. The report misconstrues Tutu and concludes that he is committed to "differential development" in a religious and political sense (which being interpreted means separate development); that he rejects "liberal" theology and politics, including notions such as "one man, one vote, election of a central government in a unitary but multiracial state." Tutu really is about Africans not uncritically accepting Western interpretations of Christian theology and ending up thinking that African Christians have nothing to contribute. He is critical of the oppression that the South African system holds for blacks. He does not indicate in his writings that his criticisms of aspects of Western theology can (by "parity of reasoning," as the report claims) be transferred to "Western liberal politicians and jurists."

28 Desmond Tutu, "Brothers and Sisters Together," address for Trans Africa, April 29, 1981.

29 Desmond Tutu, review of James Cone's *God of the Oppressed*, in *Journal of Theology for Southern Africa* 31 (June 1980), p. 74. As Cone's views

have changed, so have Tutu's views of Cone. For example, in 1989 Cone became more inclusive in his definition of blackness: "blackness symbolizes oppression and liberation in any society." See James Cone, *A Black Theology of Liberation*, 2nd edn. (Maryknoll, NY: Orbis Books, 1989), p. vii.

30   Tutu, review of Cone, p. 73.
31   Louise Kretzschmar, *Christian Faith and African Culture* (Unitra: Religious Studies Forum, 1988), p. 128, discussing Tutu's "Black Theology/African Theology – Soul Mates or Antagonists?" Tutu's article was also edited by James Cone et al., *Black Theology: A Documentary History, 1966–1979* (Maryknoll, NY: Orbis Books, 1981). Other acknowledgments of Tutu's impact include the fact that the first comprehensive book by a South African black resident on Black political opposition to apartheid (entitled *Theory and Practice of Black Resistance to Apartheid*) was banned. The book was written by Mokgethi Motlhabi, who obtained his doctorate from Boston University with the help of Tutu, to whom the book is dedicated.
32   Desmond Tutu, "Black Theology/African Theology," manuscript.
33   Cone, *Black Theology of Liberation*, pp. 94–5. Cone states that it will be necessary for whites to destroy their whiteness by becoming members of an oppressed community.
34   See James Cone, "Sanctification, Liberation, and Black Worship," *Theology Today* 35 (1978–9), pp. 139–52.
35   See James Cone, *For My People* (Maryknoll, NY: Orbis Books, 1984).
36   Cone, *Black Theology of Liberation*, p. 11.
37   James Cone, *Black Theology and Black Power* (New York: Seabury Press, 1969), p. 140.
38   Cone admits his previous failure to incorporate an international analysis of oppression in *Black Theology of Liberation*, p. xviii.
39   Desmond Tutu, "Black South African Perspectives and the Reagan Administration," address, Transafrica Forum, February 1982. This is one of Tutu's most sustained and coherent political analyses.
40   James Cone, "God is Black," in *Lift Every Voice: Constructing Christian Theologies from the Underside*, ed. Susan Brooks Thistlewaite and Mary Potter Engel (San Francisco: Harper, 1990), p. 84. Among Cone's large corpus of work, I focus on this article because here he reflects back over much of his work, as he states, "In an attempt to reconcile my Black and Christian identities" (p. 81). He goes on to state: "Were I to write an essay on 'God' today, I would seek to develop a more holistic perspective by incorporating what I have learned about divine presence from other communities of the oppressed throughout the world, particularly in Asia, Africa, and Latin America and also among women in all forms of liberation theology" (p. 83).
41   Ibid.
42   Ibid, p. 90.
43   Ibid, p. 84.

44 Ibid, p. 89.

45 Desmond Tutu, unpublished handwritten speeches and addresses, "Koinonia II."

46 See A. J. Raboteau, *Slave Religion: The "Invisible Institution" in the Ante-bellum South* (New York: Oxford University Press, 1978) for insights into the formation of Black and White Christianity. Raboteau displays how the Black Church assumes the racial classification of Black, but overcomes the power of its representation.

47 Desmond Tutu, keynote address, Allard K. Lowenstein Symposium on International Human Rights Law, April 17, 1982.

48 J. Deotis Roberts, *Liberation and Reconciliation: A Black Theology* (Philadelphia, PA: Westminster Press, 1971), p. 152.

49 J. Deotis Roberts, "Black Theology in the Making," *Review and Expositor* 70 (Summer 1973), p. 328.

50 Ibid, p. 327.

51 Ibid.

52 Maurice Wiles, "Theology and Unity," *Theology* 77:643 (January 1974), quoted in Tutu, "The Role of the Church in South Africa" (unpublished). I list these unpublished documents in my book *Reconciliation: The Ubuntu Theology of Desmond Tutu* (Cleveland, OH: Pilgrim Press, 1997).

53 See Kretzschmar, *Christian Faith*, p. xii. Kretzschmar's work is good at showing how African theology grew in the light of a determination to redress the previous neglect of relating the gospel to the broad range of African thought, tradition, and experience. She traces the work of three Christian leaders: D. D. T. Jabavu (b. 1885), Z. K. Matthews (b. 1901), and Albert John Lutuli (b. 1898).

54 Ibid, p. xii.

55 Ibid, p. 15.

56 Letters to the Editor, *Daily Dispatch*, December 11, 1984.

57 Tutu, "Whither African Theology?" p. 369.

58 See Tutu, "Black Theology/African Theology," pp. 389–90.

59 Ibid, pp. 389–90.

60 Ibid, p. 368.

61 Ibid.

62 J. C. Thomas, "What is African Theology?" *Ghana Bulletin of Theology* 4:4 (June 1973), p. 15.

63 See Tutu, "Whither African Theology?" p. 368.

64 Ibid, p. 369.

65 Ibid.

66 Tutu, "Black Theology/African Theology," pp. 391–2. In large measure Tutu is reacting here to John Mbiti's conviction that "the concerns of Black Theology differ considerably from those of African Theology. The latter grows out of our joy and experience of the Christian faith, whereas Black Theology emerges from the pains of oppression." For Tutu, Mbiti seems to imply that Black theology is perhaps not quite Christian: "One

would hope that theology arises out of spontaneous joy in being a Christian responding to life and ideas as one redeemed. Black Theology, however, is full of sorrow, bitterness, anger and hatred." See John Mbiti, "An African Views American Black Theology," *Worldview* 17:8 (August 1974), p. 43. This article is reprinted in James H. Cone and Gayraud S. Wilmore, eds., *Black Theology: A Documentary History*, Vol. 1: *1966–1979*, 2nd edn. (Maryknoll, NY: Orbis Books, 1993).

67   Tutu, "Whither African Theology?" p. 367.
68   Ibid.
69   Ibid.
70   Ibid.
71   See Tutu, "The Role of the Church in South Africa."
72   Desmond Tutu, "The Church and Human Rights in South Africa," handwritten address, University of South Africa, Center for Human Rights, May 18, 1992.
73   Desmond Tutu, "Doing Theology in a Divided Society," address, Contextual Theology, Hammanskraal, May 19, 1983.
74   Ibid.

Chapter 6
The Black Church as the Beloved Community

We disobeyed a court order. We did not take this radical step without prolonged and prayerful consideration. Planned, deliberate civil disobedience had been discussed as far back as the meeting at Harry Belafonte's apartment in March. There, in consultation with some of the closest friends of the movement, we had decided that if an injunction was issued to thwart our demonstrators, it would be our duty to violate it.

Martin Luther King, Jr.[1]

In this chapter I discuss the communal impact of the Black Church in America. The civil rights movement – a major approach to social transformation in the United States and in much of the world – was sparked by the Black Church. This fact is not celebrated as it should be, with more credit given to the Black Church for the momentum of the civil rights movement. During the 1800s and early 1900s the "social gospel" movement created activist interpretations of Christian spirituality. Christians like Walter Rauschenbusch urged Christians to apply their faith to practice in eradicating poverty, violence, and social injustice. Also, spiritual leaders like Rauschenbusch knew that the industrialization of the twentieth century required activist Christians to speak out for those not benefiting from capitalism.

African American spiritual leaders, however, were deeply troubled by how white social gospelers conveniently left out the problem of racism. It was because of this inaction that the civil rights movement, through the Black Church, came together as a united witness of communal spirituality. Because the spirituality of the Black Church is interpersonal and communal, the civil rights movement was a natural action derived from the history, worship, and theology of the Black Church. Seldom known, however, is that many of the major Black Church leaders (who *de facto* were leaders of the civil rights movement) were also inspired by communitarian spiritualities coming out of the Eastern world, such as Gandhi's *Satyagraha* movement. This leads me to believe that the communitarian sensibilities of the Black Church extend beyond the United States.

The Black Church clearly initiated the civil rights movement. The most basic civil right is the right to a civic community in which all other human rights become intelligible. Without a place in which to become a person with an identity among other people, opportunities are mere abstractions for African Americans. In destroyed urban neighborhoods and deserted rural ones, churches are often the only survivor institutions, the only remnants of what once was a rich fabric of shops, businesses, community organizations, clubs, clinics, schools, and charities. What these churches do when they are most effective is to recreate some of the conditions for civic community on the most basic level. Historically, the Black Church has worked in partnership with government agencies, local entrepreneurs, neighborhood mothers, suburban non-profit organizations, earnest seminarians, volunteer lawyers, etc. When the Black Church was successful in initiating community, it created a fragile semblance of civic community where people could learn the satisfactions of effectiveness, acceptance, and competence, even though the Black Church was obliged to create in itself the circumstances under which those satisfactions could be experienced.

The civil rights movement, led by the Black Church, sought not to access a set of opportunities that were already in existence, but the new creation of a civic community that could sustain basic opportunities for and relationships among people historically oppressed in American society and then for those oppressed in the rest of the world.[2] Around the 1950s, Black Christian communities found leaders to articulate the theological basis for the social transformation it was advocating. The one who chiefly emerged was Martin Luther King, Jr.[3] Ariel Dorfman states:

> Beyond my amazement at King's eloquence when I first heard him back in 1968, my immediate reaction was not so much to be inspired as to be puzzled, close to despair. After all, the slaying of this man of peace was answered, not by a pledge to persevere in his legacy, but by furious uprisings in the slums of black America, the disenfranchised of America avenging their dead leader by burning down the ghettos where they felt imprisoned and impoverished, using the fire this time to proclaim that the non-violence King had advocated was useless, that the only way to end inequity in this world was through the barrel of a gun, the only way to make the powerful pay attention was to scare the hell out of them. King's assassination, therefore, savagely brought up yet one more time a question that had bedeviled me, as so many other activists, in the late sixties: What was the best method to achieve radical change? Could we picture a rebellion in the way that Martin Luther King had envisioned it, without drinking from the cup of bitterness and hatred, without treating our

adversaries as they treated us? Or did the road into the palace of justice and the bright day of brotherhood inevitably require violence as its companion, violence as the unavoidable midwife of revolution?[4]

King was influenced by Christian thinkers such as Reinhold Niebuhr who applied a realistic assessment of the struggle for justice to race relations in the United States as early as *Moral Man and Immoral Society*. In a brief passage remembered mostly because King subsequently acknowledged its influence on him, Niebuhr recommends the application of Gandhi's techniques of nonviolent resistance to the problem of racial justice in America, but he cautions against mistaking the strategic decision to eschew violence for a principled reliance on the power of love.[5] Such love is not insipid or vapid, but characteristic of the Black Church's civil rights movement. The emerging practice of nonviolent resistance so characteristic of the Black Church *vis-à-vis* the Nation of Islam (or at least its earlier form) points to the desire of the Black Church to be more than a racial church.

Nonviolent resistance is a form of power. Used effectively, it is a way to acquire more power to resist those forces controlling definitions of human identity. Those who seek racial equality must remember this, because people who hold power do not surrender it due to moral suasion alone. They surrender it when they are confronted by greater power. Niebuhr states: "However large the number of individual white men who do and who will identify themselves completely with the Negro cause, the white race in America will not admit the Negro to equal rights if it is not forced to do so. Upon that point one may speak with a dogmatism which all history justifies."[6] By the time Reinhold Niebuhr died in 1971, many were pronouncing his Christian realism hopelessly flawed. What had seemed dangerous radicalism in the 1930s appeared altogether too cautious after the changes of the 1960s. The effort to gain and hold power within the existing political order, which realists saw as the basis for turning moral ideas into effective politics, seemed now to their critics a compromise with a system of domination and exploitation that had to be demolished because it could not be reformed. Power could not be wrested from the White establishment by borrowing some countervailing power. Freedom had to have a base in a power all its own – the birth of the Black Power movement.

The call for Black Power was already familiar from the latter days of King's leadership of the civil rights movement. James Cone made it the basis for a new social theology that rejected the compromises of Christian realism and provided the basis for a more radical approach to social change. Cone soon linked his theology of Black Power to a theology emerging among Catholics in Latin America, a theology of liberation that rejected the economic domination of privileged elites and called for an empowerment of the people. Over the longer run, the Latin American theorists of liberation theology, including Gustavo Gutierrez, Juan Luis Segundo, and Leonardo Boff, became the primary shapers of this theology for North Americans as well. These Latin American theologians rejected attempts to gain a share in the prevailing systems of power and authority. Christians were to free themselves through participation in base communities, where study of the Bible provided an alternative to ideological rationalizations for their suffering and powerlessness, and they could gain control of their own lives through economic self-sufficiency. The internal tasks of creating community and personal dignity among the poor replaced the reform and gradual transformation of political systems as the goal of Christian action.

While the mainstream denominations from which Niebuhr and his Christian realist contemporaries came have lost membership and influence over the last decades, Pentecostal and evangelical congregations and denominations have grown steadily. These congregations are too large and diverse a group to be easily categorized. Their theology tends to center on biblical doctrine, personal conversion, and strict standards of personal morality. Their social and political beliefs range from the radicalism of the Sojourners community in Washington, DC, to the political conservatism and commitment to free-market economics found among the new Christian right. Some of these new evangelicals reject prevailing American political and economic values with as much vigor as any liberation theologian, while others uncritically identify those values with the core of Christian faith.

Attitudes toward the history of the civil rights movement and contemporary issues in race relations are similarly diverse. Many African American congregations, of course, would characterize themselves as part of those who resisted systemic racism, and they are likely to regard the civil rights movement as an important part of their history and religious heritage. Others, however, have moved to the new evangelical churches precisely because they were alienated by the emphasis on civil rights and social action that they found in the mainstream denominations to which they once belonged. In general, the emphasis on personal conversion takes precedence over the call for social transformation, and where the latter does not entirely disappear, it is often argued or assumed that any hope for real social change depends on the change in individual lives instead of the whole community. In recent years, Black Churches have rediscovered some of the political strategies that the mainstream denominations deployed so effectively during the civil rights movement.

While this has made the Black Church a force to be reckoned with in contemporary politics, black theologians are having a difficult time today producing political theologies that could allow the full inclusion that the civil rights movement intended.

King learned from Niebuhr that politics can accomplish very little that is of real moral value, and the best way to avoid failure and disappointment is by appropriately limiting one's expectations of the political world at the outset. King learned that the hope to achieve a moral good through political strategies rests on a fundamental mistake about what politics can achieve. Contemporary political theorists who adopt this perspective include Glen Tinder.[7] Tinder argues that the appropriate political role for Christians is to keep everyone mindful of the limits of politics. Those who forget those limits may drift off into sentimental idealism when their moral aspirations are disappointed, but they are perhaps even more likely to resort to totalitarianism. Politics can sometimes prevent evil or keep it from getting worse, but it cannot do good. There is in Tinder's rigorous rejection of political idealism more than a trace of Reinhold Niebuhr's realism, though Niebuhr would insist that we balance the rejection of naive political idealism with an equally firm refusal to set prior limits on what the political struggle for justice can achieve. Niebuhr and Tinder would nonetheless agree that Christians can participate in politics if they can keep their expectations appropriately limited.

There is another strand from Church tradition that holds that Christians must altogether avoid participation in the coercive use of force that inevitably accompanies political authority. This is the historic stance of Christian pacifism and the churches of the so-called Radical Reformation. It has been ably represented in recent years by the Mennonite theologian John Howard Yoder (1929–97). Yoder understood the difference between a modern democratic politics and the authoritarian monarchies in which the Radical Reformation tradition first was formulated, and he was by no means so complete in his rejection of politics as the churches in his tradition have sometimes been. Inevitably, however, a theology that limits participation in political community focuses attention on the Christian community, seeing it as the place for nurturing virtues that cannot be brought to birth in other environments and that are, indeed, radically at risk in the realm of politics and power that lies outside.

Stanley Hauerwas also stresses the role of the Christian community of discourse in creating and sustaining Christian virtues.[8] What lies outside the Christian community is not merely a realm of force and power in which Christian values are radically threatened. Outside the

Christian community Christian virtues are simply incomprehensible. Without the Christian narrative to make sense of the ethics of non-violence and care for all life, its imperatives are drained of meaning and motivating power. Attempts to translate an ethics formed by love of God and love of neighbor through Jesus Christ into general principles of justice are doomed to failure, and an attempt at Christian politics that invests historical movements and constitutional principles with religious import the way Niebuhr's Christian realism did trivializes the Christian commitment and compromises its radical critique by accepting the rationalization of dominance that prevails in the realms of politics and economics.

Such a conviction is interesting in light of Martin Luther King's seeming passion for human rights and politics. The problematic for King, spawned from his Baptist theology in the Black Church, was a response to how Christians could turn a blind eye to the horrors of racial injustice, especially before his eyes when growing up in the South. The "other worldliness" of the Baptist theology in which there was lack of concern for earthly justice became a characteristic King sought to rectify. Joseph Washington described this characteristic:

> The hallmark of religion among Negroes has been emotionalism and other worldliness. This pattern resulted from a combination of factors – the frustration of the militant concern for equality in the fold religion, the response of the Negro to the emotionalism of the missionaries, the tendency to use religion as an escape valve from insufferable conditions, the failure to accept the Negro within the mainstream churches, to identify a few. Religion is always a means to an end, always functional in the context of the situation. So that when the socioeconomic situation changed for some Negroes, when they found life worth living through gaining responsible economic positions and diversion in social life, it follows that, like all other disinherited groups, they gradually began to orient their religious life to their new-found selfhood. This is all the de-emphasis of the "other worldly" points to – the Negro considers himself a real person, a typical American.[9]

For King, this other worldly emphasis declined during his formal education and exposure to liberal and neoliberal theologians. Concern for the existential situation in contemporary times was crucial for King. However, he was raised in a theology in which heaven was a vital reward for the faithful. "No matter how small one thinks his life's work is in terms of the norms of the world and the so-called big jobs, he must realize that it has cosmic significance if he is serving humanity and doing the will of God."[10]

King often quoted the prophets, especially Amos 5:24 ("Let justice roll down like waters, and righteousness like an ever-flowing stream")[24] and Isaiah 40:4 ("Every valley shall be exalted and every hill and mountain shall be made low. The rough places shall be made plain and the crooked places will be made straight, and the glory of the Lord shall be revealed, and all flesh shall see it to enter").[25]

> I still have a dream today that one day justice will roll down like water, and righteousness like a mighty stream. I still have a dream today that in all of our statehouses and city halls men will be elected to go there who will do justly and love mercy and walk humbly with their God. I still have a dream today that one day war will come to an end, that men will beat their swords into plowshares and their spears into pruning hooks, that nations will no longer rise up against nations, neither will they study war any more. I still have a dream today that one day the lamb and the lion will lie down together and every man will sit under his own vine and fig tree and none shall be afraid. I still have a dream today that one day every valley shall be exalted and every mountain and hill will be made low, the rough places will be made smooth and the crooked places straight, and the glory of the Lord shall be revealed, and all flesh shall see it together.[26]

Isaiah holds out a similar vision in which infant mortality will be reduced and the aged will have adequate healthcare. That is, those who are most vulnerable in society will be given the support they need. Isaiah provides a heavenly vision both for children who can grow to maturity and the elderly who can live out their lives in dignity. Isaiah's vision informs how we locate King's vision of community; namely, in concrete realities. King's vision makes us consider the content of community in all its concreteness and contemporary significance. He helps us consider also how community relates so directly to our present struggles for a more just society:

> It's all right to talk about "long white robes over yonder," in all of its symbolism. But ultimately people want some suits and dresses and shoes to wear down here. It's all right to talk about "streets flowing with milk and honey," but God has commanded us to be concerned about the slums down here, and his children who can't eat three square meals a day. It's all right to talk about the new Jerusalem, but one day, God's preacher must talk about the new New York, the new Atlanta, the new Philadelphia, the new Los Angeles, the new Memphis, Tennessee. This is what we have to do.[27]

Isaiah and King's vision continue to correlate the concreteness of human communities as they envision a particular economy for how persons should relate. Divine economics includes a system of labor in which there is mutual exchange. There will be no scapegoats in such an economy, whereas in many current human economies persons often never experience the benefit of their labor.

> They shall build houses and inhabit them;
> they shall plant vineyards and eat their fruit.
> They shall not build and another inhabit;
> they shall not plant and another eat.
>   (Isaiah 65:21, 22)

Isaiah's vision holds true for King as well, as both hold out the promise that everyone will have adequate housing and shelter. In King's context, African Americans will be able to live in the homes they have built without fear of losing them. King demonstrates this economic vision when he shares his vision for African American economy:

> Now the other thing we'll have to do is this: Always anchor our external direct action with the power of economic withdrawal. Now, we are poor people, individually, we are poor when you compare us with white society in America. We are poor. Never stop and forget that collectively, that means all of us together, collectively we are richer than all the nations in the world, with the exception of nine. Did you ever think about that? After you leave the United States, Soviet Russia, Great Britain, West Germany, France and I could name the others, the Negro collectively is richer than most nations of the world.[28]

King's economy is specific. No rampant capitalist exploitation will widen the gap between the haves and the have-nots. Labor, according to this vision, is not drudgery, but a joy. Not only will African Americans possess their own homes, they will also have the freedom and right to grow their own crops and to eat what they have produced. Like Isaiah, in King's economy there is no slave labor that provides food for the rich while keeping the poor in their place. This is why memory is so important. It calls to mind what God has done in the past. How easy it is to forget and, like the Israelites in the wilderness, to start complaining: "If only we had died by the hand of the Lord in the land of Egypt, when we sat by the fleshpots and ate our fill of bread" (Exodus 16:3). As we struggle with present realities it is easy, perhaps, to have a romantic view of the past, those "good old days" when things were better. But that they were days of slavery in Egypt or captivity in Babylon we forget. How many white people in South Africa, for example, look back to apartheid and say how much better it was then. They forget they were on the verge of a civil war that would have devastated the country. They forget the "miracle" of transition.

The whole of Israel's faith and hope is predicated on the conviction that God led their forefathers out of the slavery of Egypt into the promised land, just as he led them from the captivity of Babylon back to Jerusalem. In the same way, Christian Eucharistic faith recalls the life, death, and resurrection of Jesus Christ. "Do this in memory of me." Such memories are not simply of the past; they bring the past into the present. The death and resurrection become present to our contemporary experience. But there is more at stake in our Eucharistic faith, for we remember the death and resurrection of Jesus Christ in anticipation of the "new heaven and new earth." We "do this until he comes." In other words, it is not only the past that becomes present, so too does the future. Isaiah's vision continues:

> They shall not bear children for calamity;
> for they shall be offspring blessed by the Lord
> and their descendants as well.
>
> (Isaiah 65:23)

In Isaiah's vision, childbearing will no longer be regarded as a way to provide extra hands to deal with poverty, or as a means to ensure old-age care. Children will no longer be sold into slavery of whatever kind in order to earn money so that their parents can eke out a living. Children will no longer roam the streets in search of scraps to eat, or in search of drugs to dull pain, or in search of tourists to rob to buy food or cocaine. Children, according to this vision, will be blessed by God. They will be able to be children, and so also will their children. King provides a great example of a child being a child when he was stabbed in New York City by "a demented black woman" asking for his autograph. The *New York Times* reported that if he had sneezed after the stabbing, King would have died. After this "dark Saturday afternoon," King writes:

> They allowed me to read some of the mail that came in, and from all over the states, and the world, kind letters came in. I read a few, but one of them I will never forget. I had received one from the President and the Vice-President. I've forgotten what those telegrams said. I'd received a visit and a letter from the Governor of New York, but I've forgotten what the letter said. But there was another letter that came from a little girl, a young girl who was a student at the White Plains High School. And I looked at that letter, and I'll never forget it. It said simply, "Dear Dr. King: I am a ninth-grade student at the White Plains High School." She

said, "While it should not matter, I would like to mention that I am a white girl. I read in the paper of your misfortune, and of your suffering. And I read that if you had sneezed, you would have died. And I'm simply writing you to say that I'm so happy that you didn't sneeze."[29]

The final part of Isaiah's vision is one of harmony among God's creatures – with the serpent, the evil one, literally biting the dust. Here is a radical vision of the environment being restored to its pristine character, as bitter enemies are reconciled. Herein, King's nonviolent vision coincides with Isaiah's prophecy. King states:

> The ultimate weakness of violence is that it is a descending spiral, begetting the very thing it seeks to destroy. Instead of diminishing evil it multiplies it. Through violence you may murder the liar, but you cannot murder the lie, nor establish the truth. Through violence you may murder the hater, but you do not murder hate. In fact violence merely increases hate. So it goes. Returning violence for violence multiplies violence, adding deeper darkness to a night already devoid of stars. Darkness cannot drive out darkness; only light can do that. Hate cannot drive out hate; only love can do that.
>
> The beauty of nonviolence is that in its own way and in its own time it seeks to break the chain reaction of evil. With a majestic sense of spiritual power, it seeks to elevate truth, beauty and goodness to the throne. Therefore I will continue to follow this method because I think it is the most practically sound and morally excellent way for the Negro to achieve freedom.[30]

King thinks that nonviolence is made manifest in eternity, from which we now catch glimpses of how to live on earth. He is therefore committed to nonviolence based upon an eschatological vision in which violent reality succumbs to God's presence.[31] King had visions like the prophets of the Bible. "As I stood with them and saw white and Negro, nuns and priests, ministers and rabbis, labor organizers, lawyers, doctors, housemaids and shop workers brimming with vitality and enjoying a rare comradeship, I knew I was seeing a microcosm of the mankind of the future in this moment of luminous and genuine brotherhood."[32] Such a vision looks like Isaiah's own:

> The wolf and the lamb shall feed together,
> the lion shall eat straw like the ox;
> but the serpent – its food shall be dust!
> They shall not hurt or destroy
> on all my holy mountain, says the Lord.
> (Isaiah 65:25)

This prophetic hope is no spiritualized fantasy world, a world of make-believe, but the promise of a "transformed material world in which justice will prevail, there will be bread for all, and the human race will 'dwell securely.' " King is intensely aware of how pacifism may be perceived:

> After reading [Reinhold] Niebuhr, I tried to arrive at a realistic pacifism. In other words, I came to see the pacifist position not as sinless but as the lesser evil in the circumstances. I felt then, and I feel now, that the pacifist would have a greater appeal if he did not claim to be free from the moral dilemmas that the Christian nonpacifist confronts.[33]

King states: "My friends, the Christmas hope for peace and goodwill toward all men can no longer be dismissed as a kind of pious dream of some utopian. If we don't have goodwill toward men in this world, we will destroy ourselves by the misuse of our own instruments and our own power."[34] The Beloved Community is a hope which concerns the restoration of fertility, the yielding of the produce of the earth, so that there is enough for all. Indeed, prophetic text is, in Walter Brueggemann's words, the most extreme statement of this capacity for the recovery of creation. It is an extravagant promise which heralds the overcoming of everything that has gone wrong in creation, touching every aspect and phase of life and remaking them whole, and overcoming hostility at every level – not just in Israel or the human community, but throughout creation. Brueggemann states:

> It is clear that King claimed special experience and insight and therefore special authority that somehow was related to the powerful presence of God in his life. In some secret way never made public to us, Dr. King, like every authentic prophet, has been face to face with God's holy call.[35]

Nothing could be more embracing, so radically new, and yet so related to the world as we know and experience it. It is literally the promise of starting again, a new creation brought about by the activity of God, and yet in continuity with everything that we hold dear and for which we strive. But, we must ask, can such a promise be fulfilled? King preaches:

> Well, I don't know what will happen now. We've got some difficult days ahead. But it doesn't matter with me now. Because I've been to the mountaintop. And I don't mind. Like anybody, I would like to live a long life. Longevity has its place. But I'm not concerned about that now. I just want to do God's will. And He's allowed me to go up to the mountain. And I've looked over. And I've seen the promised land. I may not get

there with you. But I want you to know tonight, that we, as a people, will get to the promised land. And I'm happy, tonight. I'm not worried about anything. I'm not fearing any man. Mine eyes have seen the glory of the coming of the Lord.[36]

The Beloved Community provokes the question that all serious believers continually ask: is heaven not a totally unrealistic and romantic view of things, a utopian illusion that must inevitably be thwarted by social and political forces beyond our control? After all, this promise was uttered centuries ago and was repeated in the Christian scriptures, and yet the vision of a new heaven and new earth still seems beyond reach. "Lord, when will this come to pass?" is the perennial cry of believers through the centuries as they struggle to give an account of the hope that is within them. This leads to the understandings of inner and outer access to God's presence. As for inner access, King describes it thus:

At that moment I experienced the presence of the Divine as I had never before experienced him. It seemed as though I could hear the quiet assurance of an inner voice, saying, "Stand up for righteousness, stand up for truth. God will be at your side forever." Almost at once my fears began to pass from me. My uncertainty disappeared. I was ready to face anything. The outer situation remained the same, but God had given me inner calm. Three nights later, our home was bombed. Strangely enough, I accepted the word of the bombing calmly. My experience with God had given me a new strength and trust. I knew now that God is able to give us the interior resources to face the storms and problems of life.[37]

What we discover in King's dreams is the eschatological hope for the Beloved Community. I think we discover in King that these penultimate hopes for a new world of justice and peace are intrinsically connected to the ultimate hope of a new heaven and a new earth. Similar to the concept of African ancestors, the future of a new heaven and a new earth breaks into our present struggles, awakening hope and strengthening faith and love in the expectation that there is always more that God wants to give us. God is always ahead of us, always creating the new, always opening up new possibilities. So the true prophets are not awakening false expectations, but rather proclaiming that there is always more that God wants to give us, more that God wants to do. Moreover, the prophets know that unless that hope of the more is kept alive, we will simply give up and begin to accept things as they are instead of reaching out to receive the more which God has in store for us. King states:

We can remember the days when unfavorable court decisions came upon us like tidal waves, leaving us treading the waters of despair. But amid all of this we have kept going with the faith that as we struggle, God struggles with us, and that the arc of the moral universe, although long, is bending toward justice. We have lived under the agony and darkness of Good Friday with the conviction that one day the heightened glow of Easter would emerge on the horizon. We have seen truth crucified and goodness buried, but we have kept going with the conviction that truth crushed to the ground will rise again.[38]

All of this is finally based on the faithfulness of God, the God who is true and trustworthy, who calls forth from us the response of Christian community. Indeed, the word of the prophet read from the perspective of Christian faith leads us to the conclusion expressed by St. Paul that in Christ "every one of God's promises is a 'Yes.' For this reason it is through him that we say 'Amen' to the glory of God" (2 Corinthians 1:20). King states:

> What silenced me was a profound sense of awe. I was aware of a feeling that had been present all along below the surface of consciousness, passed down under the weight of concern for the movement: I had never been truly in solitary confinement; God's companionship does not stop at the door of a jail cell. I don't know whether the sun was shining at that moment. But I know that once again I could see the light.[39]

Christian hope is rooted in reality, but it is also a "hope against hope," a hope which often flies in the face of reality because it is based on the faithfulness of the God who surprises us in ways which enable us, in the end, to say "Amen." Indeed, prophetic text declares that it is a vision that only God can bring to reality. Although we are called to participate with God in the struggle for justice and peace, in the end it is God who will surprise us all by the way in which the new world is born. For it is God who finally creates the new heaven and new earth, and we participate in this birth. We participate, as King envisions, "not through violence; not through hate; no, not even through boycotts; but through love . . . But we must remember as we boycott that a boycott is not an end within itself; . . . the end is reconciliation; the end is redemption; the end is the creation of the beloved community."[40]

> Then I saw a new heaven and a new earth; for the first heaven and the first earth had passed away, and the sea was no more. And I saw the holy city, the new Jerusalem, coming down out of heaven from God, prepared as a bride adorned for her husband. And I heard a loud voice from the throne saying:

"See, the home of God is among mortals.
He will dwell with them as their God;
they will be his peoples,
and God himself will be with them;
He will wipe every tear from their eyes.
Death will be no more; mourning and crying and pain will be no more,
for the first things have passed away."

And the one who was seated on the throne said, "See, I am making all things new." Also he said, "Write this, for these words are trustworthy and true." Then he said to me, "It is done! I am the Alpha and the Omega, the beginning and the end. To the thirsty I will give water as a gift from the spring of life. Those who conquer will inherit these things, and I will be their God and they will be my children." (Revelation 21:1–7)

African American Responses to King

There have been three major responses to King's vision of a Beloved Community.

First, the Black Muslims rejected King's philosophy. The Muslim leader Elijah Muhammad emphatically stated two major points of difference: separation of the so-called Negroes and that the offer of integration is hypocritical.[41] The psychologist Kenneth B. Clark analyzed the relationship between the tactics and philosophy of Martin Luther King and the Black Muslim movement:

> Martin Luther King preaches a doctrine of "love for the oppressor" at the same time that he offers an effective social action technique of non-violent, assertive demand for civil rights. The Black Muslims preach a doctrine of black supremacy, hatred of whites, and total separation of negroes from whites, who are characterized as "blue eyed devils," morally defective and therefore incapable of offering the negro justice and equality. In spite of these apparent differences, it would be a mistake to ignore the similarities in these two movements. Each reflects the negro's basic impatience; each accepts, as a fact, the assumption that if the negro is to attain his rights, he must do so primarily, if not exclusively, through his own efforts; each is an assertive reaction against the dawdling, tortuously slow pace of desegregation by the majority of whites who seem to negroes to desire racial peace at any price; and each is in its own way militant and uncompromising.[42]

The nonviolent movement and the Black Muslim movement both represent a basic dilemma and ambivalence within the Negro people as a whole. King described Malcolm X's position of a completely separate and independent Black nation as "a strange dream."[43] The hatred and resentment espoused by the Muslims are a reflection of oppressive reality affecting all African Americans. Black Muslims are definitely opposed to passive resistance as outlined by King. C. Eric Lincoln contends "they oppose King because he emphasizes the Christian principle of loving the oppressor rather than retaliating against him. This is precisely the 'slave philosophy' the Muslims have sought to escape in their repudiation of Christianity. Hence, King represents to the Muslims a capitulation to the cunning Christian strategy of the white man."[44] Black Muslims believe that teaching the black person to defend self and dignity has nothing to do with Black supremacy. It is a passivity that robs the black person of a vital weapon in a racist society.

King received criticism from the Muslims regarding the morality of sit-ins. He and others were "accused of putting the lives of Negro children on the line 'while they sip cocktails in the lounges of Fifth Avenue.'" The Muslims boasted that they never sent their women and children into the lair of the beast.

What was King's response to the Black Muslims?

> While I strongly disagree with their separatist black supremacy philosophy, I have nothing but admiration for what our Muslim brothers have done to rehabilitate ex-convicts, dope addicts and men and women who, through despair and self-hatred, have sunk to moral degeneracy. This must be attempted on a much larger scale, and without the negative overtones that accompany Black Muslims.[45]

Black Power advocates sought to change the method and slogans of the civil rights movement. According to Stokely Carmichael and Charles Hamilton, Black Power "is a call for black people in this country to unite, to reorganize their heritage, to build a sense of community. It is a call for black people to begin to define their own goals, to lead their own organizations and to support those organizations. It is a call to reject the racist institutions and values of this society."[46] To do these things, the advocates of Black Power rejected the old slogans and "meaningless" rhetoric of the civil rights movement. "The language of yesterday is indeed irrelevant: progress, nonviolence, integration, fear of 'white backlash,' coalition."[47] These terms had to be set aside or redefined. Carmichael wrote:

> One of the tragedies of the struggle against racism is that up to this point there has been no national organization which could speak to the growing

militancy of young black people in the urban ghettos and the blackbelt South. There has been only a "civil rights" movement, whose tone of voice was adapted to an audience of middle-class whites. It served as a sort of buffer zone between that audience and angry young blacks . . . We had nothing to offer that we could see, except to go out and be beaten again . . . We had only the old language of love and suffering.[48]

In reference to the nonviolence strongly supported and advocated by King, Carmichael said: "Those of us who advocate Black Power are quite clear in our minds that a 'non-violent' approach to civil rights is an approach black people cannot afford and a luxury white people do not deserve."[49] Black Power advocates assert "there can be no social order without social justice."

The slogan "Black Power" has been closely studied by many theologians, of whom the best known is James Cone, who wrote:

> Because of King's work we are now in the beginning stages of real confrontation between black and white Americans. He may not have endorsed the concept of Black Power, but its existence is a result of his work. Black Power advocates are men who are inspired by his zeal for freedom, and Black Power is the only hope of the black church in America.[50]

Cone gives King credit for inspiring the Black Power advocates. Their inspiration led them to seek a change in methods and slogans. But if some blacks thought that King was too passive, many whites had other thoughts. White America thought that King was becoming too militant. As early as 1964, the generalized community-wide attacks on *de facto* school and housing segregation were followed by a "white backlash" of latent white prejudice. This prejudice was clearly apparent among low-income white groups, but it was not confined to this segment. In times of social strife, many liberal whites admonished blacks not to engage in disruptive and lawless demonstrations. Their argument was that such demonstrations might incite violence and reverse the progress made on the black person's behalf. They wanted King to choose only those techniques, tactics, and demonstrations which did not inconvenience the dominant White society. White people were delighted to have King speak of "loving the oppressor" in nonviolent demonstrations. This made them feel comfortable. They were upset, however, when King became an activist in sit-ins, economic boycotts, and open housing. This was too threatening, and they reacted against King, saying that he was becoming too militant.

To summarize, King's view of the civil rights movement was shaped by two concepts that characterize his life and thought: nonviolence and community. The former concept often contended with the shattering of hope in which many in the civil rights movement began to view King's utopian vision as unproductive and idealistic. King states:

> Yes, I am personally the victim of deferred dreams, of blasted hopes, but in spite of that I close today by saying I still have a dream, because, you know, you can't give up in life. If you lose hope, somehow you lose that vitality that keeps life moving, you lose that courage to be, that quality that helps you to go on in spite of all, and so today I still have a dream.[51]

However, just as the shattering of hope was not unknown to the prophets or the people of Israel, so too it was not uncommon in the trials that King faced. It is in the face of shattered hopes and dreams that King's recourse to nonviolence is made all the more powerful.

> Let us be dissatisfied until rat-infested, vermin-filled slums will be a thing of a dark past and every family will have a decent sanitary house in which to live. Let us be dissatisfied until the empty stomachs of Mississippi are filled and the idle industries of Appalachia are revitalized . . . Let us be dissatisfied until our brothers of the Third World – Asia, Africa, and Latin America – will no longer be the victim of imperialist exploitation, but will be lifted from the long night of poverty, illiteracy, and disease.[52]

In a 1959 speech to the Montgomery Improvement Association, King said:

> As victories for civil rights mount in the federal courts, the angry passion and deep prejudices . . . will be further aroused. These persons will do all within their power to provoke us and make us angry. But we must not retaliate with external physical violence or internal violence of spirit . . . As we continue the struggle for our freedom we will be persecuted, abused and called bad names. But we must go on with the faith that unearned suffering is redemptive, and love is the most durable power in all the world.[53]

This understanding of human suffering troubles scholars like Anthony Pinn, who cannot accept the idea that collective suffering on a daily basis has any value at all. For Pinn, it is necessary to explore an alternative response that uncompromisingly affirms – at all costs, including even the rejection of Christian concepts such as God – the demonic nature of collective suffering because human liberation is more important than the maintenance of any religious symbol, sign, canon, or icon.

Pinn sees nothing in history pointing toward the presence of something in the world beyond visible realities. There is no sneaking suspicion, no "smoking gun," pointing beyond humans. There is no God to hold us accountable, to work with us in moving beyond our current existential dilemmas. In the words of Oscar Wilde: "The true mystery of the world is the visible not the invisible."

"After taking a deep breath, I spoke a new word: God does not exist."[54] Even with this confession made, Pinn was still committed to doing theology, but without reliance on notions of God. He would do theology as a humanist. And as such, he was no longer talking about God (at least not in positive terms), but talking about ultimate questions of life that are not dependent on some type of "supreme reality" or "prime mover." He continued his work with this commitment: religious questions can surely be posed without the assumption of God. Pinn believes that other less visible aspects of Black religious life are ignored or marginalized because they threatened the ideological stability of the Church and by extension the thinkers who seek its sanction. The words of religious studies scholar Joseph Washington point to this assumed ontological link between African Americans and Black Christian churches:

> In the beginning was the black church, and the black church was with the black community, and the black church was the black community. The black church was in the beginning with the black people; all things were made through the black church, and without the black church was not anything made that was made. In the black church was life; and the life was the light of the black people.[55]

Washington's comments, tied in tone and form to Christian scripture, link together too intimately African American collective life and one form of religious conduct. By extension, if one is black, one is Christian; hence embracing other forms of religious experience places one outside the recognized borders of the Black family. Naturally, for Pinn, this is problematic and should give us pause, particularly for African American humanists who are excluded by such unfounded assertions. For the humanist, the question of liberation is a primary consideration. For example, suspicion concerning the Christian message was pointed out by Daniel Payne in 1839. Fearful that slaves would completely give up on the Christian faith if they were not introduced to the "true" gospel message, Payne wrote:

The slaves are sensible of the oppression exercised by their masters and they see these masters on the Lord's day worshipping in his holy Sanctuary. They hear their masters professing Christianity; they see these masters preaching the gospel; they hear these masters praying in their families, and they know that oppression and slavery are inconsistent with the Christian religion; therefore they scoff at religion itself – mock their masters, and distrust both the goodness and justice of God. Yes, I have known them even to question his existence. I speak not of what others have told me, but of what I have both seen and heard from the slaves themselves . . . A few nights ago between 10 and 11 o'clock a runaway slave came to the house where I live for safety and succor. I asked him if he was a Christian; "no sir," said he, "white men treat us so bad in Mississippi that we can't be Christians." . . . In a word, slavery tramples the laws of the living God under its unhallowed feet – weakens and destroys the influence which those laws are calculated to exert over the mind of man; and constrains the oppressed to blaspheme the name of the Almighty.[56]

Based upon Payne's depiction, it seems fairly clear that the early presence and rationale for humanism within African American communities revolved around the inadequacy of Christianity for responding to moral evil. Humanism, in turn, gives more attention to humanity's responsibility for evil in the world, hence humanity's responsibility for reorienting human destiny and fostering equality. Pinn points out that humanism continued to grow in Black communities through figures such as Frederick Douglass, Zora Neale Hurston, and W. E. B. Du Bois. One can say that humanism reaches its zenith with respect to open declarations and expression during the two periods of what has been labeled the Harlem Renaissance.

Moving into the late twentieth century, the civil rights movement's ideological underpinnings are further clarified through attention to humanist principles. Pinn cannot help but believe that the movement away from the Christian-based civil rights movement sparked by the Student Nonviolent Coordinating Committee (SNCC) and the thundering call for Black Power pointed to deep theological differences. It is more than likely that theistic motivations and explanations did not adequately address the concerns and ideas of some of the more "radical" elements of the movement. The break, Pinn argues, also marks a move away from the theism of the civil rights movement and toward materialist analysis and human-centered solutions. The late 1960s witnessed a methodological and epistemological shift within the SNCC. Gone were the integrationist goals that made it compatible with the civil rights movement; gone was its reliance upon Christian doctrine and paradigms for action. The SNCC decided that social transformation would only occur when African Americans took control of their destiny and worked toward change. Reliance on human potential for empowered praxis was heightened in ways that distinguished this phase of the SNCC's persona from the civil rights movement. Although inadequately defined in terms of social transformative thrusts and foci, Black Power – for some of its advocates – did harness rather clearly defined theological assumptions based upon humanist leanings and articulated itself in the language of self-determination.

Take, for example, the thoughts of James Forman, a member of the SNCC. In his autobiography Forman describes his "conversion" to humanism (as defined above), which did not hamper but rather informed his praxis. His work toward social transformation with the SNCC points to the nature and sustainability of humanist praxis. Such interactions are summed up by this comment: "God was not quite dead in me, but he was dying fast."[57] After returning from military service some years later, Forman came to a final conclusion concerning the existence of God:

> The next six years of my life were a time of ideas. A time when things were germinating and changing in me. A time of deciding what I would do with my life. It was also a time in which I rid myself, once and for all, of the greatest disorder that cluttered my mind – the belief in God or any type of supreme being.[58]

For Forman, humanism required a strong commitment on the part of people to change their present condition, a commitment that belief in God did not allow.

One can further trace humanism in Black thought and praxis through the Black Panther Party. The Panthers recognized that recruitment would be difficult if open hostility existed between the Party and the Black churches. Therefore, the Panthers fostered a relationship of convenience and sociopolitical necessity, but without a firm commitment to the Church's theological underpinnings. However, Huey Newton rationalized this involvement by arguing a different conception of God: God as the "unknown" whom, interestingly enough, science will ultimately resolve. In this sense, God does not exist in the affirmative; God is the absence of knowledge. According to Newton:

> So [the Panthers] do go to church, are involved in the church, and not in any hypocritical way. Religion perhaps is a thing that man needs at this time because scientists cannot answer all of the questions ... the unexplained and the unknown is God. We know nothing about God,

really, and that is why as soon as the scientist develops or points out a new way of controlling a part of the universe, that aspect of the universe is no longer God.[59]

Humanism is also found in the academic discussions of scholars such as William R. Jones. In 1973 Jones presented one of the first challenges to the Black Church tradition through humanist philosophical opinions. Jones pointed out the inconsistencies in the emerging Black theology movement, using the doctrine of God as his central concern. Although this critique of Black theology was timely and has resulted in much needed theological growth among African American theologians, what is more of concern here is his apology for Black humanism in his 1973 text and subsequent works.

Jones points out the early development of African American humanist leanings. He argues that the African American humanist project emerges not as a consequence of the Enlightenment, but rather as a direct response to a unique set of circumstances facing African American communities in the United States. Taking on the often myopic perspectives and narrow criteria established by Christian theologians for the doing of theology, Jones argues that a variety of approaches must be utilized if the liberation of African Americans is actually the central objective. Countering claims that the Black Church is the source of liberation for Black Americans, Jones asserts that the Black churches have a "checkered" past with respect to liberative praxis. Hence:

> Black humanism . . . thinks that it is unwise for the fate of black liberation to depend upon whether the black church awakens from its slumber or continues to snore, however piously and rhythmically. In this connection, the possibility must also be entertained that the emergence of black humanism as a formidable opponent may successfully prod the black church, as other secular movements have done.[60]

The Black churches, according to Jones, have harnessed the energy of their laity, yet there are many "unchurched" African Americans who might find humanism more compatible with their outlook and orientation.

Pinn's humanism has become typical of many black scholars who no longer accept Christian spirituality as normative reality. I think this is the case, however, because of a growing lack of community in the Western world. Much has been written in recent years about the loss of community and civility in American life. Because of this loss of community, locality and a sense of belonging are also lost. This leads to the conclusion that resources for the restoration of community are not readily available. Only in a very abstract way do the rights to participate in elections, enjoy public services, and receive public education constitute community for many Americans. Here, I think Martin Luther King has much to teach us in terms of the restoration of community. King's daughter, Bernice A. King, states: "It is the creation of the 'beloved community' that my father worked to attain. For him, nonviolence was the means for creating this community. Inherent in this process is reconciliation, which is the bringing together of estranged forces. Therefore, reconciliation becomes the act of creating community, which is only possible through love and nonviolence."[61]

King's Dream of the Beloved Community

I have a dream that one day men will rise up and come to see that they are made to live together as brothers. I still have a dream this morning that one day every Negro in this country, every colored person in the world, will be judged on the basis of the content of his character rather than the color of his skin, and every man will respect the dignity and worth of human personality. I still have a dream today that one day the idle industries of Appalachia will be revitalized, and the empty stomachs of Mississippi will be filled, and brotherhood will be more than a few words at the end of the prayer, but rather the first order of business on every legislative agenda.[62]

The concept of a dream corresponds in a powerful way to Martin Luther King, Jr.'s Beloved Community. Such a community spawned in the Black Church. Erskine is correct in his conclusion:

Martin King was a son of the Black church, and his theology cannot be understood without referring to those origins. Because his social activism was based on theological convictions about God and humanity, he gave particular attention to an explication of Christian faith in a situation of oppression. Faith for him was the victorious struggle against injustice and oppression of all sorts. Faith as the power of reconciliation becomes faithfulness to God as one lives out one's commitment for a restored and reconciled community. Faith in the mission to create the reconciled and restored community becomes the goal of history.[63]

King's vision of community is best characterized in his metaphor of the great world house or worldwide neighborhood, which suggests a totally integrated human family, unconcerned with human differences and devoted to the ethical norms of love, justice, and community:

We have inherited a large house, a great "world house" in which we have to live together – black and white, Easterner and Westerner, gentile and Jew, Catholic and Protestant, Moslem and Hindu – a family unduly separated in ideas, culture and interest, who, because we can never again live apart, must learn somehow to live with each other in peace.[64]

The Beloved Community was essentially "the capstone of King's thought" – "the organizing principle of all his thought and activity."[65] This beloved community would be characterized by its ultimate goal of nonviolence. King writes: "In other words, our ultimate goal is integration, which is genuine intergroup and interpersonal living. Only through nonviolence can this goal be attained, for the aftermath of nonviolence is reconciliation and the creation of the beloved community."[66]

One could say that King's Beloved Community found partial fulfillment in South Africa when Nelson Mandela and political prisoners were freed, when the first democratic elections took place in April 1994, when through the Truth and Reconciliation Commission the country was given a new future, and when Mandela became the country's first black president. It had been variously called the "Christian eschatological ideal," "the ideal corporate expression of the Christian faith," and "the mutually cooperative voluntary venture" of all moral and rational persons.[67] The Beloved Community vision was consistent with King's understanding of the Christian doctrine of the kingdom of heaven on earth, and with his view of democratic socialism as an economic and political ideology: "There is the more excellent way of love and nonviolent protest. I am grateful to God that, through the influence of the Negro church, the way of nonviolence became an integral part of our struggle."[68]

For King, this conception of community represented a peculiar blend of insights from Black culture, the Bible, liberal Christian theology and ethics, the American democratic heritage, Niebuhrian Christian realism, and Western philosophical traditions.[69] While the African American Church, the extended family network, and the Southern Black experience in which King was nurtured constituted the most important formative influences shaping his ideas about community, Boston personalism and the social gospelism of Walter Rauschenbusch provided him with the intellectual framework to articulate those ideas.[70] This must be clearly understood before King's communitarian ideal can be extended beyond the American context and perceptively related to the unique South African situation.

In King's view contemporary society had lost sight of transcendent value, adopting instead "a pragmatic test for right and wrong." In the modern world, he asserted, most people believed that "it's all right to disobey the Ten Commandments, but just don't disobey the Eleventh, Thou shall not get caught." The moral decay that King identified in modern culture could only be recovered by ethical living. "The thing that we need in the world today, is a group of men and women who will stand up for right and be opposed to wrong, wherever it is." King argued that making ethical decisions was impossible without rediscovering the transcendent values of heaven.

King charged that many people, including those who attended church every Sunday, had lost their faith in such concepts of heaven. "We must remember that it's possible to affirm the existence of God with your lips and deny his existence with your life." Returning to the biblical parable, King asserted that "we had gone a whole day's journey, and then we came to see that we had unconsciously ushered God out of the universe." The materialism of American consumer culture had caused some to lose sight of God, and King cautioned that "automobiles and subways, televisions and radios, dollars and cents, can never be substitutes for God."

King drew upon traditional African American religious ideas, particularly the notion of God acting in human history. Alluding to a verse in Psalm 23 and to a familiar hymn, he affirmed faith in the God "who walks with us through the valley of the shadow of death, and causes us to fear no evil," and in the God "who has been our help in ages past, and our hope for years to come, and our shelter in the time of storm, and our eternal home." He concluded with a rousing affirmation of God as an integral part of his life. "As a young man with most of my life ahead of me, I decided early to give my life to something eternal and absolute. Not to these little gods that are here today and gone tomorrow. But to God who is the same yesterday, today, and forever." It is through this vision that King could understand reality through nonviolence. He states:

> Here is the true meaning and value of compassion and nonviolence, when they help us to see the enemy's point of view, to hear his questions, to know his assessment of ourselves. For from his view we may indeed see the basic weaknesses of our own condition, and if we are mature, we may learn and grow and profit from the wisdom of the brothers who are called the opposition.[71]

Communal Antithesis for King

For King, the concept of community of the segregationists against which he and his fellow witnesses marched was this: the White race is genetically and spiritually superior to all others. For King and the civil rights movement, such a concept of community included only dragons.[72] It was not only a White segregationist world that offered the antithesis to true community, it was also modernity's obsession with mass destruction:

> If modern man continues to flirt unhesitatingly with war and eventually transforms his earthly habitat into an inferno such as even the mind of Dante could not imagine, it will have resulted from downright badness and also from downright stupidity.[73]

The organized principle by which to understand community for those against King was the institutionalized system of segregation and the modern decline of spirituality into individualism and materialism. King states: "One of the great problems of mankind is that we suffer from a poverty of spirit which stands in glaring contrast to our scientific and technological abundance. The richer we have become materially, the poorer we have become morally and spiritually."

> The stability of the large world house which is ours will involve a revolution of values to accompany the scientific and freedom revolutions engulfing the earth. We must rapidly begin the shift from a thing-oriented society to a person-oriented society. When machines and computers, profit motives and property rights are considered more important than people, the giant triplets of racism, materialism, and militarism are incapable of being conquered. A civilization can flounder as readily in the face of moral and spiritual bankruptcy as it can through financial bankruptcy.[74]

At the center of the antithesis to community were unhealthy hearts and souls resulting in skewed priorities and vision. King fought back with kataphatic witness to what heaven should be.

For a more explicit look at how King's vision relates both to the United States and South Africa, it is helpful to discuss the work of Lewis Baldwin, which is based upon the conviction that apartheid "in any form, rooted in the assumption that people of color are inferior to and cannot live on terms of equality with white people, is the very antithesis of the beloved community ideal." In order to see heaven's antithesis for King, one need only see any human system dependent upon hierarchical concepts of race and privilege. The power of Baldwin's work is in his application of King's ideal to South Africa and the rest of the world:

> We need to know more about how King moved beyond conceptions of "a new South" and "the American dream" to articulate a vision of "the world house." Also, we need to better understand the means by which

he sought to translate this vision of the "the world house" into practical reality. We have much to gain from studies of the relevance and applicability of King's global vision for contemporary and future human situations.[75]

Baldwin's contention is that apartheid constitutes both social evil and theological heresy because it denies at least four basic principles that formed the core of King's conception of community: (1) the impartiality of God in creating and dealing with human beings; (2) a sacramentalistic idea of the cosmos as echoed by the psalmist, "the earth is the Lord's, and the fullness thereof – the world, and they that dwell therein"; (3) a belief in the dignity and worth of all human personality; and (4) a solidaristic view of society and the world, which holds that each person is a distinct ontological entity who finds growth, fulfillment, and purpose through personal and social relationships based on the *agape* love ethic.[76]

The critical importance of the Beloved Community in King's intellectual concerns is evident from a reading of his sermons, public speeches, interviews, and writings from Montgomery to Memphis.[77] Convinced that community is the ultimate goal of human existence, King insisted that it was imperative for all persons of goodwill to struggle nonviolently against sin and the evil forces that work against harmony and wholeness in God's creation.[78] This view had powerful implications for the struggle against America's racism three decades ago, and it is relevant to the continuing efforts to destroy the last vestiges of the South African apartheid system. King refused to isolate South African apartheid from the larger, global problem of racism as promoted by white people. "In country after country," he wrote in 1967, "we see white men building empires on the sweat and suffering of colored people."

Portugal continues its practices of slave labor and subjugation in Angola; the Ian Smith government in Rhodesia continues to enjoy the support of British-based industry and private capital, despite the stated opposition of British Government policy. Even in the case of the little country of South West Africa we find the powerful nations of the world incapable of taking a moral position against South Africa, though the smaller country is under the trusteeship of the United Nations. Its policies are controlled by South Africa and its manpower is lured into the mines under slave-labor conditions.[79]

Thus, the apartheid regime in South Africa was symptomatic of a world problem; namely, the irrational preoccupation with skin color, the need for whites to dominate and control peoples of color, and the failure of persons to grasp the extent to which they are interrelated and interdependent. This perception was fundamental to King's theological, philosophical, and ethical arguments against apartheid.[80]

Baldwin's three main points for King's roots in the South African situation are as follows. First, experientially as a black person in a society founded on White supremacy and subsequently able to relate to people of color in South Africa, he was able "to identify those intellectual, moral and spiritual values so essential for their liberation and advancement." Second, "King's concern for the contributions to the movement against apartheid were in phase with his deepening and expanding involvements, coupled with his mounting interest in the oppressed worldwide." As he increasingly studied the vast sweep of humanity, and advanced his obligations as a social activist over time, King became more and more convinced that the success of blacks in America would remain questionable as long as black South Africans, and peoples of color generally, suffered on grounds of race and economics. Indeed, he came to the conclusion that African Americans and people of color in South Africa were engaged in essentially the same struggle, a conclusion that reinforced his thinking about the unity of the struggles of the oppressed on a global scale. Such a perspective came naturally for one who possessed a remarkable ability to empathize with others.[81]

Third, King's interest in and contributions to the struggle against South African apartheid linked him to a tradition of African American thought and leadership dating back to Richard Allen, Robert A. Young, and David Walker in the eighteenth and nineteenth centuries, and as recent as the Republic of the New South Africa and the Nation of Islam. King's spiritual and cultural bond with this tradition of thought and leadership, a tradition shaped primarily by Black nationalists, was his concern for the freedom and uplift of all people of African descent. This is not to say that King was a full-blown Black nationalist or a Pan-Africanist, for the range of his concern and vision (at least in his own mind and the thinking of those who have explored his life and thought) ultimately transcended such ideological categories. George M. Houser states: "Martin Luther King, Jr. was not essentially a Pan-Africanist, although his and Du Bois' positions had a great deal in common." Houser's point is questionable to the extent that King did accept aspects of the central view of Pan-Africanists; namely, that "people of African descent throughout the world have common cultural characteristics and share common problems as a result of their African origins, the similarity of their political oppression and economic exploitation by Western civilization, and the persistence and virulence of racist theories, attitudes, and behavior characterizing Western contact with people of African descent." However, King was too much of an integrationist and a believer in a common culture shared by blacks and whites in America to fit neatly into the tradition of Pan-Africanism.[82]

Notes

1 Martin Luther King, Jr., *Why We Can't Wait* (New York: Mentor Book, 1963), p. 70.
2 See Robin Lovin, "Civil Rights, Civil Society, and Christian Realism," *Religion and Values in Public Life*, Center for the Study of Values in Public Life at Harvard Divinity School, 6:2/3 (Winter/Spring 1998), p. 8.
3 It should be noted here that there were other ecumenical leaders in the civil rights movement, such as John LaFarge and John Courtney Murray for Roman Catholics, Robert Gordis and Abraham Herschel for Judaism, and Reinhold Niebuhr for Protestants. See E. J. Dionne, Jr., "Faith, Politics, and the Common Good," *Religion and Values in Public Life*, Center for the Study of Values in Public Life at Harvard Divinity School, 6:2/3 (Winter/Spring 1998).
4 Ariel Dorfman, "A Latin American Perspective on Martin Luther King, Jr.," September 5, 2003, quoted in *Dialogue* (periodical of Duke University).
5 Reinhold Niebuhr, *Moral Man and Immoral Society* (New York: Charles Scribner and Sons, 1932), especially chapter 9.
6 Ibid, chapter 9.
7 Glen Tinder, *The Political Meaning of Christianity: An Interpretation* (Baton Rouge: Louisiana State University Press, 1989).
8 It is important to note here a great debt to Stanley Hauerwas, my colleague at Duke University, who trained my theological vision as he supervised me as a PhD student.
9 Joseph Washington, *Black Religion* (Boston, MA: Beacon Press, 1964), p. 132.
10 Martin Luther King, Jr., *The Measure of A Man* (Philadelphia, PA: Christian Education Press, 1959), p. 45.
11 Martin Luther King, Jr., *Stride Toward Freedom: The Montgomery Story* (New York: Ballantine, 1958), pp. 69–70.
12 See Joseph Milburn Thompson, "Martin Luther King, Jr. and Christian Witness: An Interpretation of King Based on a Theological Model of Prophetic Witness," dissertation, Fordham University, New York, 1981.
13 Martin Luther King, Jr., *Where Do We Go from Here: Chaos or Community?* (Boston, MA: Beacon Press, 1967), pp. 76–7.
14 Martin Luther King, Jr., "The Rising Tide of Racial Consciousness," *YWCA Magazine* (December 1960), p. 3.
15 King, *Stride Toward Freedom*, pp. 116–17.
16 Ibid, p. 117.

17 Martin Luther King, Jr., *Strength to Love* (Cleveland, OH: Collins Publishers, 1963), p. 150.

18 See King, *Stride Toward Freedom*, ch. 6; "Pilgrimage to Nonviolence," *Christian Century* 77 (April 13, 1960), pp. 439–41; *Strength to Love*, ch. 17.

19 Martin Luther King, Jr., "The Unchristian Christian," *Ebony* 20 (August 1965), p. 77. See also King's "Letter From a Birmingham Jail" in *Why We Can't Wait*, p. 91.

20 See King, "The Death of Evil on the Seashore," in *Strength to Love*, pp. 58–66. King delivered this sermon on May 17, 1956 at the Episcopal Cathedral of St. John the Divine in New York City. Other King references to the Exodus are *Strength to Love*, pp. 5, 188; *Where Do We Go from Here*, pp. 124, 170; "Facing the Challenge of a New Age," *Fellowship* 23 (February 1957), p. 4; "I Have a Dream," in *Martin Luther King, Jr.: A Documentary, Montgomery to Memphis*, ed. Flip Schulke (New York: W. W. Norton, 1976), p. 213; "I've Been to the Mountain," in Schulke, *Martin Luther King*, pp. 223–4.

21 N. L. Erskine, *King Among the Theologians* (Cleveland, OH: Pilgrim Press, 1994), p. 145.

22 King, *Strength to Love*, p. 82.

23 King, *Stride Toward Freedom*, p. 182; *Strength to Love*, pp. 97, 130–1. Unfortunately, King omits "male nor female" in his allusion to Galatians. For an interesting discussion of an internal critique of King's work and the Black Church in relation to womanist theology, see Erskine, *King Among the Theologians*, pp. 159–73; *Garth Baker-Fletcher, Somebodyness: Martin Luther King, Jr. and the Theory of Dignity* (Minneapolis, MN: Fortress Press, 1993), pp. 165–93.

24 King, "I Have a Dream," p. 123; *Stride Toward Freedom*, pp. 186–7; *The Trumpet of Conscience* (New York: Harper and Row, 1967), p. 92; Kenneth L. Smith and Ira G. Zepp, Jr., *Search for the Beloved Community: The Thinking of Martin Luther King Jr.* (Valley Forge, PA: Judson Press, 1974), p. 39.

25 King, "I Have a Dream," p. 218; *Trumpet of Conscience*, p. 9.

26 King, "I Have a Dream," p. 218; *Trumpet of Conscience*, pp. 91–3.

27 Martin Luther King, Jr., *I've Been to the Mountaintop* (San Francisco: Harper, 1994), p. 16.

28 Ibid, p. 17.

29 Ibid, pp. 29–30.

30 King, *Where Do We Go from Here*, pp. 62–3; cf. *Strength to Love*, p. 37.

31 King, *Where Do We Go from Here*, p. 63.

32 Ibid, p. 9.

33 King, *Stride Toward Freedom*, p. 81; *Strength to Love*, p. 140.

34 King, *Trumpet of Conscience*, p. 67.

35 Walter Breuggemann, "How Do We Know a Prophet When We See One? Martin Luther King, Jr.," *Youth Magazine* 26 (January 1975), p. 54.

36   King, *I've Been to the Mountaintop*, pp. 33–4.

37   King, *Strength to Love*, p. 104; cf. *Stride Toward Freedom*, pp. 114–15.

38   King, *Stride Toward Freedom*, p. 171.

39   King, *Why We Can't Wait*, p. 75.

40   Martin Luther King, Jr., "Facing the Challenge of a New Age," in *Testament of Hope: The Essential Writings of Martin Luther King, Jr.*, ed. James M. Washington (San Francisco: Harper and Row, 1986), p. 140.

41   Elijah Muhammad, *Message to the Black Man in America* (Chicago: Muhammad Mosque of Islam No. 2, 1965), pp. 163–5.

42   Kenneth B. Clark, *Dark Ghetto* (New York: Harper and Row, 1965), pp. 214–19.

43   For discussion and references to King's ambivalent relationship with Malcolm X, see L. V. Baldwin, *To Make the Wounded Whole: The Cultural Legacy of Martin Luther King, Jr.* (Minneapolis, MN: Fortress Press, 1992), p. 34ff.

44   C. Eric Lincoln, *The Black Muslims in America* (Boston, MA: Beacon Press, 1961), p. 152.

45   King, *Where Do We Go from Here*, p. 148.

46   Stokely Carmichael and Charles V. Hamilton, *Black Power* (New York: Random House, 1967), p. 44.

47   Ibid, p. 50.

48   Ibid, p. 50.

49   Ibid, p. 53.

50   James Cone, *Black Theology and Black Power* (New York: Harper and Row, 1989), p. 109.

51   King, *Trumpet of Conscience*, p. 76.

52   Martin Luther King, Jr., "Honoring Dr. Du Bois," *Freedomways* 8:2 (Spring 1968), pp. 110–11.

53   Untitled Montgomery Improvement Association address, 1959, Boston University, King Collection, Box 2, I-11, Folder 2. This address mentions the type of abuse that those fighting for liberation encounter. King often had his person and character attacked, and was accused of communist leanings. See, for example, David Garrow, *The FBI and Martin Luther King, Jr.* (New York: W. W. Norton, 1981) for accounts of governmental resentment. See also Billy James Hargis, "Unmasking the Deceiver," Boston University, King Collection, Box 80, X.43.

54   Anthony Pinn, "On Becoming Humanist: A Personal Journey," *Religious Humanism: Journal of the HUUmanists* 32:1&2 (Winter/Spring 1998). I am in great debt to Pinn's reflections here and the honest challenges that he raises for us all.

55   Joseph Washington, "How Black is Black Religion?" in *Quest for a Black Theology*, ed. James J. Gardiner and J. Deotis Roberts (Philadelphia, PA: Pilgrim Press, 1971).

56   Daniel Alexander Payne, "Daniel Payne's Protestation of Slavery," *Lutheran Herald and Journal of the Franckean Synod* (August 1, 1839), pp. 114–15.

57 James Forman, "Corrupt Black Preachers," in *The Making of Black Revolutionaries* (Washington, DC: Open Hand Publishing, 1985), p. 58.
58 Ibid, "God Is Dead: A Question of Power," pp. 80–1.
59 Huey Newton, *To Die For The People: The Writings of Huey P. Newton*, ed. Toni Morrison (New York: Writers and Readers Publishing, 1995), p. 64.
60 William R. Jones, "The Case for Black Humanism," in William R. Jones and Calvin Bruce, eds., *Black Theology II: Essays on the Formation and Outreach of Contemporary Black Theology* (Lewisburg, PA: Bucknell University Press, 1978), p. 221.
61 Bernice A. King, foreword to Noel Leo Erskine, *King Among the Theologians* (Cleveland, OH: Pilgrim Press, 1994), p. x.
62 King, *Trumpet of Conscience*, pp. 77–8.
63 Erskine, *King Among the Theologians*, p. 9.
64 King, *Where Do We Go from Here*, pp. 167–8.
65 See Smith and Zepp, *Search for the Beloved Community*, p. 119; Fluker, They Looked for a City, pp. 110–28; Walter E. Fluker, "They Looked for a City: A Comparison of the Ideal of Community in Howard Thurman and Martin Luther King Jr.," *Journal of Religious Ethics* 18:2 (Fall 1990), pp. 33–50; Baldwin, *To Make the Wounded Whole*, pp. 245–313.
66 King, *Stride Toward Freedom*, p. 196.
67 Fluker, They Looked for a City, pp. 110–13.
68 King, *Where Do We Go from Here*, p. 37.
69 See Fluker, "They Looked for a City," pp. 82–8; L. V. Baldwin, *There Is a Balm in Gilead: The Cultural Roots of Martin Luther King Jr.* (Minneapolis, MN: Fortress Press, 1991), pp. 4–5, 104, 171–3; Baldwin, *To Make the Wounded Whole*, pp. 163–313; Smith and Zepp, *Search for the Beloved Community*, pp. 119–49; Kenneth L. Smith, "The Radicalization of Martin Luther King Jr.: The Last Three Years," *Journal of Ecumenical Studies* 26:2 (Spring 1989), p. 278; John J. Ansbro, *Martin Luther King Jr.: The Making of a Mind* (Maryknoll, NY: Orbis Books, 1982), pp. 29–36, 163–97.
70 See Baldwin, *There Is a Balm in Gilead*, p. 172; Fluker, *They Looked for a City*, pp. 81–128.
71 King, *Trumpet of Conscience*, p. 29.
72 For an interesting appropriation of King's nonviolent resistance for the Book of Revelation, see Brian K. Blount, "Reading Revelation Today," *Interpretation* (October 2000).
73 King, *Strength to Love*, p. 32.
74 King, *Where Do We Go from Here*, p. 186; cf. *Trumpet of Conscience*, pp. 41–2.
75 Lewis Baldwin, *Toward the Beloved Community: Martin Luther King Jr. and South Africa* (Cleveland, OH: Pilgrim Press, 1995), p. 6. (For a more extensive list of published references for how King relates to South Africa, see ibid, p. 188, n.3.)

76 See Smith and Zepp, *Search for the Beloved Community*, pp. 119–40; Fluker, *They Looked for a City*, pp. 81–172; Baldwin, *To Make the Wounded Whole*, pp. 163–313.

77 See Smith and Zepp, *Search for the Beloved Community*, p. 119.

78 See King, *Where Do We Go from Here*, pp. 173–91; *Trumpet of Conscience*, pp. 67–78; Fluker, *They Looked for a City*, pp. 120–43.

79 King, *Where Do We Go from Here*, pp. 173–4.

80 See Fluker, *They Looked for a City*, pp. 110–52.

81 See Baldwin, *There is a Balm in Gilead*, pp. 15–90; *Toward the Beloved Community*, p. 4.

82 See George M. Houser, "Freedom's Struggle Crosses Oceans and Mountains: Martin Luther King, Jr. and the Liberation Struggles in Africa and America," in *We Shall Overcome: Martin Luther King, Jr. and the Black Freedom Struggle*, ed. Peter J. Albert and Ronald Hoffman (New York: Pantheon Books, 1990), p. 183; John H. Bracey, Jr. et al., eds., *Black Nationalism in America* (New York: Bobbs-Merrill, 1970), p. xxix; Baldwin, *To Make the Wounded Whole*, pp. 163–244.

Chapter 7
Embodying African American Spirituality

Give us grace, O God, to dare to do the deed which we well know cries to be done. Let us not hesitate because of ease, or the words of [people's] mouths, or our own lives. Mighty causes are calling us – the freeing of women, the training of children, the putting down of hate and murder and poverty – all these and more.

W. E. B. Du Bois[1]

This chapter looks at the future of the Black Church in America in light of its current needs and concerns. How will current forms of Black worship styles maintain themselves and/or be transformed? What will happen to the Black Church as a larger middle class and upper middle class emerge? How will the Church change as more women take leadership? How will debates over sexual orientation affect the Black Church? And will the Black Church continue to be the major context from which major civil rights leaders emerge, especially in light of some of the more radical political voices of the Nation of Islam? The extent to which the Black Church in America continues to explore how individual and communal fulfillment are inextricably tied together is the extent to which it can continue to be a light to the nations.

This book has argued that community and communal practices such as nonviolence constitute the essence of African American spirituality. The future of the Black Church will continue to live in the argument as to how practical such a spirituality is. Although theology may still exist as an intellectual discipline, and prayer and liturgical practices are not dismissed as species of self-delusion, still the impact of the ideas elaborated by religious groups on existing social institutions and political developments is not impressive. The global North retreats into personal and privatistic spiritualities that substitute for Christianity. Stimulating communal spiritualities in a part of the world that would rather engender private religion has been the continuing nemesis to the character of African American spirituality. In fact, some argue that the Black Church will inevitably become Western and privatistic. For example, black theological constituents are thrown into disarray when addressing problematic themes of a specifically Christian view of the state, of armed service in time of war, and of development in economically developing countries.

Concerning future definitions of the Black Church, one must ask whether the Church is an abstraction or a communal entity, an idea (in the Platonic sense) or a fact in the historical order with a continuity in time? From our journey together from seeing how the Black Church survived slavery, separated into denominations, worships together, led the civil rights movement, and imagines the Beloved Community, I answer this question with eight convictions about how one is to continue imagining the communal nature of African American Christian spirituality.

1   The Black Church is willing to consult together in seeking to learn how to be more about mutuality than segregation.
2   The Black Church constitutes a communal spirituality of conversation, cooperation, and common witness based on the common recognition of the community of God.
3   The Black Church believes on the basis of the New Testament that the Church of Christ is one.
4   The Black Church recognizes that the membership of the Church should be more inclusive day by day. By virtue of baptism and faith, all Christians obtain a primary identity in which to order all other identities, including racial identity.
5   Based on inclusivity of other identities and the lack of threat of others in Christ, the Black Church can consider the relationship of the other as bettering the identity of self.
6   The Black Church recognizes racial and economic human divisions as sin.
7   Good health is a practical implication of common membership in the Black Church. Therefore, members should recognize their solidarity with each other, render assistance to each other in case of need, and refrain from such actions as are incompatible with communal relationships.
8   The Black Church enters into spiritual relationships through which healing is sought in order that communities may be built up and renewed.

With these eight convictions, two contemporary subjects need to be reimagined in order to sustain the vital witness of African American Christian spirituality. These two subjects continue to challenge the communal convictions of African American Christian spirituality and even threaten to return it to the older exclusivist arguments in which black identity should be one's primary identity. These two subjects are (1) a churchless Black Church and (2) a womanless Black Church. These are subjects that African American Christian spirituality enables us to reimagine out of the stagnant situations in which many people currently suffer. Let us look at each in turn.

A Churchless Black Church

Will the Black Church be able to adapt to the challenges ahead? In future multicultural societies, challenges unforeseen will arrive at the door of the Black Church. Can the Black Church lead in a way that demonstrates its essential nonviolent and communal spirituality? These are crucial questions to ask. The Black Church today is perceived by some to be too apologetic for its own causes and provincial, failing even to appreciate complex African American experience.[2] For example, in *Black Theology of Liberation,* James Cone threatens to destroy "God" if God is not in favor of Black liberation: "If God is not for us . . . then God is a murderer, and we had better kill God."[3] Cone suggests that the African American existential condition and its radical alteration take priority over the Black Church's symbol systems, language games, doctrinal formulations, and religious structures. Understood in this way, Cone's statement implies that the Black Church needs fresh visions of "liberation." Regrettably, for some black scholars, the Black Church has not taken Cone's advice. Rather, it has lost sight of its objective, while embracing comfortable institutional structures and traditional rhetoric and becoming theologically numb to the changing African American context.

Such black scholars think there is a need to move beyond a strictly polemical discussion of the Black Church toward a more constructive and pragmatic posture. One such move could be the rethinking of conceptions of religious experience in ways that recognize the multiplicity of religious experiences rather than typecasting African American spirituality through the Black Church. For Anthony Pinn, theology is not done through the Black Church per se, but should be done with a knowledge of and acquaintance with the variety of religious expressions in African American heritage. He seeks to think through theology as an empirical and historical discipline. Understood in this way, theology becomes a way of seeing, interpreting, and taking hold of African American experience.

This thesis is also expressed through an examination of theology's objective and goals, using Victor Anderson's notion of "cultural fulfillment." For Pinn and Anderson, the use of social sciences facilitates a better methodology for Black theology than through the simple confessional nature of the Black Church. Using these primary sources, Pinn also argues for a critical, pragmatic commitment that gives priority to experience (and the objective of fulfillment) over Church "tradition." The challenging view for Pinn is that the Black Church – its concept of God, humanity, and Christ – when construed as the normative expression of African American religion, limits the relevance and truth content of other religious experiences that are not in keeping with Church activity and doctrines. In short, for Pinn and Anderson, to hold the Black Church as normative in theological conversation and methodological formulation of African American experience is to make its principles hegemonic or closed to others with different viewpoints.

The prevailing assumption now becomes that the Black Church should no longer fully represent African American spirituality. For the emerging black religious scholar, one finds traces of a Black aesthetic forcing a dwarfed understanding of Black life and sacrificing individuality for the sake of an illusionary unified Black "faith" and life. Implicit in this critique is a crisis of faith determined by the construct of racial identity. According to Anderson:

> Talk about liberation becomes hard to justify where freedom appears as nothing more than defiant self-assertion of a revolutionary racial consciousness that requires for its legitimacy the opposition of white racism. Where there exists no possibility of transcending the blackness that whiteness created, African American theologies of liberation must be seen not only as crisis theologies; they remain theologies in a crisis of legitimation.[4]

"Racial apologetics" has been the norm for African American theological production. Cornel West sees such productions as the major African American response to racist discourse.[5] In order to move away from being a crisis of legitimation, Anderson describes the aesthetic move behind this production in terms of the Black aesthetic or Black "genius" (exceptional if not essentialized qualities) informed by African American cultural philosophies. This sense of Black genius challenges notions of White superiority by arguing for the uniqueness of African American contributions to culture as the rationale for including black Americans in the larger picture of social progress and democratic humanism.

This sense of Black creativity and legitimacy provides a vocabulary for responding to the challenges of life ahead. The problem of the churchless Black Church, however, occurs. Anderson refers to this counter-discourse (discourse against racism) as ontological blackness and no longer finds much use for the confessional cosmology of the Black Church so defined by racial identity. Although passionate and reasoned, such arguments from the likes of David Walker, Reverdy Ransom, Maria Stewart, and W. E. B. Du Bois inadvertently reinforced racial ideologies, thereby doing internal damage to Black cultural and religious criticism and limiting the life options of black Americans. African American collective identity, so defined, creates conflict to the extent that individual desires and styles do not match the Black "party line."

Anderson seeks to change this understanding of Black religious aesthetics by maintaining an optimism that speaks to the possibility of triumph over wrongdoing in tension with the recognition that the causes of injustice are long-suffering and slow to change. He sees the theoretical grounding for this stance in figures such as Cornel West and Howard Thurman. Anderson contextualizes the integrating of cultural and religious criticism. For him, the religious functions of cultural criticism are developed through a critical appeal to the theory of radical consciousness and human action of Thurman and the prophetic pragmatism and politics of difference of West. He appreciates the manner in which these thinkers promote an approach to the existential condition of black people that is aware of racism but is not subsumed by it. They acknowledge the richness and complexity of African American existence; this life is neither binary, nor communal at the expense of the individual, and nor is it radically individualistic. Black life is then understood as a mosaic, a full range of individually selected and community nurturing actions, attitudes, stances, objectives, and goals. Herein, appreciation is expressed for the human impulse toward creative transformation, or what Anderson labels "cultural fulfillment." Cultural fulfillment accentuates the communal and individual potentials and possibilities for freedom, emancipation, and transcendence. Connected to this is an appreciation of the full range of life in what Anderson embraces as the grotesqueries of Black life.

The grotesque serves as an effective counter-discourse to ontological Blackness that enlarges the scope of life by embracing both the "light" and "dark" aspects of existence insofar as it holds in tension oppositional sensations – pleasure and pain, freedom and oppression.[6] In this way, the full range of African American expression, interactions, etc., are given weight in and of themselves because difference is valued. The concept of the Black Church as the repository of such interaction is no longer needed. In this way, the grotesque can help theology free itself from the totalizing nature of racial apologetics and the classical Black aesthetic through a multilayered and humanistic agenda.

Unlike prior approaches, an understanding of the grotesquery of Black life provides a full range of Black individual and collective activities, the good and the "questionable." It provides, in short, a complete historical workup, one that does not sweep unacceptable behavior (e.g., heterosexism, sexism, classism) under the rug in the name of racial unity. The hegemony and the specific forms of power, and the established forms of discourse on power associated with it, must be deconstructed if the Black Church is to serve a fruitful purpose. In the Black Church, full expression of life must be the goal and the full range of creative possibilities must be kept in view.

Although new understandings of the Black Church have developed in recent years, still the words of Charles Long hold their relevance some thirty-five years after they were first published. Long suggests that "what we have in fact are two kinds of studies: those arising from the social sciences, and an explicitly theological apologetic tradition." He continues: "This limitation of methodological perspectives has led to a narrowness of understanding and the failure to perceive certain creative possibilities in the black community in America."[7] By this, Long means that African American experience has been a frequent topic of academic discussion, but much of this conversation misses the uniquely "religious" components of this experience because the methodological tools are limited to the social sciences – anthropology, sociology, etc. According to Long, an attempt was made to correct this through the development of Black theology, with its attention to African American history, experience, and cultural production as the substance of a unique form of theological reflection.

Yet, argues Pinn, such efforts are limited to the Christian context and apologies for the liberative content of the gospel message, and varieties of faith existing outside of this context are excluded. With time, this apologetic Black theology has come to define the discussion of uniquely religious elements within African American experience. The dilemma most relevant to Pinn's argument is the manner in which the Black Church's hegemonic tone deadens the complexity of Black religious experience. In other words, historically speaking, the professionalization of Black theology resulted in an economy of ideas and the establishment of a canon based on what was considered representative of Black religious experience.[8]

Other less visible aspects of Black religious life were ignored or marginalized because they threatened the ideological stability of the

Church and by extension the thinkers who sought its sanction.[9] By extension, if one is black, one is Christian; hence embracing other forms of religious experience places one outside the recognized borders of the Black family. For Pinn, the normative status of the Black Church is maintained by minimizing the true diversity of Black experience. Pinn argues that even some of those who seek to take seriously the theological ramifications of African American cultural production that falls outside of the Church stumble over this issue. For example, theologian Dwight Hopkins' push for a contextual expansion of resources as part of the constructive enterprise – recognition of and respect for Africanisms or "remains" – ultimately collapses.[10] In several of his works (most notably *Shoes That Fit Our Feet*) Hopkins argues that Black theology properly done must engage the full range of African American insights, including slave narratives, folktales, and the literature of figures such as Toni Morrison. In Hopkins' words: "It calls on Black Theology to set its compass for the avenues African American folk are traveling. Black Theology, then, must develop itself from beliefs deeply embedded in the very blood and bones of an African American reality. Black resources are the heart of Black Theology."[11]

This process, according to Hopkins, will bring theologians into contact with African elements deeply embedded in African American life, present in the stories of High John the Conqueror, Brer Rabbit, and other cultural heroes. Albeit important within Hopkins' work, Africanisms are only of rhetorical value for Pinn because they become dependent upon a strong Christian base that renders them relatively indefinable and without vitality or texture. According to Hopkins, "enslaved Africans took the remnants of their traditional religious structures and meshed them together with their interpretation of the Bible." Furthermore, "all this occurred in the Invisible Institution, far away from the watchful eyes of white people. Only in their own cultural idiom and political space could black slaves truly worship God."[12]

A Womanless Black Church

Alice Walker's first use of the term "womanist" occurred in her review of *Gifts of Power: The Writings of Rebecca Jackson*, a book edited by Jean McMahon Humez about the legendary nineteenth-century black Shaker.[13] Jacquelyn Grant states: "Womanists were Sojourner Truth, Jarena Lee, Amanda Berry Smith, Ida B. Wells, Mary Church Terrell, Mary McLeod Bethune, Fannie Lou Hamer and countless others not remembered in any historical study."[14] Walker's primary claim is the right of black women to name their own experience. Such a naming process does not mean that there is an exclusion of other identities – just that all voices need to be heard. This in itself raises a major future challenge for the Black Church in America.

Womanist theology – a corrective to a patriarchal Black Church – also maintains a similar perspective on the centrality and normative status of Black Church thought within theological reflection. The position taken by Cheryl Sanders during the roundtable discussion on ethics and theology in womanist perspective published in the *Journal of Feminist Studies in Religion* is representative of this orientation.[15] Womanism as defined by Alice Walker should open new approaches to religious materials, and new conceptions of liberation and community, because it provides a hermeneutic of life, a mosaic that embraces black women's diverse experiences, thoughts, and productions.[16] Yet Sanders questions womanism's usefulness: "Are we committing a gross conceptual error when we use Walker's descriptive cultural nomenclature as a foundation for the normative discourse of theology and ethics?"[17] Sanders concludes that the term denotes a primarily secular way of life that is likely to be incompatible with the Christian context of theological discussion.

There were two parallel movements in the USA: Black consciousness and feminist consciousness. Far from working together for social and political reform they viewed each other with suspicion. Sojourner Truth provides this example:

> That man over there says that women need to be helped into carriages, and lifted over ditches, and to have the best place everywhere. Nobody ever helps me into carriages, or over mud-puddles, or gives me any best place! And ain't I a woman? Look at me! Look at my arm! I have plowed and planted, and gathered into barns, and no man could head me! And ain't I a woman? I could work as much and eat as much as a man – when I could get it – and bear the lash as well! And ain't I a woman? I have borne thirteen children and seen most all sold off to slavery, and when I cried out with my mother's grief, none but Jesus heard me! And ain't I a woman?[18]

The social construction of being a woman, the image of what it was to be a woman, totally excluded black women from the movement. Black women were absent from critiques of both racism and sexism. As Alice Walker commented: "White women feminists revealed themselves as incapable as white and black men of comprehending blackness and feminism in the same body, not to mention within the same imagination."[19]

Black feminism had the challenge of critiquing racism and sexism. The setting aside of race in earlier feminism was not an innocent matter. It was an ideological decision. The manifesto of bell hooks suggests that feminism is not the answer, but rather part of the problem. The well-being of women must be considered in a wider context which includes sexism without isolating it from other material factors which determine women's lives. In Alice Walker's novel *The Color Purple* black women have no possibility of being ladylike. For example, one character, Sofia, is described standing by an ironing board with an iron in her hand. "Sofia the kind of women no matter what she have in her hand it look like a weapon."[20] Walker develops this theme of lacking ladylike qualities and redescribes the concept of the "womanly." For Walker, a womanist describes a spirit of independence that intensifies when faced with injustice.[21] A womanist becomes a black feminist or feminist of color. Walker explained that the term "womanist" was broader, more comprehensive, "More reflective of black women's culture, especially Southern culture."[22]

bell hooks was also influential in describing the emergence of womanism. "Even though there are a few black women (I am one) who assert that we empower ourselves by using the term feminism, by addressing our concerns as black women as well as our concern with the welfare of the human community globally, we have had little impact."[23] She was particularly concerned with the rejection of the term "black feminism" in the academic context.

It is because these wider concerns cannot be accommodated in a feminist theory that is inherently racist and sexist that Alice Walker has turned to the term "womanist." It is a platform from which to address issues of sex, yes, but also as hooks recommends a system of challenges such as self-development, race, class, imperialism, economic expansion, and material desires. It is because of this that womanist theology emerged in the 1980s. During this era, black women theologians could appreciate much of feminist theology, but it did not ring true to their experience. They accepted much of Black theology, but their voices were also missing. It was time for womanist theology, a distinctive theology that applied womanist perspectives to Christian theology.

Thus womanist theology benefited from those liberation theologies which preceded it. From feminist theology it has taken the criticism of oppression on the basis of sexual discrimination. From Black theology it has taken the criticism of oppression on the basis of racial discrimination. From Latin American theology of liberation it has taken the criticism of oppression on the basis of class discrimination. This leads to my first conviction: (1) The Black Church is willing to consult together in seeking to learn how to be more about mutuality than segregation. Theology has to be concerned with the mutuality of identity and not just one form of oppression but with all forms: sex, race, and class. When womanist theology appeared it inherited this conviction of mutuality, although it often presents this holistic approach through great challenge. For Marcia Y. Riggs, "one of the tasks of a womanist ethicist is to retrieve Black women's history as a source of ethical reflection."[24] For this reason stories of the discounted lives of black women such as Zora Neale Hurston must be told.[25]

Womanist theology therefore presents the experience of black women as its own tradition. There are frequent references to features of African culture which are preserved – perhaps unconsciously – and which contrast with European (and White American) culture. It is right that womanist voices, too long suppressed for sexist as well as racist reasons, should be told. Womanism gives a mutual voice to a significant part of society previously ignored, dismissed, and silenced. It explores the possibility that these experiences were not at all as they were assumed to be. The challenge for womanist theologians is in how to make their voices mutual and accessible to wider communities. This also remains the challenge of the Black Church at large in America.

In summary, the crucial issue is whether Black experience is *one* experience or a combination of many, and thus whether it leads to one theological expression or many. Charles Long writes: "The Christian faith provided a language for the meaning of religion, but not all the religious meanings of the black communities were encompassed by the Christian forms of religion."[26] These other forms of expression arose out of black people's experiences and addressed their needs. Anything less would have been religiously counterfeit.

The reconstruction of African American spirituality for these scholars thus involves a movement toward a churchless Black Church. In the current context of Black theological production, many black theologians give attention to other forms of religious expression (i.e., Africanisms), but in order only to foster better understanding of the Black Church. Again, for Anthony Pinn, the Black Church is not the only expression and representation of Black religious life. He quotes Long to make the point:

> To be sure, the church is one place one looks for religion . . . But even more than this, the church was not the only context for the meaning of religion . . . The Christian faith provided a language for the meaning of religion, but not all the religious meanings of the black communities were encompassed by the Christian forms of religion . . . Some tensions have existed between these forms of orientation and those of the Christian

churches, but some of these extrachurch orientations have had great critical and creative power. They have often touched deeper religious issues regarding the true situation of black communities than those of the church leaders of their time.[27]

If Long is correct (Pinn thinks that he is), and if African American religion is understood in terms of ultimate orientation and framed by an ultimate concern, then Pinn thinks theologians who are interested in African American experience are required to extend religious boundaries beyond the obvious and well-documented forms of Black religiosity. African American theology ought genuinely to be open to what Long has labeled "extra-church orientations."

Pragmatically oriented methodological shifts in African American theology result in a theological discourse mature and refined enough to embrace and explore the full range of Black religious experience, in all its grotesqueries. What Pinn suggests is not new. A seldom mentioned but extremely important move in this direction was provided by William R. Jones in his theological work between 1972 and 1974, most notably his 1973 text *Is God A White Racist?*[28] Jones argues for a methodological reconstruction of theology in light of inconsistencies between what black theologians theoretically claim and what is existentially present.

Jones urges theological formulations that make historical and experiential realities central. He asserts that theologies which are explicitly geared toward "liberation" from oppression are by nature extended theodicies. Therefore, a broadly conceived theodicy that is not confined to strict definitions of theodicy provides a proper methodology for liberation theologians. Jones explains that "the theologian of liberation, by definition, is committed to annihilate oppression, which is to say, to eliminate the suffering that is the heart of oppression. Thus he must provide an explanation that perceives the suffering as negative. He must show that the suffering that is oppression is not God's will or sanctioned by nature." Furthermore, "he must, in sum, de-sanctify the suffering in question, or else the oppressed will not regard their suffering as oppressive and will not be motivated to attack it. The theologian or philosopher of liberation, in short, *must* engage in the enterprise of theodicy if he is to accomplish his task."[29] For African Americans in the United States, the contextual framework for this questioning entails a response to the possibility that God is in fact a racist who is bent on their destruction. However, Jones argues black theologians have avoided the logical possibility of such a God. They have assumed that this is not the case and consequently their theological formulations "beg the question" of divine racism. The issue of divine racism is left unresolved through the conceptualization only of the Black Church *vis-à-vis* more inclusive African American spirituality.

We have attempted to see African Christian spirituality as particular and yet catholic. This means that the criticisms of Pinn and Anderson need to be addressed through a Black Church that does not exist only for itself, especially as only a racial construct. This leads to my second conviction: (2) The Black Church constitutes a communal spirituality of conversation, cooperation, and common witness based on the common recognition of the community of God. The Black Church does not need to be parochial, especially in light of the tensions that seem rampant around the world.[30] Conceived in this way, the Black Church has an obligation to uncover and invite spiritual and material meaning.

I have argued that African Christian spirituality has an obligation to respond to all questions of life and to provide a nonviolent liberative vision of community. Granted, the Black Church may find itself representing the majority of African Americans, but that does not make spirituality the possession only of those officially in Black churches. That is to say, the catholic nature of African American Christian spirituality seeks public, not private or parochial, foundations. This is my third conviction: (3) The Black Church believes on the basis of the New Testament that the Church of Christ is one. Belief based on a historic Church necessarily shows the failures of human understanding and actions. Such belief, however, does not mean that the object of belief is erroneous. Jesus prays in the New Testament that his disciples may be one (John 17). No doubt, Jesus understood the idealism of such a request. It is in such idealism as practiced by Jesus, King, and Tutu that the Black Church continues to negotiate what reality should be like. In other words, belief in Jesus' concept and practice of the Church can drive toward better realities, instead of exacerbate cultural wars. And as I sought to show through King's concept of the Beloved Community, belief in the particularity of the Church does not have to lead to ethnocentrism or religious war. Belief in Jesus shows how the Black Church is not restricted either to the language and traditions of a particular esoteric community or to the peculiar experience of unusual racial individuals who call themselves black.

The voices and critiques of the Black Church are crucial, however. They offer the reference point in which the Black Church is constantly called not to give in to the siren song of assimilating to violent worldviews that marginalize and oppress others. This is why my fourth conviction is so important: (4) The Black Church recognizes that the membership of the Church should be more inclusive day by day. By virtue of baptism and faith, all Christians obtain a primary identity in which to relate all other identities, including racial identity. The Black Church believes that Christian identity is primary and capable of relating other identities in such a way that cultural and racial wars are deemed morally wrong. Through such a perspective, the Christian identity's confession of sin reminds us all of the tendency toward such conflict of identities. One need not look too far around the world to see that the old adage remains true: yesterday's oppressed become tomorrow's oppressors. If the Black Church is not careful and disciplined, it will become too complacent, and as a result lose its critical edge of nonviolent response modeled by Jesus. African American Christian spirituality offers an ever-evolving language seeking to voice the depths of the individual and its larger self – community – to give space and meaning to the fact of oneself in the world – to identify locations, presence, meaning, and the function of the "I" in relationship to the "We."

How does the Black Church involve itself in this enterprise of better relating the I and the We? I answer with my fifth conviction: (5) Based on inclusivity of other identities and the lack of threat of others in Christ, the Black Church can consider the relationship of the other as bettering the identity of self. In other words, the beauty of the Black Church is such that its particularity is always looking for fulfillment among different communities and individuals. Therefore, those who are different (even those who are enemies) are approached through belief that God's work is always about expansion of human identity to include the other. Whenever there is no such expansion, there is the result of evil's pursuits of restricted and diminished identity. I suggest that the problem of evil provides a starting point in which particularity is seen more as a threat than the potential of celebration of God. The Black Church, in response to the tragedy of slavery in America, has resisted evil unlike any other human organization. It has maintained the conviction not to repeat the sins of the past by seeing the other as a threat. And, consequently, as I have tried to show with the civil rights movement, the Black Church sees itself as largely resisting the temptations defining others as evil. Articulating the problem of evil as a methodological option allows the Black Church to uncover issues of spirituality often missed by sociologists and anthropologists. In short, there is a substantial, yet often unspoken, rationale for ritual activity and attitudes toward the problem of evil.

The Black Church is indeed necessary for the challenges ahead. My fifth conviction helps the Black Church live into and face future identity crises – those grounded in nearsighted notions of liberation. The sixth conviction is: (6) The Black Church recognizes racial and economic human divisions as sin. This language of sin implicates most human responses to reflect upon how complicity of action often exacerbates situations. In other words, many tragic situations in human history are caused by those claiming to do good (e.g., Hitler, slave masters, etc.). This language of sin brings the continued and new awareness that what is in fact good must be tested and made available in divergent contexts. New awareness of these divergent contexts, no doubt, requires humility (a great virtue in Christian spirituality) for the benefit of sustained dialogue and the welfare of larger groups and sets of experiences. This becomes a challenge that we dismiss at our own peril.

The Full Embodiment of the Black Church

African American Christian spirituality is at heart communal in nature. Arguments by Pinn, Anderson, and womanist thinkers help us see the problem of which communities are truly included in African American spirituality. It is not only important for African Americans to seek inclusion of the other, but also it is extremely important to seek the health of the other's body. This leads to my seventh conviction: (7) Good health is a practical implication of common membership in the Black Church. Therefore, members should recognize their solidarity with each other, render assistance to each other in case of need, and refrain from such actions as are incompatible with communal relationships. Such a conviction places the Black Church in America in the crucial position of becoming an advocate of its motherland: Africa. Unfortunately, unless the Black Church seeks the health of African bodies, such health will continue to diminish.

This is what the challenge looks like for the Black Church to embody African health. More than 1.4 million Nigerian children have been orphaned by AIDS. In addition, Africa has been described by the United Nations as having one of the worst epidemics in the history of humankind (the HIV/AIDS epidemic). In a study conducted in 2001, it was reported that on average, 600 Kenyans die of AIDS every day.[31] Health and spirituality take on deep significance in Africa. Such significance requires careful spiritual reflection. The Black Church is once again called to lead a movement in which there is the opportunity for all people to work in common. Current views of African and European spirituality could be integrated to address an embodied Church through the concepts of medicine, science, holism, and spirituality. The relationship of these European and African practices shows how spirituality is interwoven into the lives of Africans and African Americans in such a way that communal sensibilities become one's worldview.

Health and healing present both a crisis and a blessing in this regard of communal spirituality. The crisis looks like this. In the West, multitudes of research studies have found that among African Americans, spirituality has been a major resource for managing illness and stressful life events. This has important implications for Western healthcare. Life expectancy for African Americans is 69 years, whereas it is 75 years for the total US population. For many health problems (especially hypertension, diabetes, infant mortality, and AIDS) the death rates are two to three times higher for African Americans than whites. More than 50 percent of newly reported HIV infections in the United States are among African Americans. In the US, 1 in 50 black men and 1 in 160 black women are HIV-positive. Although only 15 percent of the adolescent population in the United States is black, over 60 percent of AIDS cases reported in 1999 among 13–19 year olds were among blacks.[32]

The blessing is in how there should be ready inspiration and access to the world community to address systemic ills that seem to hit African and African American communities the hardest. Becky Polzer's cutting edge work on healthcare and African American spirituality helps us learn a great deal about the crisis.[33] Polzer first explores the philosophy of holism in relation to Western and African healthcare, and then examines how Western thought concerning holism has affected African American spirituality. Medicine in the West is based on several philosophies about how truth and knowledge are obtained. According to Cartesian Dualism, mind and matter are separate realities. Physical health is allocated to the physician, mental health to the psychiatrist, and the soul is assigned to the care of the clergy.

In addition, within the Western worldview, causes of disease are scientific in nature (e.g., microbial and chemical). Diagnostic methods include physical examination and the use of technological procedures. Treatment of disease consists of surgery, medications, and invasive technological procedures. The medical model has worked well in the treatment of acute illness and has greatly increased the life span of the Western population. Its drawbacks include the depersonalization of healthcare, expensive healthcare costs, the fragmentation of care (i.e., lack of communication between physician specialists), and ineffective management of chronic illness.

The closest that the Western view of health comes to the African world is through the biological concept of holism. Webster's Dictionary, after defining holistic as "relating to or concerned with wholes, or with complete systems, rather than analysis of, treatment of, or dissection into parts," offers the following as an example of holistic: "i.e., medicine is holistic as it attempts to treat both the mind and body."[34] (In 1926

Jan Christian Smuts, basing his ideas on the views of Hegel and Darwin, first coined the term "holism," which he described as the principle which makes for the origin and progress of wholes in the universe.)[35]

Polzer (a nurse herself) believes nurses have tried to approach their clinical practice from a holistic perspective.[36] An example of holism in nursing can be found in the philosophy of the Holistic Nurses Association, which states that holistic nursing recognizes that health proceeds from a balance of physical, spiritual, psychological, and social needs. The relationship between persons is dependent upon their relationship to one another, the environment, and that which gives our life meaning.[37] For nursing care to be holistic, it should incorporate all aspects of a person's needs: physiological, psychological, social, and spiritual.[38]

Another perspective on holism can be found in African traditional medicine. A stark contrast exists between Western and African culture and spirituality, which is reflected in each culture's system of healthcare. Western values espouse individualism, ownership, autonomy, independence, mastery of the environment, youth, planning and efficiency, progress, and the future. In contrast, African values emphasize affiliation, collectivity, sharing, obedience to authority, acceptance of fate, spirituality, respect for the elderly, and the past.[39] Likewise, Western spirituality emphasizes domination, the individual, and independence. In the West, religion is separate from culture; prayer is a monologue; God is related to the individual; and spirituality is optional. African spirituality emphasizes destiny, the community, and interdependence. In Africa, religion equals culture; prayer is a concert; God is related to the community; and spirituality is survival. This way of understanding the world leads to my last conviction for the Black Church: (8) The Black Church enters into spiritual relationships through which healing is sought in order that communities may be built up and renewed.

The future challenge for the embodiment of a healthy community is for the Black Church to produce healers. Healers in Sub-Saharan Africa are referred to as diviners. The Black Church will need to produce diviners for sick economies, violent societies, diseased bodies, and conflicted minds. The higher grade of practitioner is the diviner who combines spiritual and political power that enables instead of destroys. In addition, the Black Church will need to produce and encourage specialists to concentrate on particular aspects of healing, such as the relationships among Jews, Christians, and Muslims. Specialists will be needed to create a new language of religious identity that is complimentary and helps the world, instead of the derogatory language that justifies war and perpetuates violence. We will need specialists who deal with the environment, encouraging human communities to care for God's creation.

The Black Church is called to be an African healer. The African healer is expected to provide both curative and preventative healthcare. On a curative level, he or she is expected to diagnose and treat presenting symptoms. Divination plays a major role in the diagnostic process. Divination is aided by bones, sticks, spiritual voices, and other physical signs. An important diagnostic aid is also provided by dreams. Dreams are viewed as the gateway to the ancestors, as the communication channels of those past with those present. In addition to treating presenting symptoms, the African healer is also required to restore balance between the person, society, and the world. The healer therefore plays a dominant social role in the community, serving as a center of social integration and order. Part of this responsibility includes tracking down perpetrators of evil deeds. Functions extend beyond the physical world into the spiritual, where mediation between the ancestors and descendants occurs. For this reason, healing actions, whether curative or preventative, are frequently directed not at the ailing individual, but towards the healing of the community.

For African Americans, spirituality has ontological significance, as it pertains to the very question of existence or being. Because of this ontological significance, spirituality is intertwined in all aspects of life so fully that it is not always easy or possible to isolate it. There is no distinction between the sacred and the secular, between the religious and the nonreligious, between the spiritual and material areas of life. The spiritual beliefs of African Americans provide a framework for health and illness, and are a testament to the inseparability of spirituality from other aspects of life. Health and illness are a dynamic entity; they are governed by body, mind, and soul; again, without separation of the sacred and the secular. Health and illness beliefs also go far beyond a biological notion of disease.

Community is the ordering aspect of African American Christian spirituality. For African Americans, the spiritual community includes the family, the community of ancestors (deceased relatives and religious saints), and most importantly, the African American Church. The Church is the most trusted and dominant institution in the African American community, and has been regarded as a refuge from wider societal injustice. Participation in the Church provides nurturance, support, tangible assistance, a cultural identity, and a sense of belonging to both families and individuals. The Church has inspired the community to reject and subvert oppressive social, political, and economic conditions. The Black Church has served as a site for healthcare teaching and preventative screening for African Americans, as well as a site where church leaders impart religious views about health to their congregations. This interaction of the Church with social justice, politics, economics, and healthcare is another example of the integral role of spirituality in African American life.

A frequent conceptualization of African American spirituality is that it is a vital force that resides in all things, both animate and inanimate, and that permeates all affairs, human and non-human. African American spirituality also has a relational component; it is a force that connects human beings to God, the universe, and the larger community, including the community of ancestors. Because African American spirituality and religion are both so intertwined in all aspects of African American life, it is imperative that they be considered when examining the future challenges for us all.

Notes

1   W. E. B. Du Bois, *Prayers for Dark People*, ed. Herbert Aptheker (Amherst: University of Massachusetts Press, 1980), p. 21.

2   See Anthony B. Pinn, "Rethinking the Nature and Tasks of African American Theology: A Pragmatic Perspective," *American Journal of Theology and Philosophy* 19:2 (May 1998).

3   James H. Cone, *A Black Theology of Liberation*, 2nd edn. (Maryknoll, NY: Orbis Books, 1986), p. 27.

4   Victor Anderson, *Beyond Ontological Blackness: An Essay on African American Religious and Cultural Criticism* (New York: Continuum, 1995), p. 117.

5   See Cornel West, *Prophesy Deliverance* (Philadelphia, PA: Westminster Press, 1982); Anderson, *Beyond Ontological Blackness*, pp. 118–32.

6   See Anderson, *Beyond Ontological Blackness*, p. 127.

7   Charles Long, "Perspectives for a Study of Afro-American Religion in the United States," *History of Religions* 11:1 (August 1971), p. 55.

8   See Pinn, "Rethinking."

9   See Sally Cole's introduction to Ruth Landes' *The City of Women* (Albuquerque: University of New Mexico Press, 1994), pp. xxiv–xxv.

10   See Dwight Hopkins, *Shoes That Fit Our Feet: Sources for a Constructive Black Theology* (Maryknoll, NY: Orbis Books, 1993), p. 5.

11   Ibid, p. 2.

12   Ibid, p. 18. Hopkins' recent work entails an exploration of connections between cultural studies and theology, a movement away from strict attention to Church-bound theological formations. See, for example, Dwight Hopkins and Sheila Greeve Davaney, eds., *Changing Conversations: Cultural Analysis and Religious Reflection* (New York: Routledge, 1996).

13   The review is reprinted in Alice Walker, *In Search of Our Mothers' Gardens: Womanist Prose* (New York: Harcourt Brace Jovanovich, 1983), p. 80.

14 Jacquelyn Grant, *White Women's Christ and Black Women's Jesus: Feminist Christology and Womanist Response* (Atlanta, GA: Scholars Press, 1989), p. 205.
15 Roundtable, "Christian Ethics and Theology in Womanist Perspective," *Journal of Feminist Studies in Religion* 5 (Fall 1989), pp. 83–112.
16 See Walker, *In Search of Our Mothers' Gardens*, pp. xi–xii.
17 Roundtable, pp. 83, 85.
18 Mariam Schnier, *Feminism: The Essential Historical Writings* (New York: Vintage, 1972), pp. 94–5.
19 Walker, *In Search of Our Mothers' Gardens*, p. 374.
20 Alice Walker, *The Color Purple* (London: Women's Press, 1983), p. 224.
21 Ibid, pp. xi–xii.
22 Alice Walker, *Anything We Love Can Be Saved: A Writer's Activism* (London: Women's Press, 1997), p. 76.
23 bell hooks, *Talking Back: Thinking Feminist, Thinking Black* (Cambridge, MA: South End Press, 1989), p. 180.
24 Marcia Y. Riggs, "A Clarion Call to Awake! Arise! Act!" in *A Troubling in My Soul: Womanist Perspectives on Evil and Suffering*, ed. Emilie M. Townes (Maryknoll, NY: Orbis Books, 1996), p. 67.
25 See Katie G. Cannon, *Black Womanist Ethics* (Atlanta, GA: Scholars Press, 1988); "Ida B. Wells-Barnett," in Emilie M. Townes, *Womanist Justice, Womanist Hope* (Atlanta, GA: Scholars Press, 1993).
26 Charles Long, *Significations* (Minneapolis, MN: Fortress Press, 1986), p. 7.
27 Ibid.
28 William R. Jones, *Is God a White Racist? A Preamble to Black Theology* (Garden City, NY: Anchor Press/Doubleday, 1973). For a more in-depth analysis of Jones' text and larger project see my *Why, Lord?: Suffering and Evil in Black Theology* (New York: Continuum, 1995).
29 Jones, *Is God a White Racist?* pp. xix–xx.
30 See Lamin Sanneh, *Piety and Power: Muslims and Christians in West Africa* (Maryknoll, NY: Orbis Books, 1996).
31 Report on the Global HIV/AIDS Epidemic, June 2000 (UNAEDS), IMPACT – Family Health International, Population, Health and Nutrition Programs, US Agency for International Development and AIDS – All Africa.Com
32 Data provided by the US Center for Disease Control and Prevention, Harvard AIDS Institute, Henry J. Kaiser Family Foundation, and USAID.
33 Becky Polzer was my student at Duke University, and I served on her PhD committee at the University of North Carolina at Chapel Hill. Her PhD research is based at the Nursing School on African American Christian Spirituality and Diabetes.
34 *Webster's Ninth New Collegiate Dictionary* (Springfield, MA: Merriam Webster, 1991), p. 576.
35 See M. J. Owen and C. A. Holmes, "'Holism' in the Discourse of Nursing," *Journal of Advanced Nursing* 18 (1993), pp. 1688–95.

36 Polzer references the work of Owen and Holmes, "Holism."
37 See E. F. Patterson, "The Philosophy and Physics of Holistic Health Care: Spiritual Healing as a Workable Interpretation," *Journal of Advanced Nursing* 27 (1998), pp. 287–93.
38 See B. Hancock, "Are Nursing Theories Holistic?" *Nursing Standard* 14:17 (2000), pp. 37–41.
39 See K. Russell and N. Jewell, "Cultural Impact of Health-Care Access: Challenges for Improving the Health of African Americans," *Journal of Community Health Nursing* 9:3 (1992), pp. 161–9.

Timeline of the
Black Church

1526
Nearly forty years before the first permanent European settlement in North America, Spanish explorers bring enslaved Africans to what are now the Carolinas. The Africans escape in what is the first recorded slave revolt in North America.

1527
Estevan, the first identified Muslim in North America, lands in Florida as a Moroccan guide to the Spaniards. During the ensuing years of the slave trade, as many as 20 percent of West African slaves brought to North America are Muslim.

1619
Newly established English colonies in North America create a demand for laborers in the New World. At first, captured Africans are brought to the colonies as indentured servants. Once their term (3–7 years) is completed, indentured servants are allowed to live free, own land, and have indentured servants of their own. However, this system does not last long; indentured servitude gives way to lifetime slavery for Africans as the British colonies grow and the need for a permanent, inexpensive labor force increases.

1641
Massachusetts becomes the first British colony to legitimize slavery. Other states soon follow suit. Rights for free Africans are gradually restricted. By 1662 all children born to slave parents in Virginia are enslaved as well. Slavery has become a self-perpetuating system. First account of African Church member in Massachusetts.

1701
The English Crown charters the Society for the Propagation of the Gospel in Foreign Parts of the Anglican Church to convert slaves and

Native Americans to Christianity. The drive to convert slaves is not welcomed by all slaveholders. Many are unwilling to allow their slaves to receive religious instruction, fearing that they will no longer be able to claim them as property once they are baptized. In 1705 Virginia passes a law that all laborers who "were not Christians in their Native Country . . . shall be slaves. A Negro, mulatto and Indian slaves . . . shall be held to be real estate."

1738
Santa Teresa de Mose is established in Florida as a town for freed slaves who have converted to Catholicism. It becomes the first free Black town in North America.

1740
The Great Awakening, a revitalization of religious expression, sweeps the British colonies. The revival movement, unlike the earlier doctrine of the Puritans, promises the grace of God to all who experience a desire for it. Methodists and Baptists welcome African Americans to join their ranks. Open-air preaching and charismatic, passionate preachers attract throngs of participants.

1750s
Small black congregations begin to emerge in the South. They are not necessarily affiliated with a church, but are instead informal gatherings held outdoors in hush harbors. In the hush harbor both men and women are called by the spirit. Many of the male plantation preachers go on to found the first independent Black churches – women remain itinerants.

1750
Georgia legalizes slavery. It is the last colony to do so.

1758
One of the first recorded Black congregations is organized on the plantation of William Byrd in Mecklenburg, Virginia.

1773
Phillis Wheatley, a freed slave, publishes *Poems on Various Subjects, Religious and Moral*. Wheatley's former owners, the Wheatleys of Boston, had provided Wheatley with an excellent education, rare for blacks and women at the time, and encouraged her to pursue writing.

1773–5

Plantation slave preacher George Liele, the first black Baptist in Georgia, founds the Silver Bluff Baptist Church in Silver Bluff, South Carolina. The congregation includes free and enslaved blacks. One of Liele's original followers, Andrew Bryan, goes on to become ordained by the Baptist Church in 1788, and founds the Bryan Street African Baptist Church, which is later renamed the First African Baptist Church of Savannah.

1775

Society for the Relief of Free Negroes Unlawfully Held in Bondage, which in 1784 becomes known as the Pennsylvania Society for the Abolition of Slavery, is founded in Philadelphia. Quakers, who had abolished slavery among themselves nearly twenty years earlier, found the organization and revise its constitution to include a broader membership.

The American Revolution, the War of Independence from England, begins. Black soldiers fight for both the Loyalists (those loyal to England) and the Patriots. At least 5,000 black men serve in the Continental Army and fight in key battles, including Lexington, Concord, and Bunker Hill. British colonial governors try to incite slave rebellions and escapes by promising freedom to slaves who fight for the English Crown.

1776

On July 4 the Continental Congress ratifies the Declaration of Independence. It declares: "We hold these truths to be self-evident, that all men are created equal, that they are endowed by their Creator with certain unalienable Rights, that among these are Life, Liberty and the pursuit of Happiness." It does not, however, abolish slavery. Until the passage of the 13th Amendment 91 years later, the issue of slavery is left to individual states to legislate. The following year Vermont becomes the first state to abolish slavery.

1784

At the conference of Methodist Episcopal Churches in America, under the leadership of Bishop John Wesley, the Church denounces slavery and asks its members to free their slaves within 12 months. The regulations are defeated and suspended the following year.

1787

On September 17 the delegates to the Constitutional Convention vote to adopt the Constitution of the United States of America. As part of the Great Compromise between Northern and Southern states, the Constitution counts a slave as three-fifths of a free man, effectively boosting the representation of Southern states in Congress. It delays the prohibition of the slave trade, and upholds the right of slaveholders to reclaim escaped slaves.

Richard Allen and Absalom Jones establish the Free African Society, the first Black mutual aid association in Philadelphia. Although non-denominational at its inception, the Free African Society is the first step toward the establishment of an independent Black Church. Richard Allen goes on to establish the African Methodist Episcopal Church (AME), the first major Black religious institution in America. Also in 1787, Africans are removed from prayer at St. George's Church in Philadelphia.

1793

On March 14 Eli Whitney receives a patent for the cotton gin. The invention transforms cotton into a profitable crop, and reinvents the economy of the cotton-growing states in the South. Suddenly, Southern states need an unprecedented number of slaves to keep pace with cotton production. The slave population almost triples in size between 1790 and 1830.

1794

Francis Asbury dedicates Bethel Church.

1796

Black Methodists begin in New York. Request to hold separate meetings.

1799

Richard Allen ordained.

1800s

The Second Great Awakening begins. Presbyterians, Baptists, and Methodists win African American converts by the thousands. Its message of equality before God lends credence to the Abolitionist movement and leads to a coalition between black and white abolitionists.

1800

African Methodist Episcopal Church of St. John built.

1801

Black Methodists incorporate as the African Methodist Episcopal Church of New York.

1804

Slaves in Haiti, under the leadership of Toussaint L'Ouverture, revolt, kill their masters, and ultimately drive out the French to establish the first independent Black republic in the Western hemisphere. Their actions strike fear into the hearts of slaveholders in the United States and inspire the enslaved. The Haitian revolution leads to an exodus of mixed race people, mostly Catholic, to the Louisiana territories and to the eastern shore of Maryland. Vodoun takes a foothold on the mainland.

1816

Richard Allen invites black Methodist Church leaders from around the country to meet in Philadelphia to discuss forming a united African Methodist Church. Delegates vote to organize the African Methodist Episcopal Church (AME) with Allen as the founding bishop. Today, the AME Church has over a million members in the US and abroad.

1821

The American Colonization Society establishes the Black Republic of Liberia in West Africa. Founded four years earlier by Robert Finley, a white Presbyterian clergyman, the American Colonization Society and its mission to resettle free American blacks in Africa is opposed by the AME Church.
New Conference of Black Methodists founded.

1822

Denmark Vesey, a 51-year-old carpenter and former slave in Charleston, South Carolina, plans a violent revolt to set his people free. Thousands of Charleston blacks are involved, including many members of the first AME church. The rebellion unravels when slaves confess the plan to their masters. After a brief trial, Vesey and his allies are hanged, and Charleston authorities tear down the African church.

1827

Missions sent to Canada and Haiti by AME Church.

1829

Four free black women (refugees from Haiti) – Elizabeth Lange, Marie Balas, Rosine Boegue, and Almeide Duchemin Maxis – establish the nation's first permanent community of black Catholic nuns in Baltimore, Maryland. It is called the Oblate Sisters of Providence, and receives papal recognition in 1831.

1831
Nat Turner leads a two-day rebellion in Southampton County, Virginia. Turner claims the spirit of the Old Testament called on him to deliver his people. Joined by over 60 men, Turner kills around 60 whites and destroys 15 homesteads. Over 3,000 armed whites set out to end the rebellion, killing many innocent blacks along the way. Turner remains at large for two months, until he is captured, tried, and hanged. As a result of the insurgency, many Southern states forbid blacks to preach.

1834
Henry McNeal Turner is born of free parents in Newberry Court House, South Carolina. He goes on to become the first chaplain of US Colored Troops fighting for the Union and a leader in the AME for 50 years. The Black Baptist Association begins.

1838
Divided by the issue of slavery, the Presbyterian Church splits along regional lines. The Southern and Northern branches of the Church remain apart until 1983.

1839
Pope Gregory XVI condemns slavery.

1844
The Methodist Church splits into Northern and Southern congregations after argument over whether members should be allowed to own slaves.

1846
Frederick Douglass, a leading black Abolitionist, publishes the *Narrative of the Life of Frederick Douglass: An American Slave*. Douglass had been born into slavery in 1818 in Maryland. He escapes 20 years later, and begins a lifetime of speaking and writing to promote abolition and improved social and economic conditions for African Americans.

1848
Baptists split over slavery.
Black Methodists add "Zion" to their name.

1850
Born into slavery in 1797 in Kingston, New York, Sojourner Truth, known then as Isabella, is taught that slavery is part of God's natural order. Isabella accepts this until the age of 30, when she hears the voice

of God instructing her to set out on her own as a free woman. In 1843 she takes the name Sojourner Truth and travels the country preaching abolition, women's suffrage, and the gospel. She rises to national prominence, meeting with Presidents Lincoln and Grant. Her memoirs, dictated to Olive Gilbert, are published in 1850 as *The Narrative of Sojourner Truth: A Northern Slave.*

1861
Rising conflict among Northern and Southern states over slavery leads to the Civil War. Black enlistment is initially rebuffed by the Union army because of concerns that their participation will weaken Northern support for the war. Black politicians like Frederick Douglass, joined by pastors like Henry McNeal Turner, lobby passionately for Black enlistment: "We ask you to modify your laws, that we may enlist – that full scope may be given to the patriotic feelings burning in the colored man's breast."

1863
President Abraham Lincoln issues the Emancipation Proclamation freeing slaves in rebellious states. Four months later, black soldiers are allowed to join the fight. More than 180,000 African Americans serve in the Union army. Two years later, the 13th amendment to the Constitution outlaws slavery or involuntary servitude except as punishment for a crime.

1864
AME and AME Zion churches consider uniting.

1866–9
In 1866 the 14th Amendment passes. It grants citizenship to former slaves, changing them from three-fifths of a man to whole men (and women). However, women – white and black alike – remain disenfranchised when, in 1869, the 15th Amendment guarantees the right to vote to black men. Southern states respond to these Amendments with the Black Codes: state laws that regulate the day-to-day life of ex-slaves and sharply restrict their new freedoms.

1867
Springfield Baptist Church founds the Augusta Institute, one of thousands of schools begun by churches in the wake of the Civil War. The school will later become Morehouse College, named after Reverend Henry L. Morehouse.

1869–77

Between 1869 and 1877, 14 African Americans serve in the House of Representatives. Two serve in the US Senate. African American political leadership continues until 1877, the end of Reconstruction. Black Codes and the continued intimidation of black voters keep many away from the polls. It will be almost a century before blacks are once again able to fully exercise their legal right to vote.

1870

In the 1870s the Fisk Jubilee Singers of Fisk University popularized the choral arrangements of Black spirituals throughout the world, with successful tours in the United States and Europe.
The Colored Methodist Episcopal Church (CME) is founded by free blacks.

1886

First African American Roman Catholic priest: Augustus Tolton.

1894

Henry McNeal Turner says God is a Negro.
The first black woman is ordained in the AMEZ Church: Julia Foote.
National Baptist Magazine first published.

1895

The Foreign Mission Baptist Convention of the USA, the American National Baptist Convention, and the American National Educational Baptist Convention consolidate into the National Baptist Convention of the USA.

1896

The US Supreme Court upholds racial segregation. The *Plessy v. Ferguson* decision declares that "separate but equal" accommodations are constitutional. The case arises when a railroad company refuses a black passenger access to a white sleeping car. The Court rules this constitutional as long as the railroad provides equal sleeping accommodations for blacks. The ruling paves the way for the legal segregation of schools and public facilities throughout the United States. At this point, 90 percent of African Americans live in the South; 80 percent of them farm for a living.
The Church of God is formed by Charles Mason (renamed Church of God in Christ in 1897).

1897
The National Baptist publishing house is incorporated.
Elijah Muhammad (born Elijah Poole) is born in Sandersville, Georgia.
He will become leader of the Nation of Islam.

1898
The first black woman is ordained as an elder in the AMEZ Church:
Mary Jane Small.

1900–30
The first three decades of the twentieth century witness the migration
of nearly 2 million blacks to the North. African Americans leave the
South to escape harsh economic conditions, continued discrimination,
and the threat of racially motivated violence. The belief that the
North holds the key to better jobs and political rights shifts the African
American population from South to North, from the countryside to
the cities. The migration to urban areas brings about the rise of store-
front churches, often the place of worship of poor or newly formed
denominations.

1903
W. E. B. Du Bois publishes *Souls of Black Folk*.

1906
William Seymour becomes pastor of a small black Holiness mission
in Los Angeles. It later becomes known as the Azusa Street Revival,
an integrated 24-hour church, which is regarded as the genesis of the
American Pentecostal movement. Seymour's newspaper *The Apostolic
Faith* gains an international readership with up to 50,000 copies printed
per issue. The interracial period of Pentecostalism ends eight years later
with the formation of the all-white Assemblies of God.
National Primitive Baptist Convention founded.

1909–11
The NAACP is founded by a group including blacks and whites, men
and women, to combat discrimination, promote social justice, and
support the advancement of African Americans. Leading black activists
and intellectuals Ida Wells-Barnett and W. E. B. Du Bois are among
the founders. Two years later, Dr. George Edmund Haynes, the first
African American to receive a PhD from Columbia University, and
Mrs. Ruth Standish, widow of a New York City railway tycoon, found

the Urban League. Its mission is to bring educational and employment opportunities to urban blacks.

1914
Whites leave COGIC to form the Assemblies of God.

1915
National Baptist Convention of America forms.

1915–20
The Ku Klux Klan, originally founded in 1865 by Confederate veterans in Tennessee bent on resisting Reconstruction in the Confederate States, rises again. More than 4 million Americans join this anti-Catholic, anti-Semitic, anti-immigrant, and anti-black organization.

1917
The US enters World War I "to make the world safe for Democracy." The first African American to be drafted is Leo Pickney. Approximately 370,000 blacks serve. The US military is as segregated as the rest of the country, and African Americans fight in all-black regiments. Racial tension escalates at home and explodes in a rash of race riots during the so-called Red Summer of 1919.

1918
Charles Mason protests World War I.

1924
AMEZ bishop assigned to Africa.

1929
Martin Luther King, Jr. born.

1930–40s
Gospel music, influenced by the ragtime and boogie-woogie rhythms of Jazz and Blues, sweeps Black Baptist and Methodist churches. Thomas Dorsey, the Father of Gospel, organizes the first gospel choir at the Ebenezer Baptist Church in Chicago. In 1932 Dorsey writes his most famous song, "Take My Hand, Precious Lord," and co-founds the first publishing house for the promotion of Black American gospel. In 1942 the Golden Gates record "No Segregation in Heaven," a highlight in the era of *a cappella* music that dominates gospel.

1930

W. D. Fard arrives in Detroit, Michigan selling silk goods to the city's Black population and inviting them to learn about Islam. He promotes his teachings as the "natural religion" for African Americans, and offers the opportunity to break with Christianity, which some see as a vestige from the days of slavery. Fard's message of self-reliance and Black Power wins many followers, and the Nation of Islam is formed. When Fard disappears mysteriously in 1934, Elijah Muhammad assumes leadership of the Nation of Islam.

1936

Martha Keys introduces a bill at the AME General Conference in New York to ordain women.

1937

Howard Thurman, a Baptist pastor and educator, travels to India to learn firsthand about Mahatma Gandhi's philosophy of non-violence as an agent of social change. He introduces Gandhi's teachings to students at Howard and Boston Universities, including James Farmer, founder of the Congress of Racial Equality (CORE), and Martin Luther King, Jr.

1941

The December 7 attack by the Japanese on Pearl Harbor provokes the US to enter the war. As in World War I, blacks serve in segregated units.

1946

COGIC headquarters constructed.

1948

Rebecca Glover is ordained in the AME Church.

1954

By 1954, 65 percent of all African Americans live in urban areas. It is the first time in America's history that the majority of blacks live outside the South, and marks the completion of the population shift begun during the Great Migration. Leaving the South, however, did not guarantee leaving discrimination behind. The status of blacks as Americans facing discrimination on a daily basis remains much the same. They live in substandard housing. Black workers continue to be concentrated in less-skilled jobs. They are the last hired; the first to be fired. The average income of an African American family is only three-fifths of that of a

white family. These conditions set the stage for the urban riots of the
1960s.

In the landmark *Brown v. Board of Education*, the Supreme Court
reverses *Plessy v. Ferguson*, declaring that "separate but equal" public
education is unconstitutional. In the coming years, civil rights activists
will chip away the remaining vestiges of legal discrimination, from
segregated buses and restaurants to voting rights.

1955

On December 1, Rosa Parks, a 43-year-old black woman, refuses to
give up her seat on a Montgomery, Alabama city bus to a white man.
Her arrest sparks a black boycott of the city buses. Martin Luther King,
Jr., a relatively unknown 26-year-old Baptist minister, becomes the
spokesperson and organizer of the boycott and is catapulted into
national prominence. He is elected head of the Montgomery Improvement Association. In 1956 the Supreme Court declares that segregation
on buses is unconstitutional, and buses throughout the US are forced to
desegregate. The Montgomery Bus Boycott ends.

1956

Colored Methodist Episcopal Church changes to Christian Methodist
Episcopal Church (CME).

1957

Martin Luther King, Jr. and other Southern black ministers found
the Southern Christian Leadership Conference (SCLC) to bring about
the end of segregation. The SCLC adopts nonviolent protest as the
cornerstone of its strategy and builds alliances with local community
organizations across the South. King heads the SCLC and builds it into
a powerful civil rights organization.

Start of the Interdenominational Theological Center in Atlanta.

1958

By 1958 unemployment is 14.4 percent for blacks and 6.9 percent
for whites. The economic indicators for black Americans lead some to
argue that the 1954 school desegregation had made little difference
to the majority of African Americans living outside the South. Indeed,
the benefits of desegregation flowed first to the black upper classes: by
the end of the decade, there would be at least 25 black millionaires, and
more than 400 who earned 50,000 dollars a year. Some 10 percent
of black Americans earned between 15,000 and 50,000 dollars a year.
At the time, their achievements were lauded as a sign that things had

improved. Nevertheless, the black upper classes contributed (in time and money) to the civil rights effort: for them, times may have gotten better, but things had gotten worse.

1959
Walter Eugene King takes the Yoruba name Adefunmi and becomes a Santeria priest. He forms the Shango Temple in New York City. Over the years, the Shango Temple distances itself from the Santeria community, stressing ritualism and nationalism in lieu of the Catholic-Yoruba synthesis of Santeria. In 1964 Adefunmi changes the temple name to the Yoruba Temple.

1960
Black college students found the Student Nonviolent Coordinating Committee (SNCC). The organization is dedicated to ending segregation and giving young blacks a stronger voice in the civil rights movement. SNCC members demonstrate the efficacy of nonviolent sit-ins, a tactic that is soon taken up by other civil rights groups. SNCC members participate in the Freedom Rides – trips taken on interstate buses to challenge the segregation of restrooms, restaurants, and waiting rooms of bus stations. After the Freedom Rides, the SNCC focuses on voter registration. Friction between the SNCC and SLCC develops, and by 1965 some SNCC members question the effectiveness of nonviolent activism, precipitating a dramatic shift in SNCC practices.
AME General Conference approves ordination of women as deacons and elders.
First black Roman Catholic cardinal elected: Laurean Rugambwa.
The Nation of Islam expands to a membership of 100,000 with Elijah Muhammad at the helm. The Nation's spokesperson, Malcolm X, travels the country on speaking tours. His enraged eloquence and message of self-defense and Black nationalism reflect the anger and alienation of many urban blacks, drawing huge crowds and converts.

1961
Start of the Progressive National Baptist Convention.
Charles Mason dies.
Official manual of COGIC written.

1962
First African bishop elected in the Episcopal Church: John Burgess in the diocese of Massachusetts.

1963
Martin Luther King, Jr. writes "Letter from a Birmingham Jail."
May 10: settlement reached to desegregate facilities such as lunch counters and increase jobs for blacks.
June 11: President Kennedy announces civil rights plan.
June 12: Medgar Evers assassinated.
August 28: Martin Luther King, Jr. gives the "I Have a Dream" speech in front of the Lincoln Memorial as part of the March on Washington. Over 250,000 people participate, making it the largest protest assembly in the country's history. In his speech, King lays out a vision of an America that will "rise up and live out the true meaning of its creed: 'We hold these truths to be self-evident; that all men are created equal.'"
September 15: The black Sixteenth Street Baptist Church in Birmingham, Alabama is bombed while Sunday school is in session, and four young girls are killed. Thousands of mourners, white and black, attend the funeral services. Four suspects are soon identified, but FBI Director J. Edgar Hoover blocks their prosecution. Alabama Attorney General Bill Baxley reopens the case in 1971, and Robert Edward Chambliss is convicted of one count of murder. The case is opened again in 1997, and two aging former Klansmen, Thomas Blanton, Jr. and Bobby Frank Cherry, are sentenced to life in prison.
November 22: John F. Kennedy assassinated.

1964
Martin Luther King, Jr. wins the Nobel Peace Prize. He issues the "Letter from a Birmingham jail."
In the wake of President Kennedy's assassination, the Civil Rights Act of 1964 is passed. The Act effectively desegregates public facilities, stating: "All persons shall be entitled to the full and equal enjoyment of the goods, services, facilities, privileges, advantages, and accommodations of any place of public accommodation . . . without discrimination or segregation on the ground of race, color, religion, or national origin."
Carrier Hooper, the first woman in the AME Church to run for bishop.
Malcolm X leaves the Nation of Islam.
July 2: Civil Rights Act signed.
July 21: Freedom Summer Campaign in Mississippi.

1965
Congress passes the Voting Rights Act, which prohibits racial discrimination in voting practices. The Act bans the literary tests and poll taxes used since Reconstruction to prevent blacks from voting. The Act comes on the heels of a major march from Selma to Montgomery in support of

voting rights led by Martin Luther King, Jr. The march begins in Selma with a few thousand participants, and concludes in Montgomery with approximately 25,000 supporters.

The Bethel Church (now known as Mother Bethel) is designated a shrine by the Department of the Interior.

The National Baptist Convention, USA Inc., accepts the first ordained woman. Trudy Trimm becomes the first female pastor.

February 21: Malcolm X is assassinated. He had left the Nation of Islam and taken the name Malik el-Hajj Shabazz. His murder shortcircuits what could have been a multiracial Islamic coalition working for civil rights. Malcolm's work helped "so-called Negroes" in the United States to realize that they are an African people, and helped Africans on the continent understand their relationship to black Americans.

Watts Riots.

1966

Bobby Seale and Huey Newton co-found the Black Panthers in Oakland, California. Unlike the civil rights activists who preach nonviolence, the Black Panthers authorize the use of violence as self-defense. The first point of their founding 10-Point Platform reads: "We want freedom. We want power to determine the destiny of our Black Community. We believe that black people will not be free until we are able to determine our destiny." The Black Panthers gain notoriety for patrolling the streets in black berets, black jackets, and armed with weapons. Their message of self-determination and power wins thousands of followers throughout the country.

Full inclusion of women clergy in CME Church.

Martin Luther King, Jr. takes a stand against the Vietnam War because it is sapping resources from domestic social programs. His action sets him against President Lyndon Johnson, who has been an ally.

The SNCC, now headed by Stokley Carmichael, rejects its historical strategy of nonviolence to embrace a doctrine of Black Power, which emphasizes Black nationalism and self-reliance. Violence is accepted as a legitimate form of self-defense. CORE endorses Black Power. The SCLC and NAACP do not.

The National Council of Churches forms an ad hoc committee (National Committee of Negro Churchmen: NCNC) to address Black Power in light of the Christian gospel.

1967

Maulana Karenga, an African American activist, creates Kwanzaa, a celebration held annually between Christmas and New Year's Day, to "restore and reaffirm African heritage and culture." It is based on seven principles that reinforce family, community, and culture among African Americans.

The NCNC holds its first national conference on Black Power.

The NCNC is changed to the National Committee of Black Churchmen (NCBC).

1968

Adam Clayton Powell, Jr., pastor of the Abyssinian Baptist Church, the largest congregation in New York City, says that nonviolence is no longer the most effective civil rights strategy.

April 4: Martin Luther King, Jr. is shot while standing on a hotel balcony in Memphis, Tennessee. He dies later at a hospital. Conspiracy theories about his assassination abound. His death provokes riots in 14 cities, and national mourning. Designation of end of civil rights movement.

The Roman Catholic Church in the US declares war on racism.

The Constitutional Convention of COGIC is held.

1969

Civil rights leader James Forman reads the Black Manifesto at Riverside Church in New York City. Forman demands $500 million in reparations from American churches for their role in perpetuating slavery. While Forman receives some funds, including $15,000 from the mostly white Washington Square United Methodist Church in Newark, NJ, his success lies primarily in initiating a national debate about the responsibility of churches for their past positions on slavery.

Sister M. Martin de Porres Grey organizes 155 women from 79 national and international congregations to form the National Black Sisters' Conference (NBSC). The NBSC speaks out about racism and sexism found in society and the church.

James H. Cone, a professor at Union Theological Seminary, publishes his seminal *Black Theology and Black Power*. The book links Jesus' struggle against human oppression with the African American struggle against racial oppression.

The NCBC begins dialogue with African theologians and issues statement on Black theology.

1970

The Society for the Study of Black Religion begins for black scholars.

Nana Adefunmi and a few families create Oyotunji Village in Sheldon, South Carolina. They want to institutionalize a Yoruba way of life and fully break from Santeria by establishing a community for people deeply committed to Yoruba.

The CME National Headquarters are established in Memphis.

James Cone publishes A *Black Theology of Liberation*, the first systematic presentation of Black theology.

1971
Jesse Jackson's Operation Push begins.

1975
Upon the death of Elijah Muhammad, his son W. D. Muhammad takes over the Nation of Islam leadership. He changes the structure to adhere more closely to orthodox Islam and renames the organization the World Community of Al-Islam. Louis Farrakhan is the organization's international spokesperson until 1977, when he breaks with W. D. Muhammad to revive the Nation of Islam and continue the traditions of Elijah Muhammad.

1977
Alex Haley's *Roots*, an epic that follows seven generations of a family from Africa to Arkansas, breaks the TV ratings record established by *Gone With the Wind* when 130 million Americans tune in to the mini-series.

1978
The seven largest Black Christian denominations organize the Congress of National Black Churches.

1979
Womanist theology begins in published format.

1980s
Black church burnings in the United States.

1984
Jesse Jackson becomes the first black candidate to run for president of the United States. He wins 3.5 million primary votes. He runs again in 1988, and is endorsed by more than 90 percent of black clergy, and wins 6.1 million votes.

1987
Womanist theology first used as formal discourse.

1988

Barbara Harris, first woman and African American woman elected in the Anglican communion in diocese of Massachusetts.
National Missionary Baptist Convention of America separates from the National Baptist Convention of America.

1989

Black Church week of prayer for healing of AIDS.

1990s

Black middle-class movement back to Black churches.
Megachurches and prosperity movement.

1991

Vinton Anderson, AME bishop, is first black president of the World Council of Churches.

1993

Thomas Dorsey, the Father of Gospel Music, dies at age 93 in Chicago.
Pope John Paul II apologizes for the Catholic Church's historical support of the African slave trade.
The National Council of Churches holds the National Black Church Environmental and Economic Justice Summit.

1995

In Washington, DC between 400,000 and 1 million black men join the Million Man March organized by the Nation of Islam's Louis Farrakhan.
South Africa's Truth and Reconciliation Commission is set up under the 1995 Promotion of National Unity and Reconciliation Act to investigate crimes committed during the apartheid era.

1996

South Africa's Truth and Reconciliation Hearings begin in April 1996 amid a swarm of international television cameras. The hearings that follow, chaired by Archbishop Desmond Tutu, see victims of the apartheid authorities, their widows and their mothers, break down in tears as they give their testimony. F. W. De Klerk appears before the commission in August 1996, and begs forgiveness for the years of apartheid rule. In a breakthrough for the commission, top apartheid-era police general Johan van der Merwe admits in October 1996 that he ordered sabotage attacks, including blowing up the Johannesburg headquarters of the South African Council of Churches in 1988.

1997

South Africa's Truth and Reconciliation Commission announces in June that Winnie Madikizela-Mandela is being subpoenaed to appear in connection with amnesty applications by her former guards, nicknamed the Mandela United Football Club. Led by her, they stand accused of kidnap and murder. Madikizela-Mandela, giving evidence for the first time to a commission hearing in Johannesburg in December, describes evidence against her as "ludicrous" and says the commission is a "mud-slinging exercise." Former South African president P. W. Botha ignores a summons to appear before the commission in December 1997. "Clearly the appeals of various people – including the president of this country – have not prevailed and Mr. P. W. Botha has seen fit not to appear," says Archbishop Tutu. "We will let the law take its course."

1998

In testimony in March on the death of black leader Steve Biko in 1977, police officers who interrogated him admit they beat him, but still say his death was accidental.

The Interfaith Pilgrimage of the Middle Passage sets out from Massachusetts to trace the historical route of the slave trade between Africa and America. The pilgrimage brings together participants of different faiths, genders, and races on a journey of healing.

South African scientist Daan Goosen tells the Truth and Reconciliation Commission in June 1998 that the apartheid government considered trying to develop a bacteria which would kill only blacks.

Former law and order minister Adriaan Vlok tells the commission in July that he received orders from former South African president P. W. Botha to engineer the bombing of the South African Council of Churches in 1988. The commission finds that testimony from Adriaan Vlok that South Africa's last white president, F. W. de Klerk, knew of illegal operations against black groups, contradicts accounts given to the commission by Mr. de Klerk himself. The commission hears testimony from Dr. Wouter Basson in July, who headed a government chemical and biological weapons program during the apartheid era. The commission officially ends its work after more than two years of hearings and investigations into human rights violations committed during the apartheid era. Former South African president P. W. Botha is found guilty in August of contempt for ignoring a summons to appear before the commission to answer allegations that he led a state-sponsored strategy to silence and harass anti-apartheid activists while in office. His lawyers appeal against the fine and suspended one-year jail sentence. A leaked document from the commission in October implicates the African

National Congress (ANC) in human rights abuses and torture. A day before it is due to be released, the report is legally challenged by F. W. de Klerk, forcing the commission to remove a section that implicated him in a series of bombings in the 1980s. Just hours before the final report is to be published the ANC fails in a court bid to prevent its publication.

October 29: President Nelson Mandela receives the Truth and Reconciliation Commission Report.

1999

Henry Lyons, president of the National Baptist Convention, USA, resigns, convicted of money laundering.

2000

First woman bishop elected in the AME Church.

2003

Cardinal Francis Arinze of Nigeria becomes a strong contender to succeed Pope John Paul II.

2004

March 7–13: Black Church Week of Prayer for the Healing of AIDS.

The senior Nigerian Anglican archbishop, Peter Akinola, commends US President George W. Bush for standing against same-gender marriages during his campaign for reelection.

2005

April 4: Retired Anglican Archbishop Desmond Tutu calls for the Catholic Church to appoint an African as its new pope. "We hope the cardinals when they meet will follow the first non-Italian pope by electing the first African pope," said Tutu on SABC TV at a press conference in his Cape Town home. Nigeria's Cardinal Francis Arinze, number four in the church hierarchy, was seen as the best hope for a pope from the third world. He would have been the first African pope since Gelasius I in AD 496.

In Britain, John Sentamu, bishop of Birmingham, succeeds David Hope as archbishop of York. Sentamu was born in Uganda.

Websites for Historic Black Denominations

African Methodist Episcopal Church	www.amecnet.org
African Methodist Episcopal Zion Church	www.theamezionchurch.org
Christian Methodist Episcopal Church	www.c-m-e.org
Church of God in Christ	www.cogic.org
National Baptist Convention of America, Unincorporated	www.nbcamerica.net
National Baptist Convention, USA Inc.	www.nationalbaptist.org
Progressive National Baptist Convention	www.pnbc.org

Bibliography

Black Church Studies

Albert, P. J. and Hoffman, R. (1993). *We Shall Overcome: Martin Luther King, Jr., and the Black Freedom Struggle.* New York: Da Capo Press.

Anderson, Victor (1995). *Beyond Ontological Blackness: An Essay on African American Religious and Cultural Criticism.* New York: Continuum.

Ayres, A. (ed.) (1993). *The Wisdom of Martin Luther King, Jr.* New York: Penguin.

Bailey, Randall C. and Jacquelyn C. Grant (eds.) (1994). *The Recovery of Black Presence: An Interdisciplinary Exploration.* Nashville, TN: Abingdon.

Baker-Fletcher, Garth (1993). *Somebodyness: Martin Luther King Jr., and the Theory of Dignity.* Minneapolis, MN: Fortress Press.

—— (1996). *Exodus: An African American Male Journey.* Minneapolis, MN: Fortress Press.

—— (1998). *Black Religion after the Million Man March.* Maryknoll, NY: Orbis Books.

Baldwin, L. V. (1991). *There Is a Balm in Gilead: The Cultural Roots of Martin Luther King, Jr.* Minneapolis, MN: Fortress Press.

—— (1992). *To Make the Wounded Whole: The Cultural Legacy of Martin Luther King, Jr.* Minneapolis, MN: Fortress Press.

Banks, J. A. (1996). "The Canon Debate: Knowledge Construction and Multicultural Education." In J. A. Banks (ed.) *Multicultural Education, Transformative Knowledge, and Action: Historical and Contemporary Perspectives.* New York: Teachers College.

Baraka, Imamu Amiri (1999). *The Leroi Jones/Amiri Baraka Reader*, ed. William J. Harris, 2nd edn. New York: Thunder's Mouth.

Barndt, Joseph (1991). *Dismantling Racism: The Continuing Challenge to White America.* Minneapolis, MN: Augsburg.

Bennett, L., Jr. (1964). *What Manner of Man: A Memorial Biography of Martin Luther King, Jr.* New York: Johnson.

—— (1969). *The Shaping of Black America.* Chicago: Johnson.

Bentley, William H. and Ruth Lewis Bentley (1990). "Reflections on the Scope and Function of a Black Evangelical Black Theology." In Kenneth S. Kantzer and Carl F. H. Henry (eds.) *Evangelical Affirmations.* Grand Rapids, MI: Academie.

Billingsley, A. (1992). *Climbing Jacob's Ladder: The Enduring Legacy of African-American Families*. New York: Simon and Schuster.

Bodo, John R. (1966). "Prayer for a Church Anniversary," *Theology Today*, 23:2 (July): 181–2.

Bradley, L. Richard (1971). "The Curse of Canaan and the American Negro." *Concordia Theological Monthly* 42:2 (February): 100–10.

Branch, T. (1988). *Parting the Waters: America in the King Years, 1954–63*. New York: Simon and Schuster.

Brown, Hubert L. (1976). *Black and Mennonite: A Search for Identity*. Scottdale, PA: Herald.

Burrow, Rufus (1994). *James H. Cone and Black Liberation Theology*. Jefferson, NC: McFarland.

Calloway-Thomas, C. and Lucaites, J. L. (eds.) (1993). *Martin Luther King, Jr., and the Sermonic Power of Public Discourse*. Tuscaloosa: University of Alabama Press.

Carson, C. (ed.) (1992–2000). *The Papers of Martin Luther King, Jr. (Vols. 1–4)*. Berkeley: University of California Press.

Chapman, Mark L. (1996). *Christianity on Trial: African-American Religious Thought Before and After Black Power*. Maryknoll, NY: Orbis Books.

Collins, D. R. (1986). *Not Only Dreamers: The Story of Martin Luther King, Sr. and Martin Luther King, Jr*. Elgin, IL: Brethren.

Cone, James H. (1984). *For My People: Black Theology and the Black Church*. Maryknoll, NY: Orbis Books.

—— (1985). "Black Theology in American Religion." *Journal of the American Academy of Religion* 53 (December): 755–71.

—— (1986). *Speaking the Truth: Ecumenism, Liberation, and Black Theology*. Grand Rapids, MI: Eerdmans.

—— (1989). *Black Theology and Black Power*. New York: Harper and Row.

—— (1990). *A Black Theology of Liberation*. Maryknoll, NY: Orbis Books.

—— (1991a). *Martin and Malcolm and America: A Dream or a Nightmare*. Maryknoll, NY: Orbis Books.

—— (1991b). *The Spirituals and the Blues: An Interpretation*. Maryknoll, NY: Orbis Books.

—— (1997). *God of the Oppressed*, revd. edn. Maryknoll, NY: Orbis Books.

Cone, James H. and Gayraud S. Wilmore (1993a). *Black Theology: A Documentary History, Vol. 1: 1966–1979*, 2nd edn. Maryknoll, NY: Orbis Books.

—— (1993b). *Black Theology: A Documentary History, Vol. 2: 1980–1992*. Maryknoll, NY: Orbis Books.

Cooper-Lewter, Nicholas and Henry H. Mitchell (1986). *Soul Theology: The Heart of American Black Culture*. Nashville, TN: Abingdon.

Cummings, George (1992). *Common Journey: Black Theology and Latin American Liberation Theology*. Maryknoll, NY: Orbis Books.

Davies, Alan (1988). *Infected Christianity: A Study of Modern Racism*. Montreal: McGill-Queens.

Davis, Francis (1995). *The History of the Blues: The Roots, the Music, the People from Charley Patton to Robert Cray*. New York: Hyperion.

Downing, J. L. (1986). *To See the Promised Land: The Faith Pilgrimage of Martin Luther King, Jr.* Macon, GA: Mercer University Press.

Early, Gerald (1999). "Devil in a Blues Dress." *Books and Culture* 5:5 (September/October).

Ellis, Carl F. (1996). *Free at Last? The Gospel in the African-American Experience*. Downer's Grove, IL: InterVarsity Press.

Erskine, N. L. (1994). *King Among the Theologians*. Cleveland, OH: Pilgrim Press.

Evans, James (1992). *We Have Been Believers: An African-American Systematic Theology*. Minneapolis, MN: Fortress Press.

—— (1997). *We Shall Be Changed: Social Problems and Theologial Review*. Minneapolis, MN: Fortress Press.

Fager, Charles E. (1967). *White Reflections on Black Power*. Grand Rapids, MI: Eerdmans.

Felder, Cain Hope (ed.) (1991). *Stony The Road We Trod: African American Bible Interpretation*. Minneapolis, MN: Fortress Press.

Fordan, Theodus (1992). *Contribution of Black Theology to Contemporary Thought*. New York: Vintage.

Fulop, Timothy and Albert Raboteau (1986). *African American Religion*.

Garrow, D. J. (1986). *Bearing the Cross: Martin Luther King, Jr. and the Southern Christian Leadership Conference*. New York: William Morrow.

Hayes, Diana L. (1996). *And Still We Rise: An Introduction to Black Liberation Theology*. Mahwah, NJ: Paulist Press.

Hodgson, Peter C. (1974). *Children of Freedom: Black Liberation in Christian Perspective*. Minneapolis, MN: Fortress Press.

Hood, Robert (1990). *Must God Remain Greek? Afro Cultures and God-Talk*. Minneapolis, MN: Fortress Press.

Hooks, B. (1994). *Teaching to Transgress: Education as the Practice of Freedom*. New York: Routledge.

—— (1998). "The Chitlin Circuit." In S. Barboza (ed.) *The African American Book of Values*. New York: Doubleday.

Hopkins, Dwight N. (1989). *Black Theology, USA and South Africa: Politics, Culture, and Liberation*. Maryknoll, NY: Orbis Books.

Hopkins, Dwight N. and George Cummings (eds.) (1991). *Cut Loose Your Stammering Tongue: Black Theology in the Slave Narratives*. Maryknoll, NY: Orbis Books.

Ivory, Luther D. (1997). *Toward a Theology of Radical Involvement: The Theological Legacy of Martin Luther King, Jr.* Nashville, TN: Abingdon.

Jones, LeRoi [Imamu Amiri Baraka] (1963). *Blues People: Negro Music in White America*. New York: William Morrow.

Jones, Major (1974). *Christian Ethics for Black Theology: The Politics of Liberation*. Nashville, TN: Abingdon.

—— (1987). *The Color of God: The Concept of God in Afro-American Thought*. Macon, GA: Mercer.

Jones, William R. (1973). *Is God a White Racist? A Preamble to Black Theology*. New York: Doubleday.

Jordan, R. L. (1982). *Black Theology Exposed*. New York: Vantage.

Kapur, S. (1992). *Raising Up a Prophet: The African-American Encounter with Gandhi*. Boston, MA: Beacon Press.

Kelsey, George (1965). *Racism and the Christian Understanding of Man*. New York: Charles Scribner's Sons.

King, C. S. (1983). *The Words of Martin Luther King, Jr*. New York: Newmarket.

—— (1993). *My Life with Martin Luther King, Jr*., revd. edn. New York: Holt.

King, Martin Luther, Jr. (1958). *Stride Toward Freedom: The Montgomery Story*. New York: Ballantine.

—— (1963a). *Strength to Love*. Philadelphia, PA: Fortress Press.

—— (1963b). *Why We Can't Wait*. New York: Signet.

—— (1967). *Where Do We Go from Here: Chaos or Community?* Boston, MA: Beacon Press.

—— (1986). *A Testament of Hope: The Essential Writings of Martin Luther King, Jr*., ed. James Washington. New York: Harper and Row.

King, Martin Luther, Sr. (1980). *Daddy King: An Autobiography*. New York: William Morrow.

Lincoln, C. E. (ed.) (1970). *Martin Luther King, Jr.: A Profile*, revd. edn. New York: Hill and Wang.

—— (ed.) (1974). *The Black Experience in Religion*. New York: Doubleday.

Lincoln, C. E. and Mamiya, L. H. (1990). *The Black Church in the African American Experience*. Durham, NC: Duke University Press.

Lischer, Richard (1995). *The Preacher King: Martin Luther King, Jr. and the Word that Moved America*. New York: Oxford University Press.

Lovell, John, Jr. (1972). *Black Song: The Forge and the Flame: The Story of How the Afro-American Spiritual Was Hammered Out*. New York: Macmillan.

McCray, Walter Arthur (1979). *Black Folks and Christian Liberty: Black, Christian, and Free to be Cultural and Social*. Chicago: Black Light Fellowship.

Mafico, T. L. J. (1997). "Tapping Our Roots." In A. Wimberly (ed.) *Honoring African American Elders: A Ministry in the Soul Community*. San Francisco: Jossey-Bass.

Mays, Benjamin (1969). *The Negro's God: As Reflected in His Literature*. New York: Atheneum.

Miller, K. D. (1992). *Voice of Deliverance: The Language of Martin Luther King, Jr. and Its Sources*. New York: Free Press.

Mitchell, Henry H. (1975). *Black Belief*. New York: Harper and Row.

Mitchell, Henry H. and Nicholas Cooper Lewter (1986). *Soul Theology: The Heart of American Black Culture*. New York: Harper and Row.

Moyd, Olin P. (1979). *Redemption in Black Theology*. Valley Forge, PA: Judson Press.

Oates, S. B. (1982). *Let the Trumpet Sound: The Life of Martin Luther King, Jr*. New York: Mentor.

Pannell, William (1993). *The Coming Race Wars: A Cry for Reconciliation.* Grand Rapids, MI: Zondervan.

Paris, P. J. (1985). *The Social Teaching of the Black Churches.* Philadelphia, PA: Fortress Press.

—— (1995). *The Spirituality of African Peoples: The Search for a Common Moral Discourse.* Minneapolis, MN: Fortress Press.

Pinn, Anthony B. (1995). *Why, Lord?: Suffering and Evil in Black Theology.* New York: Continuum.

Pinn, Anthony B. and Anne Pinn (2002). *Introduction to Black Church History.* Minneapolis, MN: Fortress Press.

Potter, Ronald (1995). "Christian Apologetics in the African-American Grain." In Timothy R. Philips and Dennis L. Okholm (eds.) *Christian Apologetics in the Postmodern World.* Downer's Grove, IL: InterVarsity Press.

Raboteau, A. J. (1978). *Slave Religion: The "Invisible Institution" in the Antebellum South.* New York: Oxford University Press.

Roberts, J. Deotis (1971). *Liberation and Reconciliation: A Black Theology.* Louisville, KY: Westminster Press.

—— (1974). *A Black Political Theology.* Louisville, KY: Westminster Press.

—— (1983). *Black Theology Today: Liberation and Contextualization.* Lewiston, NY: Edwin Mellen.

—— (1987). *Black Theology in Dialogue.* Louisville, KY: Westminster Press.

Skinner, Tom (1968). *Black and Free.* Grand Rapids, MI: Zondervan.

—— (1970). *How Black is the Gospel?* Philadelphia, PA: J. B. Lippincott.

Southern, Eileen (1983). *The Music of Black Americans: A History*, 2nd edn. New York: Norton.

Spencer, Jon Michael (1990). *Protest and Praise: Sacred Music of Black Religion.* Minneapolis, MN: Fortress Press.

—— (ed.) (1992). *Sacred Music of the Secular City: From Blues to Rap.* Durham, NC: Duke University Press.

Thurman, Howard (1949). *Jesus and the Disinherited.* Nashville, TN: Abingdon.

—— (1954). *The Creative Encounter.* New York: Harper.

—— (1971). *The Search for Common Ground.* New York: Harper and Row.

Usry, Glenn and Craig S. Keener (1996). *Black Man's Religion: Can Christianity be Afrocentric?* Downer's Grove, IL: InterVarsity Press.

Walker, Theodore, Jr. (1991). *Empower the People: Social Ethics for the African-American Church.* Maryknoll, NY: Orbis Books.

Walker, Wyatt Tee (1979). *Somebody's Calling My Name: Black Sacred Music and Social Change.* Valley Forge, PA: Judson Press.

Wamba, P. (1999). *Kinship: A Family's Journey in Africa and America.* New York: Dutton.

Watley, W. D. (1985). *Roots of Resistance: The Nonviolent Ethic of Martin Luther King, Jr.* Valley Forge, PA: Judson Press.

West, Cornel (1982). *Prophesy Deliverance! An Afro-American Revolutionary Christianity.* Louisville, KY: Westminster Press.

—— (1988). *Prophetic Fragments.* Grand Rapids, MI: Eerdmans.

Williams, J. (1987). *Eyes on the Prize: America's Civil Rights Years, 1954–1965.* New York: Penguin.

Wilmore, Gayraud (1982). *Last Things First.* Minneapolis, MN: Fortress Press.

—— (1983). *Black Religion and Black Radicalism,* 2nd edn. Maryknoll, NY: Orbis Books.

Wilmore, G. S. (ed.) (1989). *African American Religious Studies: An Interdisciplinary Anthology.* Durham, NC: Duke University Press.

Witvliet, Theo (1987). *The Way of the Black Messiah: The Hermeneutical Challenge of Black Theology as a Theology of Liberation.* Oak Park, IL: Meyer Stone Books.

X, Malcolm and Alex Haley (1966). *The Autobiography of Malcolm X.* New York: Grove Press.

African Spirituality, Theology, and Philosophy

Adeyamo, Tokunboh (1979). *Salvation in African Tradition.* Nairobi: Evangel.

African Philosophy [serial] (1998–). Cambridge, MA: Carfax.

Amirtham, Samuel and John S. Pobee (eds.) (1986). *Theology by the People: Reflections on Doing Theology in Community.* Geneva: World Council of Churches.

Appiah-Kubi, Kofi and Sergio Torres (eds.) (1979). *African Theology en Route.* Maryknoll, NY: Orbis Books.

Baeta, C. G. (ed.) (1968). *Christianity in Tropical Africa.* New York: Oxford University Press.

Becken, Hans-Jurgen (ed.) (1973). *Relevant Theology for Africa.* Mapumulo: Lutheran Publishing House.

Bediako, Kwame (1993). "Cry Jesus! Chrisian Theology and Presence in Modern Africa." *Vox Evangelica* 23: 7–25.

—— (1995). *Christianity in Africa: The Renewal of a Non-Western Religion.* Maryknoll, NY: Orbis Books; Edinburgh: Edinburgh University Press.

Boesak, Allan Aubrey (1984). *Black and Reformed: Apartheid, Liberation, and the Calvinist Tradition.* Maryknoll, NY: Orbis Books.

—— (1986). *Farewell to Innocence: A Social, Ethical Study on Black Theology and Power.* Maryknoll, NY: Orbis Books.

Boesak, Willa (1995). *God's Wrathful Children: Political Oppression and Christian Ethics.* Grand Rapids, MI: Eerdmans.

Bosch, D. (1990). *Transforming Mission.* Maryknoll, NY: Orbis Books.

Boulaga, Eboussi F. (1984). *Christianity without Fetishes: An African Critique and Recapture of Christianity.* Maryknoll, NY: Orbis Books.

Bourdillon, M. F. C. (1991). *Religion and Society: A Text for Africa.* Gweru: Mambo Press.

Bryant, R. (1975). "Toward a Contextualist Theology in Southern Africa." *Journal of Theology for Southern Africa* 11: 11–19.

Bujo, B. (1990). *African Christian Morality.* Nairobi: St. Paul.

—— (1992). *African Theology in Its Social Context*. Maryknoll, NY: Orbis Books.

Chalmers, John A. (1878). *Tiyo Soga: A Page of South African Mission Work*. Edinburgh: Andrew Elliot; London: Hodder and Stoughton; Glasgow: David Bryce; Grahamstown, Cape Colony: James Hay.

Chidester, David (1989). "Worldview Analysis of African Indigenous Churches." *Journal for the Study of Religion* 2:1 (March): 15–27.

Chikane, Frank (1985). "The Incarnation in the Life of the People of South Africa." *Journal of Religion in Southern Africa* 51: 37–50.

Chirenje, Murenje J. (1987). *Ethiopianism and Afro-Americans in Southern Africa, 1883–1916*. Baton Rouge: Louisiana State University Press.

Clingman, S. (ed.) (1991). *Regions and Repertoires: Topics in South African Politics and Culture*. Johannesburg: Ravan.

Coetzee, P. H. and A. P. J. Roux (eds.) (1998). *The African Philosophy Reader*. New York: Routledge.

Cox, James L. (ed.) (1998). *Rites of Passage in Contemporary Africa*. Cardiff: Cardiff Academic Press.

Cumpsty, John S. (1991). *Religion As Belonging: A General Theory of Religion*. New York: University Press of America.

de Gruchy, J. W. (1979). *The Church Struggle in South Africa*. Grand Rapids, MI: Eerdmans.

—— (1986). *Theology and Ministry in Context and Crisis*. London: Collins.

de Gruchy, J. W. and Charles Villa-Vicencio (1983). *Apartheid is a Heresy*. Grand Rapids, MI: Eerdmans.

de Haas, M. (1989). "Towards a Common South African Identity." Unpublished paper given at South African Perceptions Forum, Durban Metropolitan Chamber of Commerce, August 2.

Dickson, Kwesi (1984). *Theology in Africa*. Maryknoll, NY: Orbis Books.

Dwane, S. (1988). "Gospel and Culture." *Journal of Black Theology in South Africa* 1: 18–25.

Dyrness, William (1990). *Learning about Theology from the Third World*. Grand Rapids, MI: Academie.

—— (1994). *Emerging Voices in Global Christian Theology*. Grand Rapids, MI: Zondervan.

English, Parker and Kibujjo Kalumba (eds.) (1996). *African Philosophy: A Classical Approach*. Upper Saddle River, NJ: Prentice-Hall.

Ephirim-Donkor, A. (1997). *African Spirituality: On Becoming Ancestors*. Trenton, NJ: Africa World Press.

Eze, Emmanuel Chukwudi (ed.) (1998). *African Philosophy: An Anthology*. Malden, MA: Blackwell.

Fabella, Virginia and Mercy Amba Oduyoye (eds.) (1988). *With Passion and Compassion: Third World Women Doing Theology*. Maryknoll, NY: Orbis Books.

Fashole-Luke, Edward et al. (eds.) (1978). *Christianity in Independent Africa*. London: Rex Collings.

Gbadegesin, Segun (1991). *African Philosophy: Traditional Yoruba Philosophy and Contemporary African Realities.* New York: P. Lang.

Geertz, G. (1983). *Local Knowledge: Further Essays in Interpretive Anthropology.* New York: Basic Books.

Gluckman, M. (1965). *Custom and Conflict in Africa.* Oxford: Blackwell.

Goba, B. (1980). "Doing Theology in South Africa: A Black Christian Perspective." *Journal of Theology for Southern Africa* 31: 23–35.

—— (1986). "The Black Consciousness Movement: Its impact on Black Theology." In I. J. Mosala and B. Tlhagale (eds.) *The Unquestionable Right To Be Free.* Maryknoll, NY: Orbis Books.

—— (1988). *An Agenda for Black Theology.* Johannesburg: Skotaville.

Goody, J. (1962). *Death, Property and the Ancestors: Mortuary Customs of the Lodagaa (West Africa).* London: Tavistock.

Guma, Mongezi and Leslie Milton (eds.) (1997). *An African Challenge to the Church in the 21st Century.* Cape Town: Salty Print.

Hastings, Adrian (1989). *African Catholicism: Essays in Discovery.* Philadelphia, PA: Trinity Press International.

Healey, Joseph and Donald Sybertz (1996). *Towards an Africa Narrative Theology.* Maryknoll, NY: Orbis Books.

Hountondji, Paulin J. (1996). *English African Philosophy: Myth and Reality,* trans. Henri Evans and Jonathan Rée. Bloomington: Indiana University Press.

Jahn, J. (1961). *Muntu: An Outline of the New African Culture.* New York: Grove.

Kretzschmar, Louise (ed.) (1988). *Christian Faith and African Culture.* Unitra: Religious Studies Forum.

Kuckertz, H. (ed.) (1981). *Ancestor Religion in Africa.* Cacadu, Transkei: Lumko Missiological Institute.

Kurewa, John Wesley Zwomunondiita (1995). *Biblical Proclamation for Africa Today.* Nashville, TN: Abingdon.

Makhubu, Paul (1988). *Who Are the Independent Churches?* Johannesburg: Skotaville.

Makinde, M. Akin (1988). *African Philosophy, Culture, and Traditional Medicine.* Athens: Ohio University Center for International Studies.

Makobane, Mohlomi et al. (eds.) (1995). *The Church and African Culture.* Germiston: Lumko.

Maluleke, Tinyiko S. (1996). "Black and African Theologies in the New World Order: A Time to Drink from our Own Wells." *Journal of Theology for Southern Africa* 96 (November): 3–18.

—— (1998). "African Traditional Religions in Christian Mission and Christian Scholarship: Reopening a Debate that Never Started." *Religion and Theology: A Journal of Contemporary Religious Discourse* 5:2: 121–35.

Masolo, D. A. (1994). *African Philosophy: In Search of Identity.* Bloomington: Indiana University Press; Edinburgh: Edinburgh University Press.

Mbiti, John S. (1970). *Concepts of God in Africa.* New York: Praeger.

—— (1971). *New Testament Eschatology in an African Background: A Study of the Encounter Between New Testament Theology and African Traditional Concepts*. Oxford: Oxford University Press.

—— (1977). "Christianity and African Culture." *Journal of Theology for Southern Africa* 20 (September): 26–40.

—— (1986). *Bible and Theology in African Christianity*. Nairobi: Oxford University Press.

—— (1990a). *African Religions and Philosophy*. Portsmouth, NH: Heinemann.

—— (1990b). *Introduction to African Religion*. New York: Praeger.

Mofokeng, T. (1983). *The Crucified among the Crossbearers*. Kampen: Uitgeversmaatschappij J. H. Kok.

Mokgoba, S. M. (1985). "Christianity in an African Context." *Journal of Theology for Southern Africa* 52: 5–16.

Mosala, Itumeleng J. (1983). "African Traditional Beliefs and Christianity." *Journal of Theology for Southern Africa* 39:43 (June): 15–24.

—— (1986). *The Unquestionable Right To Be Free: Black Theology from South Africa*. Maryknoll, NY: Orbis Books.

—— (1989). *Biblical Hermeneutics and Black Theology in South Africa*. Grand Rapids, MI: Eerdmans.

Mugambi, J. N. K. (ed.) (1992). *Critiques of Christianity in African Literature*. Nairobi: East African Educational Publishers.

Muzorewa, Gwinyai H. (1987). *The Origins and Development of African Theology*. Maryknoll, NY: Orbis Books.

Nolan, Albert (1988). *God in South Africa: The Challenge of the Gospel*. London: CIIR.

Oduyoye, Mercy Amba (1986). *Hearing and Knowing: Theological Reflections on Christianity in Africa*. Maryknoll, NY: Orbis Books.

—— (1992a). *Leadership Development in the Methodist Church Nigeria: 1842–1962*. Ibadan, Nigeria: Sefer.

—— (1992b). *The Wesleyan Presence in Nigeria, 1842–1962: An Exploration of Power, Control and Partnership in Mission*. Ibadan, Nigeria: Sefer.

—— (1995). *Daughters of Anowa: African Women and Patriarchy*. Maryknoll, NY: Orbis Books.

Oduyoye, Mercy Amba and Musimbi R. A. Kanyoro (eds.) (1990). *Talitha, Qumi! Proceedings of the Convocation of African Women Theologians*. Millville, NJ: Daystar Press.

—— (eds.) (1992). *The Will to Arise: Women, Tradition, and the Church in Africa*. Maryknoll, NY: Orbis Books.

Ogbonnaya, A. Okechukwu (1994). *On Communitarian Divinity: An African Interpretation of the Trinity*. New York: Paragon House.

Okere, Theophilus (1983). *African Philosophy: A Historico-Hermeneutical Investigation of the Conditions of Its Possibility*. Lanham, MD: University Press of America.

Oladipo, Caleb Oluremi (1992). *The Development of the Doctrine of the Holy Spirit in the Yoruba (African) Indigenous Christian Movement*. New York: P. Lang.

Oladipo, Emmanuel (1993). "The 1993 Laing Lecture: First Response." *Vox Evangelica* 23: 27–8.

Onunwa, Udobata (ed.) (1992). *African Spirituality: An Anthology of Igbo Religious Myths*. Darmstadt: Thesen.

Oosthuizen, G. C. (ed.) (1986). *Religion Alive: Studies in the New Movement and Indigenous Churches in Southern Africa*. London: Hodder and Stoughton.

Oosthuizen, G. C. et al. (eds.) (1994). *Afro-Christianity at the Grassroots: Its Dynamics and Strategies*. New York: E. J. Brill.

Osei, G. K. (1971). *The African Philosophy of Life*. London: African Publication Society.

Otene, M. (1983). *To Be With Christ, Chaste, Poor and Obedient: An Essay in a Bantu Spirituality of the Vows*. Nairobi: St. Paul.

Padilla, C. R. (1978). "The Contextualization of the Gospel." *Journal of Theology for Southern Africa* 24: 12–30.

Parratt, John (ed.) (1987). *A Reader in African Christian Theology*. London: SPCK.

—— (1995). *Reinventing Christianity: African Theology Today*. Grand Rapids, MI: Eerdmans.

Pato, Luke (1989). *Towards an Authentic African Christianity*. Unitra: Religious Studies Forum.

—— (1990). "The African Independent Churches: A Socio-Cultural Approach." *Journal of Theology for Southern Africa* 72 (September): 24–35.

Pauw, B. A. (1975). *Christianity and Xhosa Tradition: Belief and Ritual among Xhosa-speaking Christians*. New York: Oxford University Press.

Peterson, Kirsten Holst (ed.) (1987). *Religion, Development and African Identity*. Uppsala: Scandinavian Institute of African Studies.

Pobee, John S. (1979). *Toward an African Theology*. Nashville, TN: Abingdon.

—— (1987). *Who are the Poor? The Beatitudes as a Call to Community*. Geneva: World Council of Churches.

—— (1991). *Religion and Politics in Ghana*. Accra: Asempa Publishers.

—— (ed.) (1992a). *Exploring Afro-Christology*. New York: P. Lang.

—— (1992b). *Skenosis: Christian Faith In An African Context*. Gweru: Mambo Press.

—— (1995). "Afro-Anglicanism: Quo Vadimus?" *Anglican Theological Review* 77 (4).

Pobee, John S. and Samuel Amirtham (eds.) (1986). *Theology by the People: Reflections on Doing Theology in Community*. Geneva: World Council of Churches.

Pobee, John S. and Carl F. Hallencreutz (1986). *Variations in Christian Theology in Africa*. Nairobi: Uzima Press.

Pobee, John S. and Bärbel von Wartenberg-Potter (1986). *New Eyes for Reading: Biblical and Theological Reflections by Women from the Third World*. Geneva: World Council of Churches.

Ranger, Terence et al. (eds.) (1996). *Culture, Identity and Politics: Ethnic Minorities in Britain*. Sydney: Avebury.

Rasmussen, Ane Marie Bak (1996). *Modern African Spirituality: The Independent Holy Spirit Churches in East Africa, 1902–1976.* London: British Academic Press.

Ruch, E. A. and K. C. Anyanwu (1981). *African Philosophy: An Introduction to the Main Philosophical Trends in Contemporary Africa.* Catholic Book Agency.

Sanneh, Lamin (1983). *West African Christianity: The Religious Impact.* Maryknoll, NY: Orbis Books.

—— (1989). *Translating the Message: The Missionary Impact on Culture.* Maryknoll, NY: Orbis Books.

Saunders, C. C. (1970). "Tile and the Thembu Church: Politics and Independency on the Cape Eastern Frontier in the Late Nineteenth Century." *Journal of African History* 11:4: 553–70.

Sawyerr, Harry (1968). *Creative Evangelism: Towards A New Christian Encounter With Africa.* London: Lutterworth Press.

Schreiter, R. J. (1980). "Issues Facing Contextual Theologians Today." *Verbum SVD* 21: 267–78.

—— (ed.) (1991). *Faces of Jesus in Africa.* Maryknoll, NY: Orbis Books.

Sebidi, L. (1986). "The Dynamics of the Black Struggle and Its Implications for Black Theology." In I. J. Mosala and B. Tlhagale (eds.) *The Unquestionable Right to be Free.* Maryknoll, NY: Orbis Books.

Serequeberhan, Tsenay (ed.) (1991). *African Philosophy: The Essential Readings.* New York: Paragon House.

Setiloane, G. (1978). "How the Traditional World View Persists in the Christianity of the Sotho-Tswana." In E. Fashole-Luke et al. (eds.) *Christianity in Independent Africa.* London: Rex Collings.

Shorter, Aylward (ed.) (1986). *African Christian Spirituality.* London: G. Chapman.

Sindima, Harvey, J. (1994). *Drums of Redemption: An Introduction to African Christianity.* London: Greenwood Press.

Sölle, D. (1987). "The Moment of Truth: The Kairos Document from Africa." *Concilium* 192: 116–23.

Speaking For Ourselves: Members of African Independent Churches Report on their Pilot Study of the History and Theology of their Churches (1985). Braamfontein: Institute for Contextual Theology.

Sundkler, Bengt G. M. (1948). *Bantu Prophets in South Africa.* London: Lutterworth Press.

—— (1958). "The Concept of Christianity in the African Independent Churches." Seminar program, University of Natal.

Tlhagale, B. (1985). "Culture in an Apartheid Society." *Journal of Theology for Southern Africa* 51: 27–36.

Tlhagale, B. and Itumeleng Mosala (eds.) (1987). *Hammering Swords into Ploughshares: Essays in Honor of Archbishop Mpilo Desmond Tutu.* Grand Rapids, MI: Eerdmans.

Tutu, Desmond (1982). *Crying in the Wilderness: Struggle for Justice in South Africa.* Grand Rapids, MI: Eerdmans.

—— (1994). *The Rainbow People of God*. New York: Doubleday.

—— (1999). *No Future Without Forgiveness*. New York: Doubleday.

Williams, Donovan (1978). *Umfundisi: A Biography of Tiyo Soga 1829–1871*. Alice: Lovedale Press.

Wimberly, A. S. (ed.) (1997). *Honoring African American Elders: A Ministry in the Soul Community*. San Francisco: Jossey Bass.

—— (2001). "Discovering Communal Vitality in African Rituals: Seeing and Hearing God Through Zimbabwean Christians." *Religious Education* (summer).

Wiredu, Kwasi (1980). *Philosophy and an African Culture*. New York: Cambridge University Press.

—— (1992). *Person and Community: Ghanaian Philosophical Studies I*. Washington, DC: Council for Research in Values and Philosophy.

—— (1996). *Cultural Universals and Particulars: An African Perspective*. Bloomington: Indiana University Press.

Wright, Richard A. (1977). *African Philosophy, An Introduction*. Washington, DC: University Press of America.

Young, Josiah U. (1986). *Black and African Theologies*. Maryknoll, NY: Orbis Books.

—— (1993). *African Theology: A Critical Analysis and Annotated Bibliography*. London: Greenwood Press.

Index